Short Studies in Private International Law

Short Studies in Private International Law are short-book publications devoted to topics in private international law, in particular international and European civil procedure. The volumes can be a result of papers presented at conferences but can also consist of short monographs or edited volumes on private international law, aimed to inform academics and practitioners timely of recent developments. The hardcover books are compact volumes of 100–150 pages and are characterized by fast, global electronic dissemination, standard publishing contracts, standardized manuscript preparation and formatting guidelines, and expedited production schedules.

More information about this series at http://www.springer.com/series/15450

Vesna Lazić · Steven Stuij
Editors

Brussels Ibis Regulation

Changes and Challenges of the Renewed Procedural Scheme

ASSER PRESS

Springer

Editors
Vesna Lazić
Private International Law, Research Department
T.M.C. Asser Institute
The Hague
The Netherlands

and

Utrecht University
Utrecht
The Netherlands

and

University of Rijeka
Rijeka
Croatia

Steven Stuij
Private International Law, Research Department
T.M.C. Asser Institute
The Hague
The Netherlands

and

Erasmus School of Law
Rotterdam
The Netherlands

The contributions to this book are based on the papers presented during the conference "International Civil Procedure and Brussels Ibis" held at the T.M.C. Asser Institute on 19 March 2015, celebrating the Institute's 50th anniversary. The contribution written by V. Lazić and S. Stuij replaces the paper presented by P. Beaumont, whose views are not reflected in that contribution.

ISBN 978-94-6265-146-3 ISBN 978-94-6265-147-0 (eBook)
DOI 10.1007/978-94-6265-147-0

Library of Congress Control Number: 2016951661

Published by T.M.C. ASSER PRESS, The Hague, The Netherlands www.asserpress.nl
Produced and distributed for T.M.C. ASSER PRESS by Springer-Verlag Berlin Heidelberg

Printed on acid-free paper

This Springer imprint is published by Springer Nature
The registered company is Springer Science+Business Media B.V.
The registered company address is: Van Godewijckstraat 30, 3311 GX Dordrecht, The Netherlands

Contents

Chapter 1
The Revised Lis Pendens Rules in the Brussels Ibis Regulation

Christian Heinze and Björn Steinrötter

Abstract In line with the old adage "something old, something new, something borrowed, something blue, and a silver sixpence in her shoe", the lis pendens rule is shining in a new light since the recast of Brussels I Regulation. That old wedding saying also sums up quite well the way the lis pendens rule was retained, reorganized and amended.

Keywords Brussels Ibis regulation · Lis pendens · Exclusive jurisdiction · Choice of court agreement · Jurisdiction agreement · Forum non conveniens · Torpedo action

Contents

The paper is based on a presentation by the first author in the TMC Asser Instituut in The Hague on 19 March 2015.

C. Heinze · B. Steinrötter (✉)
Faculty of Law, Leibniz University of Hanover, Königsworther Platz 1,
30167 Hannover, Germany
e-mail: bjoern.steinroetter@iri.uni-hannover.de

C. Heinze
e-mail: christian.heinze@iri.uni-hannover.de

V. Lazić and S. Stuij (eds.), *Brussels Ibis Regulation*, Short Studies in Private International Law, DOI 10.1007/978-94-6265-147-0_1

1.1 Introduction

As is well known, the revised[1] Brussels I Regulation (hereafter referred to as "Brussels Ibis Regulation") shall apply only to legal proceedings instituted, to authentic instruments formally drawn up or registered and to court settlements approved or concluded on or after 10 January 2015 (Article 66, 81 Brussels Ibis Regulation). For legal proceedings instituted earlier, the previous version[2] of the Brussels I Regulation (hereafter referred to as "Brussels I Reg") continues to apply. Although more evolutionary than revolutionary as a whole, the new version of the Regulation is substantially different from the previous text in several aspects.

This contribution deals with the *lis pendens* rules[3] as one of these aspects.[4] These rules ought to prevent or resolve conflicts of international jurisdiction when there are legal actions (potentially) pending in different states. As this is of paramount importance to the operation of the Regulation, the provisions of this part of the Regulation have to be interpreted broadly.[5] This avoids parallel proceedings

[1] Regulation (EU) No 1215/2012 of the European Parliament and of the Council of 12 December 2012 on jurisdiction and the recognition and enforcement of judgements in civil and commercial matters, OJ L 351, p. 1; see Crawford/Carruthers 2013, p. 89; Dickinson/Lein (eds.) 2015; see also Alio 2014, p. 2395; Cadet 2013, p. 218; Domej 2014, p. 508; Hau 2014, p. 1417; Hay 2013, p. 1; v. Hein 2013, p. 97; Lenaerts and Stapper 2014, p. 280; Mari and Pretelli 2013/14, p. 211; Moses 2014, p. 1; Nielsen 2013, p. 503; Pohl 2013, p. 109; Queirolo 2013/14, p. 113; Schramm 2013/14, p. 143; Seatzu 2013/14, p. 175; with regard to the proposal see Heinze 2011a, p. 581; Illmer 2011, p. 645; Magnus and Mankowski 2011, p. 252.

[2] Council Regulation (EC) No 44/2001 of December 2000 on jurisdiction and the recognition and enforcement of judgements in civil and commercial matters, OJ L 12, p. 1.

[3] Chapter II, Section 9 of both the respective EU legislative acts; see also recitals 15 Brussels I Reg and 21–24 Brussels Ibis Regulation.

[4] See in particular Lazic 2013, p. 5 and also Auernig 2015, p. 6; Dittrich 2014, p. 219 et seq.; Heckel 2012, p. 272; Hohmeier 2014, p. 217; Mankowski 2015, p. 17; Queirolo 2013/14, p. 127 et seqq.; Wagner 2015, p. 50 et seqq.; Zhang 2014, p. 1.

[5] Rogerson 2015, paras 11.01, 11.03.

and—as a consequence—irreconcilable judgements. Furthermore, in principle an autonomous interpretation of these provisions is mandated.[6]

The Brussels Ibis Regulation deals with four different scenarios: One has to distinguish whether legal proceedings are pending in Member States (Articles 29–31) or third States (Articles 33–34) and whether proceedings involve the same cause of action (Articles 29, 33) or related actions (Articles 30, 34). As the latter probably will be of limited practical relevance,[7] the following remarks concentrate on the "same cause of action"-scenarios.

The following text firstly analyses the *lis pendens* rule in favour of the court first seised to decide about jurisdiction (2.). This is followed by remarks on the new *lis pendens*-mechanism for actions pending in third States (3.), the reversal of the general *lis pendens* rule in favour of the court chosen in a jurisdiction agreement (4.) and, finally, on notification obligations (5.). The authors summarise the main findings in the end (6.).

1.2 Something Old: Court First Seised Has Priority to Decide About Jurisdiction

1.2.1 Basic Rule: Strict First-in-Time Approach

Pursuant to Article 29(1) Brussels Ibis Regulation the court first seised with the action is given priority where proceedings involving the same case of action[8] and between the same parties are brought in the courts of different Member States. Any other court shall stay its proceedings of its own motion until the jurisdiction of the court first seised is established. Once jurisdiction is established, any other court shall decline jurisdiction in favour of the court first seised, Article 29(3) Brussels Ibis Regulation.

Article 29(1),(3) Brussels Ibis Regulation thus reflect the situation under the provisions of Article 27(1),(2) Brussels I Regulation. As was well established under the old law, the court second seised must not review the jurisdiction of the court first seised,[9] even if the duration of proceedings before the court first seised is excessively long.[10]

6 Different opinion with regard to the term "same cause of action" in third State cases Weber 2011, p. 634: recourse to the understanding of the term in the national law of the respective Member State.

7 Cf. Magnus and Mankowski 2010, p. 19; see also Rogerson 2015, para 11.30 et seqq.; EJC 6.12.1994—Case C-406/92 (Tatry), E.C.R. 1994, I-5439, paras 51–58.

8 Regarding the term "same cause of action" see ECJ 8.12.1987—Case C-144/86 (Gubisch), E.C.R. 1987, 4861, paras 14–19. Two causes of action do not need to be identical to fulfill the prerequisities of the term. This is also true regarding negative declaratory actions, EJC 6.12.1994—Case C-406/92 (Tatry), E.C.R. 1994, I-5439, para 45.

9 See ECJ 27.6.1991—Case C-351/89 (Overseas Union Insurance Ltd), E.C.R. 1991, I-3317, para 26.

10 ECJ 9.12.2003—Case C-116/02 (Gasser), E.C.R. 2003, I-14693, para 73.

1.2.2 Exceptions

As the first seised-rule is fundamental for the operation of the Regulation, only few exceptions are made to this basic principle.

1.2.2.1 ECJ Case *Weber*: Exclusive Jurisdiction

First of all, the strict first seised-rule does not apply if jurisdiction of the court second seised is exclusive, i.e. based on Article 24 Brussels Ibis Regulation (Article 22 Brussels I Regulation).[11] In its judgement in *Weber*, the ECJ decided that

> in a situation such as that issue in the main proceedings, if the court first seised gives a judgement which fails to take account of Art. 22 (1) of Brussels I Reg, that judgement cannot be recognised in the Member State in which the court second seised is situated.[12]

At first sight, this result seems to be a predictable consequence from the fact that Article 35(1) Brussels I Regulation (Article 45(1)(e)(ii) Brussels Ibis Regulation) excludes recognition and enforcement of a potential judgement of the court first seised, thereby ruling out a potential conflict of judgements. At the same time, however, this decision may also be regarded as a modification of the former "strictly formal" reading of the *lis pendens* provisions by the ECJ:

> In those circumstances, the court second seised is no longer entitled to stay its proceedings or to decline jurisdiction, and it must give a ruling on the substance of the action before it in order to comply with the rule on exclusive jurisdiction.[13]

Although the decision concerned Article 22 No. 1 Alt. 1 Brussels I Regulation (Article 24 No. 1 Alt. 1 Brussels Ibis Regulation), it can be applied to all grounds of exclusive jurisdiction in Article 22 Brussels I Regulation (Article 24 Brussels Ibis Regulation).[14]

As a consequence of this decision, the court first seised will probably be under an obligation to stay its proceedings in order to avoid parallel proceedings.[15] This, however, does not follow from Article 31(2) Brussels Ibis Regulation applied by analogy.[16] Not only did the *Weber* case deal with the previous version of the

---

[11] ECJ 3.4.2014—C-438/12 (Weber), ECLI:EU:C:2014:212, paras 55–56; see Nordmeier 2015, p. 120; see also the "transformation" of the Weber-decision by the German BGH, 13.8.2014—V ZB 163/12; cf. before the Case Weber ECJ 27.6.1991—Case C-351/89 (Overseas Union Insurance Ltd), E.C.R. 1991, I-3317, para 26.

[12] ECJ 3.4.2014—C-438/12 (Weber), ECLI:EU:C:2014:212, para 55.

[13] ECJ 3.4.2014—C-438/12 (Weber), ECLI:EU:C:2014:212, para 56.

[14] Nordmeier 2015, 125; Wagner 2015, p. 51.

[15] Different opinion in this respect Wagner 2015, p. 51.

[16] Same view Nordmeier 2015, p. 125.

Regulation, which did not contain such a provision. More importantly, the conclusion in *Weber* is based on the rationale of exclusive jurisdiction in general.[17] In order to establish exclusive jurisdiction of the court second seised, a *prima facie* assessment by the court first seised seems appropriate.[18]

Within its (narrow) scope of exclusive jurisdiction based on Article 24 Brussels Ibis Regulation (Article 22 Brussels I Regulation), the ruling in *Weber* limits potential abuse, in particular the "torpedo"-scenario where one party may approach notoriously slow working courts just to delay proceedings. The strict application of the first seised rule seems to be inappropriate if the court second seised is competent pursuant to exclusive jurisdiction rules as the—in these cases—particularly close connection between the matter in dispute and the place of jurisdiction deserves special protection.[19]

It has to be noted that Article 24 Brussels Ibis Regulation establishes exclusive jurisdiction only in favour of Member States' courts. If there is exclusive jurisdiction of a third State's court, Article 33(1) Brussels Ibis Regulation applies.[20] Exclusive jurisdiction is then a (significant) factor the court of the Member State has to take into consideration within its discretionary powers under Article 33(1) Brussels Ibis Regulation (see explicitly recital 24[2] Brussels Ibis Regulation).

1.2.2.2 Exclusive Jurisdiction Agreements

The second exception concerns jurisdiction agreements. Article 31(2) Brussels Ibis Regulation[21] states that "where a court of a Member State in which an agreement as referred to in Article 25 confers exclusive jurisdiction[22] is seised, any court of another Member State shall stay the proceedings until such time as the court seised on the basis of the agreement declares that it has no jurisdiction under the agreement."[23] Recital 22 sentence 4 Brussels Ibis Regulation adds that courts designated in the choice of forum clauses do not only decide about the effectiveness of the agreement, they also decide to what extent the respective clauses apply to the pending case. If the court seised based on the agreement declares that it has jurisdiction, the other courts must decline jurisdiction.[24]

---

[17] Cf. Heinze and Dutta 2005, p. 227 regarding exclusive jurisdiction in third States.

[18] Regarding exclusive jurisdiction agreements see 1.4.

[19] Cf. Nordmeier 2015, p. 127.

[20] In detail below 1.3.2.

[21] See also recital 22 Brussels Ibis Regulation.

[22] Note Article 25(1) sentence 2 Brussels Ibis Regulation.

[23] Reversing ECJ 9.12.2003—Case C-116/02 (Gasser), E.C.R. 2003, I-14693, para 54.

[24] See in detail below 1.4.2–1.4.3 (in particular to a *prima facie* evaluation of the court first seised).

1.2.3 Consequences of a Strict Priority Rule

The strict priority of the court first seised and the broad understanding of "the same cause of action"[25] in the case law of the Court of Justice have far-reaching implications, in particular regarding abusive procedural tactics ("torpedo"). Beyond potential delay by such tactics, as decisions of the court first seised on jurisdiction are binding on any court second seised[26] and there used to be no exceptions for abuse,[27] any court first seised which has not been chosen by the parties might even be more likely to strike down jurisdiction agreements.[28]

The Brussels Ibis Regulation solves these problems with regard to (exclusive) choice of court agreements only.[29] In these cases, prorogated courts are given priority to decide about jurisdiction, Article 31(2) Brussels Ibis Regulation.[30] For the remaining cases Article 29(2) Brussels Ibis Regulation establishes only a weak "notification obligation" (upon request of another court).[31]

1.2.4 Possible Alternatives to the Status Quo

This raises the question of whether the EU legislator could have done a better job in adopting a general solution. The EU Commission had proposed a provision under which the "court first seised shall establish its jurisdiction within six months except where exceptional circumstances make this impossible."[32] It is questiona-

[25] ECJ 8.12.1987—Case C-144/86 (Gubisch), E.C.R. 1987, 4861, paras 15–19; EJC 6.12.1994—Case C-406/92 (Tatry), E.C.R. 1994, I-5439, paras 40–45, 47–48.

[26] ECJ 15.11.2012—Case C-456/11 (Gothaer Allgemeine Versicherung), ECLI:EU:2012:10989, para 41: "Thus, a judgment by which a court of a Member State has declined jurisdiction on the basis of a jurisdiction clause, on the ground that that clause is valid, binds the courts of the other Member States both as regards that court's decision to decline jurisdiction, contained in the operative part of the judgment, and as regards the finding on the validity of that clause, contained in the *ratio decidendi* which provides the necessary underpinning for that operative part."

[27] ECJ 9.12.2003—Case C-116/02 (Gasser), E.C.R. 2003, I-14693, para 53: "Finally, the difficulties (...) stemming from delaying tactics by parties who, with the intention of delaying settlement of the substantive dispute, commence proceedings before a court which they know to lack jurisdiction by reason of the existence of a jurisdiction clause are not such as to call in question the interpretation of any provision of the Brussels Convention, as deduced from its wording and its purpose."

[28] Domej 2014, p. 531.

[29] Note the new case law of the ECJ concerning exclusive jurisdiction rule since ECJ 3.4.2014—C-438/12 (Weber), ECLI:EU:C:2014:212; see 2.2.1.

[30] See 1.4.2.

[31] See 1.5.

[32] Proposal for a Regulation of the European Parliament and the Council on jurisdiction and the recognition and enforcement of judgments in civil and commercial matters (Recast), COM(2010) 748 final, p. 35; on the proposal see Weller 2012a, p. 42 et seq.

ble whether this approach—that did not include any sanction—could have prevented torpedo tactics.[33] The proposal was that the court first seised should provide information about how much time will be needed to make a decision upon request by another court of a Member State. Although this mechanism of notifying a delay could urge the courts to speed up decision-making,[34] that approach was deleted in the proposal of Council and Parliament.[35]

De lege ferenda is has also been proposed to go even beyond the Commission's notification obligation and provide that each court of first instance should be under an obligation to decide on jurisdiction within six months. The respective period would start to run when the court is seised.[36] If necessary, in particular where complex cases are pending, courts could extend the six months period by court order for another six months. Where jurisdiction is established in "six plus six months" from the date the court was seised, other courts must decline jurisdiction. Where jurisdiction is not established within this time, however, the court first seised forfeits jurisdiction if one party brings an action in another court competent within three months after expiration of the "six plus six period".[37] A further six months should be allowed for any appellate court. In comparison with the Commission's proposal, this approach might have been more effective to fight torpedo actions.

On the other hand, any more or less rigid time limits might be regarded as illusionary, taking into account different working speed of courts in the different Member States. Arguably, even forfeiting jurisdiction might not necessarily be regarded as a "sanction" by courts.[38] Moreover, this would constitute a significant interference with national procedural autonomy which the Member States are unlikely to accept.[39]

1.3 Something New Part I: Lis Pendens Rule for Actions Pending in Third States

1.3.1 Starting Point

The effect of lis pendens in a third state was raised in *Owusu*[40] Under the previous EU jurisdiction regime the question had arisen how Member States courts have to

---

[33] For a positive assessment Rogerson 2015, para 11.11.

[34] Domej 2014, p. 532; cf. Heinze 2011a, p. 597; sceptical Lazic 2013, p. 10; Weller 2012a, p. 43.

[35] Cf. Doc. 10609/12 JUSTCIV 209 CODEC 1495 and C7-0433/2010-2010/0383 (COD); see Heinze 2011a, p. 598 et seq.; Weller 2012b, p. 332.

[36] Heinze 2011a, p. 598 et seqq.

[37] Critical insofar Weller 2012a, p. 43.

[38] Weller 2012a, p. 43.

[39] Rogerson 2015, para 11.15.

[40] ECJ 1.3.2005—Case C-281/02 (Owusu), E.C.R. 2005 I-1383, paras 47–52; see Heinze and Dutta 2005, p. 224.

deal with situations in which the same cause of action is already pending in a court of a non-EU Member State at the time a court of a Member State is seised in compliance with Brussels I Regulation. May the court of a Member State stay its proceedings in such a scenario? Since the respective question referred to the ECJ did not need to be answered in Owusu the particular case, practitioners fell back on national law.[41] The national rules are, however, different in the different Member States.

For example, under German[42] and Dutch[43] law courts stay their proceedings if the foreign final judgement is likely to be recognized. In other legal systems (in particular in common law countries such as England and Ireland) foreign *lis alibi pendens* is (only) one factor in a comprehensive *forum non conveniens*[44] analysis.

1.3.2 Recast—Basic Principles

As part of the recast of Brussels I Regulation the EU legislator created separate *lis pendens* rules for actions pending in third States.[45] While Article 33 Brussels Ibis Regulation refers to "the same cause of action" (cf. Article 29), Article 34 Brussels Ibis Regulation deals with "an action which is related to the action in the court of the third State" (cf. 30). As it is uncertain whether the latter provision has significant practical relevance[46] and Article 34 is quite similar in its structure to Article 33, the following remarks concentrate on Article 33.

The wording of Article 33 Brussels Ibis Regulation reads as follows:

> (1) "Where *jurisdiction is based on Article 4 or on Articles 7, 8 or 9* and proceedings *are pending* before a court of a third State *at the time when a court in a Member State is seised* of an action involving the same cause of action and between the same parties as the proceedings in the court of the third State, the court of the Member State *may stay* the proceedings if:
>
> (a) it is expected that the court of the third State will give a judgment *capable of recognition* (...) in that Member State[47]; and
> (b) the court of the Member State is satisfied that a *stay is necessary for the proper administration of justice*.[48]

[41] Heckel 2012, p. 276 and 278; v. Hein 2013, p. 106; Magnus 2011, p. 680; Magnus and Mankowski 2011, p. 287. This may be different however if there are *lis pendens* provisions in international conventions (e.g. Article 31[2] CMR) which may take precedence over the secondary law pursuant to Article 71 Brussels I Reg/Brussels Ibis Regulation.

[42] § 261 (3) ZPO.

[43] Article 12 Dutch Wetboek van Burgerlijke Rechtsvordering.

[44] Regarding this doctrine see Barret 1947, p. 380; Childress 2012, p. 157.

[45] For doubts concerning the need for such harmonisation see Nielsen 2012, p. 263.

[46] Cf. Magnus and Mankowski 2010, p. 19.

[47] Recital 23 Brussels Ibis Regulation: "(...) under the law of that Member State (...)".

[48] Note with regard to an "action which is related to the action in the court of the third State" the further condition in Article 34(1) lit. a Brussels Ibis Regulation.

(2) The court of the Member State *may continue the proceedings at any time* if:

(a) the proceedings in the court of the third State are themselves stayed or discontinued;
(b) it appears to the court of the Member State that the proceedings in the court of the third State are unlikely to be concluded within a reasonable time; or
(c) the continuation of the proceedings is required for the proper administration of justice.

(3) The court of the Member State *shall dismiss the proceedings* if the proceedings in the court of the third State are concluded and have resulted in a judgment capable of recognition and, where applicable, of enforcement in that Member State.
(4) The court of the Member State shall apply this Article on the application of one of the parties or, where possible under national law, of its own motion."[49]

The term "proper administration of justice" is defined in recital 24:

"When taking into account the proper administration of justice, the court of the Member State concerned should assess *all the circumstances of the case* before it. Such circumstances may include connections between the facts of the case and the parties and the third State concerned, the stage to which the proceedings in the third State have progressed by the time proceedings are initiated in the court of the Member State and whether or not the court of the third State can be expected to give a judgment within a reasonable time.

That assessment may also include consideration of the question whether the court of the third State has exclusive jurisdiction in the particular case in circumstances where a court of a Member State would have exclusive jurisdiction."[50]

According to its wording, Article 33 Brussels Ibis Regulation (as well as Article 34 Brussels Ibis Regulation) applies only when jurisdiction is based on Articles 4, 7, 8 or 9 Brussels Ibis Regulation. In other cases, arguably except Article 6 Brussels Ibis Regulation, where national law applies, consideration of pendency in third States is inadmissible.[51]

For the operation of Article 33, it does not matter whether the jurisdiction of the court in the third State is exclusive or non-exclusive.[52] However, pursuant to recital 24(2) Brussels Ibis Regulation, a third State's exclusive jurisdiction deserves special attention.

There is no strict obligation for the courts to stay their proceedings if the requirements of Article 33(1) are met.[53] Rather the courts are left with considerable judicial discretion. This does not only hold true for establishing the rather openly worded requirements of this provision ("proper administration of justice") but concerns also the legal consequences ("may").[54] Moreover, as many relevant

[49] Accentuation by the authors.

[50] Accentuation by the authors.

[51] Domej 2014, p. 538.

[52] Wagner 2015, p. 51.

[53] The same applies to Article 34 Brussels Ibis Regulation.

[54] Critical Magnus and Mankowski 2011, p. 288 et seq. regarding the (even wider) version of the proposal.

aspects are already caught by the prerequisites of Article 33 required to open the discretion to stay, it is difficult to establish a clear division between the prerequisites of a stay and the factors of the court's discretion.

1.3.3 Open Questions

1.3.3.1 Order of Being Seised

Article 33 has been understood to apply only when the court of the Member State is second seised, not when it is first seised.[55] In the latter case, it has been observed that national law continues to apply.[56] This interpretation has been doubted, as the English text is not entirely clear. It reads "when a court in a Member State *is seised*",[57] which is arguably open to an interpretation that Article 33 Brussels Ibis Regulation also applies when the court of the Member State is seised first.[58] At closer sight, however, it seems likely that this is only an inaccuracy in the English text. In comparison to Article 34 No. 1 lit. a of the Commission's proposal[59] which stated that the court of the third State must have been "seised first in time", the final English text of the recast Regulation is admittedly less clear. Nevertheless, the French,[60] German,[61] Italian,[62] Spanish[63] and Dutch[64] versions support the view that Article 33 applies only when the Member State's court is the court second seised.

55 Cadet 2013, p. 220; Heckel 2012, p. 272; Pohl 2013, p. 112.

56 Wagner 2015, p. 52.

57 Accentuation by the authors.

58 Rogerson 2015, para 11.79 et seqq.; see also Magnus 2014, p. 800 et seq.; regarding the COM proposal Magnus 2011, p. 681.

59 Proposal for a Regulation of the European Parliament and the Council on jurisdiction and the recognition and enforcement of judgments in civil and commercial matters (Recast), COM(2010) 748 final, p. 38.

60 "(…)au moment où une juridiction d'un État membre est saisie d'une demande entre les mêmes parties ayant le même objet et la même cause que la demande (…)".

61 "(…) bei Anrufung eines Gerichts eines Mitgliedstaats (…) ein Verfahren vor dem Gericht eines Drittstaates anhängig (…)".

62 "(…)al momento in cui l'autorità giurisdizionale di uno Stato membro è investita di una causa tra le medesime parti, avente il medesimo oggetto e il medesimo titolo del procedimento promosso (…)".

63 "(…) el momento en que se ejercita una acción ante un órgano jurisdiccional de un Estado miembro con el mismo objeto, la misma causa y las mismas partes que en un procedimiento (…)".

64 "(…) op het moment dat een vordering wordt aangebracht bij een gerecht in een lidstaat tussen dezelfde partijen een vordering aanhangig is voor een gerecht van een derde land (…)".

1.3.3.2 Is the Court Allowed to Consider Substantive Law Aspects?

It is unclear whether it is necessary, appropriate or at least allowed under Article 33 that the second seised Member State court takes into account aspects of substantive law (such as the applicable substantive law, shorter limitation periods etc.) in its discretionary decision about a stay or whether the court is restricted to genuinely procedural aspects (e.g. availability of proof and witnesses, but also the safeguard of fundamental procedural guarantees under Article 6 ECHR[65]).[66]

At first glance, it seems that substantive interests cannot be taken into consideration. This seems to result, inter alia, from the fact that recitals 23 and 24 do not explicitly refer to such aspects. In fact, the recitals concentrate on typical matters of judicial administration (recognition and enforcement of judgements; exclusive jurisdiction). On the other hand, the wide wording of recitals 23 ("in particular") and 24 ("the court [...] should assess all the circumstances") could cover also considerations of substantive law. In essence, this question might be part of a broader debate to what extent the interpretation of the Brussels jurisdiction rules is or should be influenced by substantive law aspects.

1.3.3.3 "Proper Administration of Justice", Forum Non Conveniens and Reflexive Effect

A further question is whether the open words "proper administration of justice"[67] imply application of the *forum non conveniens* doctrine[68] or something similar. The doctrine of *forum non conveniens*, traditionally applied in common law countries, allows a court (whose jurisdiction is established under the applicable jurisdictional rules) to decline to hear a case if it finds that it is an inappropriate forum (or that another forum would be more appropriate).[69] After all, it is a mechanism of "judicial fine tuning".[70]

Even if aspects of jurisdiction and *lis alibi pendens* are undeniable linked with each other,[71] the doctrine of *forum non conveniens* has traditionally been regarded with scepticism in the Brussels regime.[72] Not only has it been feared that it would

---

[65] For a discussion of the relevance of Article 6 ECHR in this context Auernig 2015, p. 9.

[66] For the debate see Heinze 2011b, p. 950 and Weber 2011, p. 637.

[67] Lazic 2013, p. 21: "(...) rather vague notion (...)".

[68] See Barret 1947, p. 380; Childress 2012, p. 157.

[69] See in particular *Spiliada Maritime Corporation* v. *Cansulex*, (1987) 1 AC 460 (House of Lords); Brand 2002, p. 471.

[70] Blobel 2005, p. 140.

[71] Weber 2011, p. 635.

[72] Also sceptical Magnus and Mankowski 2011, p. 288 et seq; cf. ECJ 1.3.2005—Case C-281/02 (Owusu), E.C.R. 2005 I-1383, paras 41, 43; see Heinze and Dutta 2005, p. 224; open to this "legal safety valve" v. Hein 2013, p. 106.

undermine the principles of predictability and legal certainty,[73] principles which the ECJ has cherished highly,[74] it has also been stated that *forum non conveniens* ideas do not fit in the EU jurisdiction context at all.[75]

In spite of all these objections, it cannot be denied that the wording of recitals 23 ("flexible mechanism"), 24 ("assess all the circumstances of the case") and Article 33 ("may") makes use of much more flexible notions of jurisdiction. It may thus be argued that the *lis pendens* rule for actions pending in third States introduces some of the elements of the *forum non conveniens* doctrine—considerations of expediency and equity[76]—into the Brussels Ibis Regulation, albeit not the entire doctrine itself.[77]

Moreover, courts can also consider the ideas of the doctrine of reflexive effect within their discretion to stay (see recital 24[3] Brussels Ibis Regulation).[78] This theory is based on reciprocity, self-restraint and comity. It encourages courts to decline their jurisdiction when, under a reflexive application of their own jurisdictional rules, even if these do not apply to the case directly, there would be exclusive jurisdiction in a third State.[79]

It is, after all, undisputed that the term "proper administration of justice" might be difficult to prove.[80] Still, it may be hoped that the autonomous interpretation by the ECJ can gradually increase the certainty of application of this rule.[81]

1.3.3.4 "Same Cause of Action"

Another question is how the words "same cause of action" in Article 33 Brussels Ibis Regulation are to be interpreted. *Prima facie* it is conceivable of applying either the interpretation developed by the ECJ on Article 29[82] or to resort to national law. As Article 33 Brussels Ibis Regulation is—unlike Article 29 Brussels Ibis Regulation—not linked with EU rules on recognition of third State

---

73 Cf. ECJ 1.3.2005—Case C-281/02 (Owusu), E.C.R. 2005 I-1383, paras 41, 43.

74 Cf. ECJ 9.12.2003—Case C-116/02 (Gasser), E.C.R. 2003, I-14693, para 51; ECJ 27.4.2004—Case C-159/02 (Turner), E.C.R. 2004, I-3565, paras 25, 29–31.

75 Blobel 2005, p. 142; Magnus and Mankowski 2010, p. 10; Weber 2011, p. 636 et seq.

76 Cf. Heckel 2012, p. 280.

77 Rogerson 2015, para 11.78; Crawford/Carruthers 2013, p. 93: "(…) an unusual notion in a civilian inspired instrument".

78 Cf. Zhang 2014, p. 3 et seq.; in general disapproved of Magnus and Mankowski 2010, p. 5 et seq.: "inadvisable".

79 Zhang 2014, p. 3 et seq.

80 Magnus and Mankowski 2011, p. 271.

81 Rogerson 2015, para 11.78.

82 ECJ 8.12.1987—Case C-144/86 (Gubisch), E.C.R. 1987, 4861, paras 14–19; EJC 6.12.1994—Case C-406/92 (Tatry), E.C.R. 1994, I-5439, paras 29–48.

judgements, it may be argued that the "same cause of action" is defined by the national law, which applies also to the recognition of third states' judgments. On the other hand, given its reluctance to accept an interpretation of EU provisions from a national law perspective, it may be that the ECJ will prefer extending its autonomous interpretation of the same term in Article 29 to Article 33 Brussels Ibis Regulation, even if the provisions stand in a different context.

1.3.3.5 (Expectation of) Recognition of Third State Decisions

As concerns the expectation of recognition of third State decisions, divergence is unavoidable as recognition of third State decisions depends on national law.[83] This could only be avoided by adopting EU-provisions dealing with recognition of third State decisions *de lege ferenda*.[84]

1.3.3.6 Jurisdiction Pursuant to Articles 10–25 Brussels Ibis

Article 33 pre-empts national *lis pendens* provisions if jurisdiction is based on Articles 4, 7, 8, 9 Brussels Ibis Regulation. As concerns Articles 10–25 Brussels Ibis, it is unclear whether an action pending in a third state may influence the exercise of jurisdiction under these provisions. Arguably consideration of pendency in third States is inadmissible in these cases.[85]

1.3.3.7 "Pending"

The term "pending" has to be given an autonomous interpretation in the light of Article 32, recital 21 sentences 2, 3 Brussels Ibis Regulation.[86]

1.3.3.8 Suspension of Prescription

If proceedings in a Member State are initiated, Article 12 lit. d Rome I Reg determines the law applicable to suspension of prescription periods (i.e. substantive law governing the issue, e.g. contract).

---

[83] Auernig 2015, p. 8.

[84] Cf. Heckel 2012, p. 279 et seq.

[85] Domej 2014, p. 538.

[86] Lazic 2013, p. 19; Nielsen 2013, p. 518.

1.3.4 Conclusions

On the whole, the new provisions are to be welcomed.[87] Given the intensive debate about the protection of jurisdiction agreements, it is unclear why a solution similar to Article 31(2)–(4) Brussels Ibis Regulation was not adopted in the context of Article 33 (respectively Article 34) Brussels Ibis Regulation.[88] Probably the EU hoped to solve this problem by ratifying the Hague Choice of Court Convention.

1.4 Something New Part II: Priority for the Court Chosen to Decide on Jurisdiction

1.4.1 Starting Point

After the ECJ held in *Gasser* that the *lis pendens* rule in Article 27 Brussels I Regulation

> must be interpreted as meaning that a court second seised whose jurisdiction has been claimed under an agreement conferring jurisdiction must nevertheless stay proceedings until the court first seised has declared that it has no jurisdiction,[89]

a controversial discussion began. In this debate, which lasted for years, the focus has been on the disadvantages resulting from a strict *lis pendens* rule.[90] While such a rule fosters legal certainty, prevents parallel proceedings and attests every Member State court the same expertise, it may suffer from abuse.

Claimants acting in bad faith could take the case to a typically slow court not having jurisdiction, thereby blocking proceedings in the competent court and trying to force a settlement in the meantime (so called "torpedo"). Needless to say that these abusive litigation tactics had the negative side effect that the will of the parties as articulated in their jurisdiction agreement could not adequately be implemented in practice. The predictability of jurisdiction (that choice of court agreements should increase) was compromised by such abuse.[91]

As the Court of Justice had also ruled out anti-suit injunctions[92] as a potential antidote,[93] even where abusive behaviour was debatable,[94] the discussion concen-

[87] Magnus and Mankowski 2011, p. 287.

[88] Rogerson 2015, para 11.82.

[89] ECJ 9.12.2003—Case C-116/02 (Gasser), E.C.R 2003, I-14693, para 54.

[90] See above in general 1.2.3.

[91] Mankowski 2015, p. 17.

[92] This is a court order that aims to prevent an opposing party from seising another forum or continuing a respective proceeding.

[93] ECJ, 10.2.2009—Case C-185/07 (Allianz, Generali/West Tankers), E.C.R. 2009, I-663, para 34.

[94] ECJ 27.4.2004—Case C-159/02 (Turner), E.C.R. 2004, I-3565, para 31.

trated on means to enhance the effectiveness of jurisdiction agreements.[95] Against this background, the recast of the Brussels I Regulation provides for an exception to the general *lis pendens* rule.

1.4.2 Recast—Basic Principles

As a starting point, jurisdiction agreements have no legal effect if the rule on exclusive jurisdiction in Article 24 Brussels Ibis Regulation applies.[96] In this regard, ECJ Case *Weber*[97] regarding *lis pendens* between Member States' courts and Article 33(1), recital 24(2) Brussels Ibis Regulation[98] concerning third States' courts have to be kept in mind. Moreover, Article 31(1) Brussels Ibis Regulation preserves the basic *prior tempore* rule of Article 29(1) Brussels Ibis Regulation for the (rather rare) cases where pending actions fall within the exclusive jurisdiction of several courts.

As an innovation of the Brussels I recast, Article 31(2) and recital 22 Brussels Ibis Regulation give precedence to the courts of a Member State[99] chosen by an exclusive[100] jurisdiction agreement over other courts (apart from exclusive jurisdiction pursuant to Article 24 Brussels Ibis Regulation), even if the other court has been seised first.[101] This is an explicit exception to the basic *lis pendens* rule.[102] The precedence of the prorogated court was established in order to prevent parties from taking the case to a typically slow court not having jurisdiction where they

---

[95] Proposal for a Regulation of the European Parliament and the Council on jurisdiction and the recognition and enforcement of judgments in civil and commercial matters (Recast), COM(2010) 748 final, p. 9.

[96] Queirolo 2013/2014, p. 130 et seq.

[97] Below 1.2.2.1.

[98] Below 1.3.2.

[99] Jurisdiction agreements in favour of third State courts are subject to the discretionary rules of Article 33, 34 Brussels Ibis Regulation; see Mankowski 2015, p. 23 et seq.; Rogerson 2015, para 11.82; Zhang 2014, p. 4 et seqq.; cf. also Magnus 2011, p. 680 et seq.; Schaper and Eberlein 2012, p. 43. The *ratio decidendi* of ECJ 9.11.2000—Case C-387/98 (Coreck) E.C.R. 2000, I-9337, para 19 seems to suggest such a discretionary power. A question not settled in the recast is how to proceed in a case in which a court of a third State is prorogated but not seised yet. It seems reasonable to apply national law (Pohl 2013, p. 112). However, one has to take into consideration that a derogation of jurisdiction grounds based on Brussels Ibis Regulation in the light of the *effet utile* principle might be inadmissible.

[100] Note the legal presumption in Article 25(1) sentence 2 Brussels Ibis Regulation.

[101] See also Article 29(1) Brussels Ibis Regulation: "Without prejudice to Article 31(2) (…)".

[102] Note Wagner 2015, p. 51, whereas this exception of the priority rule does not cover "related actions" (Article 30 Brussels Ibis Regulation).

apply for a declaration that the claimed right does not exist[103] (so called "torpedo").[104] In the former version of the Brussels I Regulation, a comparable concept of precedence for the prorogated court to assume its jurisdiction under the choice of court agreement could be found in Article 23(3) Brussels I Regulation only.[105]

In a broader context, one may characterise the new provisions of Article 31(2)–(4) as "something borrowed" since Article 31(2)–(4) Brussels Ibis Regulation are similar, though not identical to Article 6 Hague Choice of Court Convention.[106], [107] This provision reads as follows:

> A court of a Contracting State other than that of the chosen court shall suspend or dismiss proceedings to which an exclusive choice of court agreement applies unless a) the agreement is null and void under the law of the State of the chosen court; b) a party lacked the capacity to conclude the agreement under the law of the State of the court seised; c) giving effect to the agreement would lead to a manifest injustice or would be manifestly contrary to the public policy of the State of the court seised; d) for exceptional reasons beyond the control of the parties, the agreement cannot reasonably be performed; or e) the chosen court has decided not to hear the case.

In contrast to Article 6 Hague Choice of Court Convention, the obligation to stay for courts not chosen does not allow[108] these courts "to decide on the validity of the agreement and on the extent to which the agreement applies to the dispute" (recital 22 sentence four Brussels Ibis Regulation). This difference to the Hague approach may be regarded, if we want to carry to analogy to the wedding proverb further, as "something blue" as it is a specific feature of the EU provision. Whether this monopolisation of the decision on validity of the jurisdiction agreement with the chosen court is a limitation of the principle of mutual trust[109] or not[110] need not be decided here.

---

[103] Negative declaratory action ("negative Feststellungsklage"); see ECJ 25.10.2012—Case C-133/11 [Folien Fischer AG], para 55.

[104] Pohl 2013, p. 111.

[105] Auernig 2015, p. 8.

[106] Convention on Choice of Court Agreements, concluded 30 June 2005; available online at: http://www.hcch.net/upload/conventions/txt37en.pdf.

[107] Crawford and Carruthers 2013, p. 91; v. Hein 2013, p. 104; Hess 2011, pp. 127 and 129.

[108] Contrary to Article 6 lit. a, b Hague Choice of Court convention, Article 31(2) Brussels Ibis Regulation provides that the non-chosen court must stay proceedings until the chosen court has established jurisdiction, whereas Article 6 lit. a of the Convention permits the non-chosen court to determine the validity and effect of a jurisdiction agreement. in this respect the approaches of the two instruments are different; see Beaumont and Mc Eleavy 2011, para 8.122.

[109] Pohl 2013, p. 111.

[110] Radicati di Brozolo 2010, p. 123: "(…) perfectly compatible with the spirit of mutual trust (…)".

Once a court chosen in a jurisdiction agreement has established its jurisdiction on the basis of the choice of court agreement,[111] the court first seised must decline jurisdiction pursuant to Article 31(3) Brussels Ibis Regulation. The court chosen in the jurisdiction agreement may conduct its proceedings even if it is the court second seised and irrespective of whether the non-designated court has already decided on the stay of proceedings (recital 22 sentence 5). The (allegedly) derogated court may continue its proceedings if the "chosen" court decides that the choice of court agreement is void.[112]

There are, however, some reverse exceptions, for which the general rule of Article 29 et seq. Brussels Ibis Regulation continues to apply. This is the case first when conflicting exclusive choice of court agreements exist (recital 22 sentence 6, 7), secondly, where the defendant has entered appearance in the court not chosen (Article 31[2] in connection with Article 26 Brussels Ibis Regulation) and thirdly where the jurisdiction agreements are invoked to the detriment of the "weaker" party and the jurisdiction clause is therefore ineffective (Article 31[4] Brussels Ibis Regulation).

1.4.3 Open Questions

The main advantage of the new *lex lata* in comparison to the previous legal situation is that it strengthens jurisdiction agreements and the parties' reasonable expectations when they formed this agreement.[113] Nevertheless, some open questions remain.[114]

1.4.3.1 Preventing "Reversed Torpedoes" by Prima Facie Examination?

First, one may ask whether the court first seised may scrutinise whether "an agreement as referred to in Article 25 [which] confers exclusive jurisdiction" as required by Article 31(2) Brussels Ibis Regulation actually exists. Under the present wording, such a reading is possible.[115] On the other hand, recital 22 sentence 4 assigns the competence to decide about the *validity* of the agreement to the

---

[111] This does not apply if the alleged chosen court is competent due to another jurisdiction rule. In this respect, the ordinary *lis pendens* mechanism applies; v. Hein 2013, p. 104; Nielsen 2012, p. 268.

[112] Magnus 2014, p. 798; Mankowski 2015, p. 23.

[113] Heinze 2011a, p. 588; Radicati di Brozolo 2010, p. 123.

[114] See Heinze 2011a, p. 588 et seqq.

[115] Hohmeier 2014, p. 218; Lazic 2013, p. 14.

designated court. Still, it has been argued that recital 22 does not concern the pre-stages of a jurisdiction agreement, permitting it for the court not chosen to scrutinise the question whether the parties *factually consented* to the contract.[116] On the other end of the spectrum, it may be pointed out that recital 22 sentences 4 and 5 and the *ratio legis* of Article 31(2) Brussels Ibis Regulation may be understood to militate against any competence of the court not chosen to rule on the existence, validity and scope of the jurisdiction agreement.[117]

This position, in turn, could result in a wasteful duplication of proceedings and abusive tactics in those instances where an "innocent" party has to establish that it is not bound[118] by a jurisdiction agreement in the (allegedly) chosen court first before being permitted to seise the competent court.[119] It would be quite easy to prolong proceedings via the assertion "we have made a valid agreement" and the presentation of a form that, at first glance, meets (or even does not meet) the requirements of Article 25(1) sentence 3 Brussels Ibis Regulation.[120] In other words, since Article 31(2) Brussels Ibis Regulation does not give a clear answer for such scenarios, there is a risk of a "reversed torpedo"[121] or at least a risk of legal uncertainty.[122]

Possible Solutions *de Lege Ferenda*

There are different approaches how to resolve this problem *de lege ferenda*. To put it briefly[123]: A first option would be to follow the model of Article 6 Hague Choice of Court Convention. Under this approach, a court other than the chosen one would not be excluded from ruling on the validity of the agreement, capacity of the parties etc. Rather, the existence of a jurisdiction agreement would in effect only release the court designated in an exclusive choice of court agreement from its obligation to stay proceedings under the *lis pendens* rule.

A second option would be to allow the (allegedly) chosen court to deviate from the *lis pendens* rule "only where there is no room for any doubt as to the

116 Hohmeier 2014, p. 218.

117 *Mankowski*, RIW 2015, 17, 21.

118 E.g. a party rightfully challenges the agreement.

119 Doubting the empirical evidence of abuse Heinze 2011a, p. 588 et seq.

120 AG Léger 9.9.2003, Case C-116/02 (Gasser), ECLI:EU:C:2003:436, para 74; cf. also Domej 2014, p. 535; v. Hein 2013, p. 104 et seq.; Hohmeier 2014, p. 219. The Heidelberg Report suggested that creating a standard form of choice of court agreement could minimise the risk of abuse (Report on the Application of regulation Brussels I in the Member States [Heidelberg Report], Study JLS/C4/2005/03, Final Version September 2007, para 494); sceptical Magnus and Mankowski 2010, p. 14: "device for the knowing only".

121 Pohl 2013, p. 112.

122 Heinze, 2011a, p. 590: "battle of forms"; Mankowski 2015, p. 21.

123 Heinze 2011a, p. 591 et seqq.

jurisdiction of the court second seised"[124] and when the court first seised comes to the same result. Such an approach, however, could lead to inconsistent application and finally to a race to a first judgement on jurisdiction.

A third idea[125] would impose on the court first seised a duty to clarify within a certain time whether the defendant submits to its jurisdiction. This court shall transfer the case *ex officio* to the chosen one and stay its proceedings if no such declaration is made. The parties could continue proceedings at the court first seised only if the choice of court agreement was found to be void.

A further and (from the authors perspective) arguably best option would be to spell out in Article 31(2) Brussels Ibis Regulation explicitly the requirements which trigger priority of the chosen court. A possible wording has already been proposed by the lead author elsewhere[126] as follows:

> "With the exception of agreements governed by Sects. 3, 4 and 5 of this Chapter, where jurisdiction is contested on the basis of an exclusive choice of court agreement which
>
> a) meets the formal requirements of Article 25 and
> b) to which the parties have consented or in which they have succeeded according to the applicable national law,
>
> the courts of the Member State first seised shall stay proceedings once the courts of the Member State designated in the agreement have been seised of proceedings to determine, as their main object or as an incidental question, whether the agreement confers exclusive jurisdiction to them. Once this jurisdiction is established, the court first seised shall decline jurisdiction. This paragraph shall not apply if jurisdiction is not contested within three months of the defendant having been served with the document instituting the proceedings."

Solving the Problem *de Lege Lata*

Allowing a Narrow Prima Facie Evaluation Seems Preferable

In order to solve the problem *de lege lata* it seems convincing to allow the court first seised a *prima facie* evaluation of the effectiveness of the choice of court agreement.[127] Otherwise, the court first seised would have to stay its proceedings

---

[124] Opinion of AG Léger 9.9.2003 – Case C-116/02 (Gasser), ECLI:EU:C:2003:436, para 82; similar Fentiman 2005, p. 256.

[125] Magnus and Mankowski 2010, p. 19.

[126] See in detail Heinze 2011a, p. 593 et seqq.; cf. also Article 1448 French Code de procedure civile: "Lorsqu'un litige relevant d'une convention d'arbitrage est porté devant une juridiction de l'Etat, celle-ci se déclare incompétente sauf si le tribunal arbitral n'est pas encore saisi et si la convention d'arbitrage est *manifestement nulle ou manifestement inapplicable*" (accentuation by the authors).

[127] Domej 2014, p. 536; Garcimartin 2015, para 11.50; v. Hein 2013, p. 105 takes the view that unsubstantiated statements cannot "activate" Article 31(2) Brussels Ibis Regulation; at least open for such a view Magnus and Mankowski 2011, p. 280; different opinion Mankowski 2015, p. 22; Nielsen 2013, p. 520; Nielsen 2012, p. 268; Radicati di Brozolo 2010, p. 124: "no exception".

even in cases where it is quite clear, perhaps even beyond doubt that there is no jurisdiction agreement or that such an agreement is manifestly void. It would be contradictory to leave the court first seised the room to become active in a case of conflicting agreements but not in the case of evidently void or even non-existent agreements. Another argument is that the Brussels Ibis Regulation seems to abandon the previous formal approach and rather aims at integrating more elements of equity into the formal analysis. This is particularly evident in the term "proper administration of justice" and the judicial discretion regarding a stay of proceedings in third State situations.[128]

Defining the Scope of Scrutiny

If we accept the idea that a certain *prima facie* evaluation should be permitted for the court first seised, the question arises how to define this power of scrutiny of the court first seised. In general, one may easily agree that the scope ought to be rather narrow, as otherwise the reform of the *lis pendens* rules in the context of choice of court agreements would be rendered ineffective.

What complicates the answer in detail is however the fact that demarcations between formal and substantive validity are difficult.[129] Thus, one cannot simply propose to give the authority to the court first seised to decide about formal but not about substantive validity. As a possible solution, it seems advisable to grant a margin of judicial scrutiny to the court first seised only in cases of manifest invalidity, inexistence or inapplicability of the respective clause. In all other cases a power of scrutiny should be denied. To put it more precisely: the starting point should be that jurisdiction is contested and that the defendant offers evidence that another court of a Member State is seised on the basis of a choice of court agreement. This could be done by presenting respective copies.[130] Moreover, a possible means of direct communication between the courts involved would be desirable.[131]

The court first seised should then be allowed to review *only* whether the formal requirements of Article 25 Brussels Ibis Regulation are met and exceptions under Article 31(4) do not apply.[132] One may restrict this right by reducing the review to a first glance impression, namely without obtaining further evidence. If the non-chosen court cannot rule out that a jurisdiction clause exists after this first glance, it should stay its proceedings and wait for the decision of the prorogated court.[133] This seems to be an effective but not an exuberant standard of review as the final

[128] See 3.2–3.3.

[129] Auernig 2015, p. 7; Garcimartin 2015, para 9.69.

[130] Garcimartin 2015, para 11.50.

[131] Garcimartin 2015, para 11.50.

[132] Similar in his results Hohmeier 2014, p. 219; cf. Pohl 2013, p. 112 at footnote 43; less far-reaching cf. Domej 2014, p. 534.

[133] Different opinion Garcimartin 2015, para 11.52: "(…) ask the parties to provide further information or (…) communicate directly with the designated court."

scrutiny is reserved to the chosen court. Nevertheless, satisfaction of the formal prerequisites laid down in 23 Brussels I Regulation (Article 25 Brussels Ibis Regulation) constitutes an indication or even a presumption of the existence of consent itself.[134] This approach could also make it more acceptable to grant priority to the (presumably) chosen court with regard to third party cases, as third parties could at least argue that those minimum requirements are not fulfilled.[135] Besides, a limitation to those aspects reduces the risk of conflicting judgements.[136]

On the other hand, it would be too far-reaching to allow the court first seised the power to check whether the parties have actually consented or whether they have succeeded in the position of an earlier party to the jurisdiction agreement according to the applicable national law. As the court has to determine the applicable law in accordance with Article 25(1) sentence 1 Brussels Ibis and thus resort to the (private international)[137] law of the chosen court's Member State (cf. recital 20 Brussels Ibis Regulation), succession into earlier parties' rights and obligations is quite a complex[138] assessment which should be reserved to the chosen court. The same applies to the *detailed* examination of whether the requirements of Article 25 Brussels Ibis have been met and of the exact scope of the agreement.

1.4.3.2 Time Limits or Preclusions?

The defendant must contest[139] jurisdiction of the court first seised in compliance with Articles 31(2) and 26 Brussels Ibis Regulation, which deal with tacit prorogation (submission by appe-arance). If the defendant contests jurisdiction "in time", it is unclear what happens if the defendant does not seise the chosen court (even until appellate procedure). Article 31(2) Brussels Ibis Regulation does not stipulate a time limit. Merely contesting jurisdiction does not force the court first seised

---

[134] Pro presumption Garcimartin 2015, para 9.36 with further references.

[135] Heinze 2011a, p. 594.

[136] This seems, however, reasonable *de lege ferenda*, see Heinze 2011a, p. 595.

[137] Skeptical Hay 2013, p. 3: The reference to the conflict of law rules would not make any sense, as the chosen forum must be a Member State that has to apply Rome I Regulation, which is why this legal act a priori could have been set by the EU legislation. However, Article 1(2) lit. e Rome I Reg provides that choice of court agreements do not fall within the scope of this Regulation. Nevertheless, it is preferable to apply the Rome I Regulation by virtue of analogy in case the previous provisions (Article 27 et seqq. EGBGB from a German perspective) are not in force anymore (cf. Staudinger and Steinrötter 2015, p. 4). Otherwise, national conflict of law rules apply.

[138] Certainly, in practice the law of the chosen court often converges with the law of the choice of court agreement, Garcimartin 2015, para 9.63.

[139] The court does not have an *ex officio* obligation in this respect; cf. Magnus 2011, p. 678 et seq.

to stay its proceedings.[140] If one party contests jurisdiction without seising the designated court, the Brussels Ibis Regulation allows the derogated court to decide about the effectiveness of the jurisdiction agreement.[141] If the defendant seises the chosen court late, for example in the appellate procedure, in principle the not chosen court must still stay its proceedings.[142] In such a situation, it has been proposed that the court first seised can resort to its national rules on preclusion.[143], [144]

1.4.3.3 Decision of the Derogated Court

If the derogated court decides the case in spite of the jurisdiction agreement or in the opinion that it is void, it is likely that the chosen court has to recognise this decision.[145] As the Brussels Ibis Regulation does not provide for sanctions for non-compliance with the obligations to stay proceedings or to decline jurisdiction, a decision by the derogated court will probably have to be recognised in compliance with Article 45 Brussels Ibis Regulation. In this respect, a (at least theoretical) risk of abuse remains,[146] which could only be overcome by creating an unwritten exception to recognition on the basis of the purpose of Article 31(2) Brussels Ibis Regulation.

1.4.3.4 Conclusions

The exception to the *lis pendens* provisions in favour of exclusive choice of court agreements is likely to reduce the risk of abusive litigation tactics such as the institution of proceedings for negative declaratory relief. There is still little room for a "reversed torpedo". One may minimise this risk by granting the courts first seised a power of *prima facie* evaluation of the effectiveness of the jurisdiction agreement. This scrutiny should include a first glance-review whether the formal requirements of Article 25 Brussels Ibis are met and exceptions under Article 31(4) do not apply. The allegedly derogated court shall be competent not to stay its proceedings only if there is no doubt about the fact that those requirements are not

140 Queirolo 2013/2014, p. 133 seems to tend as well in this direction. In the opinion of Garcimartin 2015, para 11.56 the court first seised may allow the contesting defendant in the light of the *effet utile*-principle to seise the designated court within "a reasonable period of time". At the same time, the non-chosen court could stay its proceedings.

141 Domej 2014, p. 533; Mankowski 2015, p. 19.

142 Auernig 2015, p. 8; Domej 2014, p. 533; Mankowski 2015, p. 23.

143 E.g. § 296 ZPO.

144 Mankowski 2015, p. 19; skeptical Domej 2014, p. 533 et seq.

145 Mankowski 2015, p. 21; uncertain Rogerson 2015, para 11.27.

146 Garcimartin 2015, para 11.53.

fulfilled. If there is any doubt, it must stay its proceedings and wait for the decision of the allegedly prorogated court.

1.5 Something New Part III: Notification and Recording Obligations

Finally, upon request by a court seised of the dispute, any other court seised shall immediately inform the former court of the date when it was seised.[147] Although an example of judicial cooperation and coordination, practice will show how effective this mechanism will work. Problems could occur with regard to reviewing or even correcting powers of the court that obtained the information.[148] Moreover courts have an obligation to record the relevant pending date pursuant to Article 32(2) Brussels Ibis Regulation.

1.6 Summary

1.6.1 Overview

In the light of the English wedding saying one finds "something old" (the general priority rule as such is maintained), "something new" (*lis pendens* rules for actions pending in third States are introduced; courts chosen by a jurisdiction agreement take precedence over the general *lis pendens* rule; notification and recording obligations are introduced), "something borrowed" (the concept of Article 31[2]–[4] Brussels Ibis Regulation is similar to Article 6 Hague Choice of Court Convention) and "something blue" (the EU specific principle of mutual trust is stressed) in the Brussels Ibis Regulation.

1.6.2 Overall Assessment of the Recast Version of the Lis Pendens System

All in all, the modifications of the *lis pendens*-system are—along with the judgement of the ECJ in *Weber*[149]—undoubtedly an improvement. Namely the reversal

[147] Article 29(2), 32 Brussels Ibis Regulation; cf. also Article 31 of the Commission's proposal, which laid down certain obligations to cooperate and inform the other courts involved in the interplay between proceedings as to the substance and an application for provisional measures.

[148] Rogerson 2015, paras 11.01, 11.28.

[149] See 1.2.2.1.

of the general *lis pendence* rule in favour of jurisdiction agreements is to be welcomed, as this is likely to reduce the risk of abusive litigation tactics. The same applies to the new third State provisions. Certainly, the new system is much more complex[150] than the previous one. The cost is, however, justified.

1.6.3 Open Questions

However, *de lege lata* there are some open questions left. According to the view advanced here (and restricted to the main issues) they may be answered as follows:

- The term "proper administration of justice" (Article 33[1] lit. b Brussels Ibis Regulation) introduces some of the aspects of the *forum non conveniens* analysis (considerations of expediency and equity) in the Brussels Ibis Regulation.
- In order to prevent "reversed torpedo actions" it seems reasonable to grant the first seised (allegedly) derogated court *prima facie* scrutiny powers regarding the choice of court agreement. This evaluation should contain a first glance-review whether the formal requirements of Article 25 Brussels Ibis Regulation are met and exceptions under Article 31(4) Brussels Ibis Regulation do not apply. If the court first seised has any doubts, it must stay its proceedings and wait for the decision of the (allegedly) prorogated court.
- As Article 31(2) Brussels Ibis Regulation does not stipulate a time limit for the defendant seising the chosen court (even until appellate procedure), it may be considered to apply national rules on preclusion.

References

Alio T (2014) Die Neufassung der Brüssel I-Verordnung. Neue Juristische Wochenschrift, pp 2395–2400

Auernig K (2015) First come, first serve? Gerichtsstandsvereinbarungen und Anhängigkeit nach der neuen EuGVVO. ecolex 26:6–9

Barret EL (1947) The doctrine of forum non conveniens. Californian Law Rev 35:380–422

Beaumont PR, Mc Eleavy PE (2011) Private International Law A.E. Anton. Scottish Universities Law Institute, Edinburgh

Blobel F (2005) Unzulässigkeit der forum non conveniens-Doktrin im Europäischen Zivilprozessrecht – EuGH, Urteil vom 1. März 2005, Rs. C-281/02 – Owusu. Gemeinschafts Privat Recht, pp 140–142

Brand RA (2002) Comparative forum non conveniens and the Hague convention on jurisdiction and judgments. Texas Int Law J 37:467–498

Cadet F (2013) Main features of the revised Brussels I regulation. Europäische Zeitschrift für Wirtschaftsrecht, pp 218–223

Childress DEIII (2012) Forum conveniens: the search for a convenient forum in transnational cases. Virginia J Int Law 53:157–180

[150] This is demonstrated clearly by the scheme described below: 6.3.

Crawford EB, Carruthers JM (2013) Brussels Ibis—the Brussels regulation recast: closure (for the foreseeable future). Scotts Law Times 12:89–95
Dittrich L (2014) Auswirkung der EuGVVO-Reform auf Gerichtsstandsklauseln und Schiedsverfahren. Europäisches Wirtschafts- und Steuerrecht, pp 217–220
Domej T (2014) Die Neufassung der EuGVVO, Quantensprünge im europäischen Zivilprozessrecht. Rabel J Comp Int Private Law 78(3):508–550
Fentiman R (2005) Comment on case C-116/02 (Gasser). Common Market Law Rev 42:241–259
Garcimartin P (2015) Prorogation of jurisdiction—choice of court agreements and submission (Arts. 25–26); Lis Pendens and related actions (Arts. 29–34). In: Dickinson A, Lein E (eds) The Brussels I regulation recast. Commentary. Oxford University Press
Hau W (2014) Brüssel Ia-VO – Neue Regeln für die Anerkennung und Vollstreckung ausländischer Entscheidungen in Zivil- und Handelssachen. Monatsschrift fr Deutsches Recht 68:1417–1421
Hay P (1-2013) Notes on the European Union's Brussels-I "Recast" Regulation. Eur Legal Forum 13:1–36
Heckel M (2012) Beachtung ausländischer Rechtshängigkeit in Drittstaatenfällen – ein Beitrag zu Art. 34 EuGVO-E. Gemeinschafts Privat Recht, pp 272–282
Heinze C (2011a) Choice of court agreements, coordination of proceedings and provisional measures in the reform of the Brussels I regulation. Rabel J Comp Int Private Law 75(3):581–618
Heinze C (2011b) Surf global, sue local! Der europäische Klägergerichtsstand bei Persönlichkeitsrechtsverletzungen im Internet. Europäische Zeitschrift für Wirtschaftsrecht, pp 947–951
Heinze C, Dutta A (2005) Ungeschriebene Grenzen für europäische Zuständigkeiten bei Streitigkeiten mit Drittstaatenbezug. Praxis des Internationalen Privat- und Verfahrensrecht (vol):224–230
Hess B (2011) Die Reform der EuGVVO und die Zukunft des Europäischen Zivilprozessrechts. Praxis des Internationalen Privat- und Verfahrensrecht, pp 125–130
Hohmeier (2014) Zur Privilegierung ausschließlicher Zuständigkeitsvereinbarungen durch die Brüssel Ia-VO. Internationales Handelsrecht 14:217–225
Illmer M (2011) Brussels I and arbitration revisited—The European Commission's Proposal COM (2010) 748 final –. Rabel J Comp Int Private Law 75:645–670
Lazic V (2013) The revised Lis Pendens-rule in the Brussels jurisdiction regulation. Revija za evropsko pravo XV:5–26
Lenaerts K, Stapper T (2014) Die Entwicklung der Brüssel I-Verordnung im Dialog des Europäischen Gerichtshofs mit dem Gesetzgeber. Rabel J Comp Int Private Law 78:252–293
Magnus U, Mankowski P (2010) Brussels I on the verge of reform—a response tot he green paper on the review of the Brussels I regulation. Zeitschrift fr Vergleichende Rechtswissenschaft 109:1–41
Magnus U (2011) Gerichtsstandsvereinbarungen im Vorschlag zur Reform der EuGVO. In: Kronke H, Thorn K (eds) Grenzen überwinden—Prinzipien bewahren. Festschrift für Bernd von Hoffmann zum 70. Geburtstag. Gieseking, Bielefeld
Magnus U, Mankowski P (2011) The proposal for the reform of Brussels I—Brussels Ibis ante portas. Zeitschrift fr Vergleichende Rechtswissenschaft 110:252–301
Magnus U (2014) Gerichtsstandsvereinbarungen unter der reformierten EuGVO. In: Witzleb N, Ellger R, Mankowski P, Merkt H, Remien O (eds) Festschrift für Dieter Martiny zum 70. Geburtstag. Mohr Siebeck, Tübingen
Mankowski P (2015) Der Schutz von Gerichtsstandsvereinbarungen vor abredewidrigen Klagen durch Art. 31 Abs. 2 EuGVVO n.F. Recht des Internationalen Wirtschaft, pp 17–24
Mari L, Pretelli I (2013/2014) Possibility and terms for applying the Brussels I regulation (recast) to extra-EU disputes. In: Yearb Private Int Law 15:211–253
Moses M (2014) Arbitration/litigation interface: The European debate. Northwest J Int Law Bus 35(1):1–47

Nielsen P (2012) The recast of the Brussels I regulation. In: Bonell MJ (ed) Liber amicorum Ole Lando. Marie-Louise Holle; Peter Arnt Nielsen. Djøf, København, pp 257–276
Nielsen P (2013) The new Brussels I regulation. Common Market Law Rev 20:503–528
Nordmeier CF (2015) Verfahrenskoordination nach Art. 27 EuGVVO bei ausschließlichen Gerichtsständen – zugleich zur Reichweite des Art. 22 Nr. 1 EuGVVO. Praxis des Internationalen Privat- und Verfahrensrecht (vol):120–121
Pohl M (2013) Die Neufassung der EuGVVO – im Spannungsfeld zwischen Vertrauen und Kontrolle. Praxis des Internationalen Privat- und Verfahrensrecht 33:109–114
Queirolo I (2013/2014) Choice of court agreements in the new Brussels I-bis regulation: a critical appraisal. In: Yearb Private Int Law 15:113–142
Radicati di Brozolo LG (2010) Choice of court and arbitration agreements and the review of the Brussels I regulation. Praxis des Internationalen Privat- und Verfahrensrecht, pp 121–128
Rogerson P (2015) Lis Pendens and related actions (Arts. 29–34). In: Dickinson A, Lein E (eds) The Brussels I regulation recast. Commentary. Oxford University Press
Schaper M, Eberlein C-P (2012) Die Behandlung von Drittstaaten-Gerichtsstandsvereinbarungen vor europäischen Gerichten – de lege lata und le lege ferenda. Recht des Internationalen Wirtschaft, pp 43–49
Schramm D (2013/2014) Enforcement and the abolition of exequatur under the 2012 Brussels I regulation. Yearb Private Int Law 15:143–174
Seatzu F (2013/2014) A plea for civil remedy: the municipal implementation of fundamental rights provisions in the framework of regulation (EU) No 1215/2012. Yearb Private Int Law 15:175–210
Staudinger A, Steinrötter B (2015) Das neue Zuständigkeitsregime bei zivilrechtlichen Auslandssachverhalten. JuS (full name) 55:1–8
von Hein J (2013) Die Neufassung der Europäischen Gerichtsstands- und Vollstreckungsverordnung. Recht des Internationalen Wirtschaft 59:97–111
Wagner R (2015) Die Brüssel Ia-Verordnung. Praktisch bedeutsame Unterschiede zur Vorfassung. Transportsrecht, pp 45–56
Weber J (2011) Universal jurisdiction and third states in the reform of the Brussels I regulation. Rabel J Comp Int Private Law 75:619–644
Weller M (2012a) Der Kommissionsentwurf zur Reform der Brüssel I-VO. Gemeinschafts Privat Recht, pp 34–44
Weller M (2012b) Der Ratsentwurf und der Parlamentsentwurf zur Reform der Brüssel I-VO. Gemeinschafts Privat Recht, pp 328–333
Zhang H (2014) The new Lis Pendens regime in the regulation Brussels I Bis and the challenge met by Chinese jurisdiction. doi:10.17103/reei.28.13

Chapter 2
The Party Autonomy Paradigm: European and Global Developments on Choice of Forum

Xandra Kramer and Erlis Themeli

Abstract One of the pillars of international commercial litigation is party autonomy as it has developed over the past fifty years. In Europe, the Brussels regime established considerable freedom for parties to select the court that would have jurisdiction. The enforceability of choice of court agreements has gained ground in many countries worldwide, and the freedom to select the competent forum is exercised widely in commercial practice. Early in 2015, the new Brussels Ibis Regulation became applicable, altering the rules on choice of court. These amendments, particularly the exception to the lis pendens rule, aim at increasing the efficiency of choice of court agreements and at preventing torpedo litigation tactics. This year also marks the entry into force of the Hague Choice of Court Convention that had been adopted ten years earlier. The present paper explores the concept and development of the party autonomy paradigm from the perspective of different disciplines, and discusses the empirical evidence available on the use of party autonomy in commercial practice. It also examines the main changes brought about by the Brussels I recast and the entry into force of the Hague Choice of Court Convention, and analyses these against the background of the party autonomy paradigm, as well as their contribution to effective litigation.

Keywords Choice of forum · Party autonomy · Efficiency · Lis pendens · Competition of courts · Brussels Ibis Regulation · Hague Choice of Court Convention

X. Kramer (✉) · E. Themeli
Erasmus School of Law, Erasmus University Rotterdam, Rotterdam, The Netherlands
e-mail: kramer@law.eur.nl

E. Themeli
e-mail: themeli@law.eur.nl

V. Lazić and S. Stuij (eds.), *Brussels Ibis Regulation*, Short Studies in Private International Law, DOI 10.1007/978-94-6265-147-0_2

Contents

2.1 Introduction

The year 2015—commemorating the 50th anniversary of the T.M.C. Asser Institute, to which this paper is dedicated—is an important one for party autonomy in international litigation. On 10 January 2015, the Brussels Ibis Regulation, replacing the Brussels I Regulation, became applicable. One of the main objectives of the recast of the Brussels I Regulation was to strengthen the effect of choice of court agreements, also in view of their practical importance in commerce.[1] On 1 October 2015, the Hague Choice of Court Convention finally entered into force, ten years after it had been adopted. The Convention currently applies between Mexico, the EU Member States (with the exception of Denmark) and Singapore. A number of other countries are expected to join the Convention in the near future. Both instruments have been developed with the objective of supporting the enforcement of choice of court agreements, and thus increasing the legal certainty and efficiency of international litigation.

Over the last several decades, party autonomy has come to be increasingly important in private international law, and has become the new paradigm, both for international jurisdiction and choice of law, in particular—but not limited to—commercial relationships. In Europe, the gradual development of the possibility of selecting the court that would have jurisdiction if a dispute were to arise or has arisen between commercial parties had already started at the beginning of the last century. It is now widely accepted in most parts of the world. Party autonomy in commercial litigation has also been intensified, due to the popularity of arbitration.

[1] See the Green Paper on the review of Council Regulation (EC) No 44/2001 on jurisdiction and the recognition and enforcement of judgments in civil and commercial matters, COM(2009) 175 final, p. 5.

In Europe, almost fifty years ago the Brussels Convention, and meanwhile the Regulation, rooted party autonomy firmly by ensuring the enforceability of choice of court agreements. On the global level, the Hague Choice of Court Convention would have the same potential if it were to be ratified by a substantial number of countries.

The aim of this paper is to explore the party autonomy paradigm in private international law—and choice of court in particular—from different perspectives, and to assess the European and global regulatory developments in this regard. Section 2.2 views the essence and value of party autonomy from various disciplines, including a psychological, sociological, and economic perspective, as well as in the context of private international law and litigation. On the basis of the available empirical data, certain conclusions are drawn with regard to the relevance and exercise of party autonomy by way of choice of court in practice. In Sect. 2.3, the new rules of the Brussels Ibis Regulation regarding choice of court are discussed, in particular with a view to enhancing the enforceability of choice of court agreements, and to increasing efficiency in international litigation. Section 2.4 sketches the background and basic rules of the Hague Choice of Court Convention and the interaction with the Brussels I Regulation. The paper concludes that party autonomy in private international law is inspired and supported by other disciplines. The available data show that parties value and often make use of their freedom to select the competent court, although the rationale behind their choices is not always evident. The Brussels regime has matured over the last several decades, and the recent amendments to the Brussels Ibis Regulation are generally to be welcomed. The entry into force of the Hague Choice of Court Convention is a landmark in the development towards a global enforceability of choice of court agreements relating to the benefit of international commercial practice.

2.2 A Paradigm on Party Autonomy

2.2.1 Party Autonomy Through the Lens of Other Disciplines

During the last fifty years, legal scholarship and regulations have afforded contractual parties more freedom to choose how to govern their contracts and rights. Closely related to freedom,[2] party autonomy is a key element that has character-

[2] It has been suggested that party autonomy can play a role in implementing fundamental freedoms in the EU. If a fundamental freedom is respected in one country but not in another, an interested person can choose the law of the country that better respects the freedom, and can later ask the other countries to respect that freedom by virtue of mutual recognition. See Weller 2015, pp. 75–77.

ised private international law in recent years.[3] While being related with other terms like private autonomy and individual autonomy,[4] party autonomy is used mainly to describe the possibility that parties to a contract have to choose the mechanisms and the location where their disputes will be resolved and/or the law that will be applicable to a contract or other legal relationship.[5] Party autonomy is the joint product of two or more parties. A choice of court made by one person is an expression of that person's individual autonomy, and the parties' autonomy is created only in conjunction with the individual autonomy of another person. Therefore, party autonomy is in essence the combination of joint individual autonomy, which is expressed in a choice of court or law.[6] From a psychological perspective, freedom is relative to each party and to the social setting of the subject. In some settings, the boundary between the individual's decision-making sphere and that of society is not evident. It is unclear where the group ends and where the individual begins. In these instances, it becomes more difficult to determine who is making the choice.[7] To illustrate this, one might consider a party that wants to make a choice of forum, but the community where that party conducts its business and interactions suppresses or distorts the freedom to make that choice.[8] A number of industries and branch organisations require their members to use certain fora, and in this manner they suppress their members' party autonomy. It is understandable that while parties are allowed a formal freedom, their social setting might require a certain conformity, and thus in fact distort their party autonomy.

Party autonomy has a sociological connotation as well, and, in a certain manner, it relates to historical events like the Scottish Enlightenment and the French Revolution. These events introduced and further developed the notions of *laissez-faire* and individual freedom in many aspects of life. While in England these movements inspired the creation of the 'freedom of contract' theory,[9] which holds that parties are free to stipulate their own contractual terms without the interference of the state, in Germany they created the idea of a liberalistic process.[10] The

---

[3] The term 'party autonomy' is a recent one, but the practice of choosing a court for resolving disputes seems to be an ancient invention, dating back to Ptolemaic Egypt (Symeonides 2013, p. 875). Without disputing the authenticity of the claim, it can be said that sporadic and isolated choice of court agreements, where party autonomy is used, does not constitute an established practice that endures over time and becomes a legal institution.

[4] Both are considered to be the base of private law (Smits 1998, p. 330).

[5] Rühl 2007, Choice of Law and Choice of Forum in the European Union: Recent Developments. Social Science Research Network, p. 4. http://papers.ssrn.com/sol3/papers.cfm?abstract_id=1604615. Accessed 6 October 2016.

[6] Symeonides 2013, pp. 882–885.

[7] Schwartz 2000, p. 84.

[8] Forced choice or related phenomenon can be conscious, as in the case of a party that knows that even though s/he has unlimited freedom to choose, in fact, the choices s/he can make are limited. Unconscious forced choice occurs when a party is not aware of all the available possibilities (Salecl 2012, 2009, p. 168).

[9] Low 2013, p. 365.

[10] Evro 2014, pp. 389–396.

core of this idea was that individuals were free in relation to the government, and at liberty to use their independence within certain boundaries. In civil procedure, this allowed parties to choose their own procedural steps, which included the choice of court, and to dispose their procedural rights as they wished. On the one hand, the liberalistic process implied that the state was neutral and passive, and the conflict between the parties was decided on what they presented, without considering the material truth. On the other hand, the parties were considered equal and able to protect themselves, which in fact was not true.

The liberalistic process idea described above implies that parties have the same bargaining power and the same qualities in creating and expressing their choice of court. In a perfect world, parties would be equal, and their choice of court would be the result of a combined effort to find an optimal solution. While a perfect distribution of power and quality between parties is ideal in principle, in reality it is not. In many cases, one of the parties has more bargaining power than the other, or is more qualitative, or both. This means that the weaker party's autonomy is distorted, if not neutralised, and the result of the negotiation largely reflects the will of the stronger party.[11] Of course, this creates social as well as economic problems, which governments try to avoid. In response to this problem, a social process idea was developed in Germany.[12] According to this notion, the court, and legal systems in general, should not be neutral, but should assist in and take into consideration the creation of equality in the community. To achieve this, weaker parties are offered special protection in procedures, which includes limiting the party autonomy in instances where weaker parties might be endangered by the superiority of the other party.[13] This means that parties can exercise their party autonomy only in cases where their bargaining power is evidently not unbalanced. It does not mean that the bargaining power should be equal, but that the difference should not be such as to allow one party to impose its will on the other. This protection of weaker parties has gained firm ground in European private international law, as is noteworthy in, among other things, the Brussels Ibis Regulation, which strictly limits the effect of a choice of court made by the stronger party in consumer, insurance, and employment contracts.[14]

---

[11] Symeonides 2013, p. 885.

[12] The social process idea was a response to the prepotency of stronger parties. Their power was manifested not only during the negotiation phase but also in the due course of the process. By dragging out the process, or by forcing costs to escalate, stronger parties weaken the chances of weaker parties having a successful outcome. According to the notion of social process, civil procedure should take this into account, and thus provide for a shorter process and for the protection of negotiation processes, as well as give judges the discretion to evaluate the social consequences of his/her decisions. Evro 2014, pp. 396–399.

[13] Eidenmüller 2011, p. 721.

[14] See Article 25(4) read together with Articles 15, 19, and 23 of the Brussels Ibis Regulation. In relation to choice of law, see Articles 6(2) and 8(1) Rome I Regulation on consumer and employment contracts, and to a lesser extent Articles 5(2) and 7(3) Rome I Regulation on passenger transport and insurance contracts.

Viewed from an economic standpoint, party autonomy is considered to increase efficiency,[15] since parties that have multiple options are better able to allocate their resources and serve their needs. If the parties' choice does not reduce the welfare of third parties, the result will be Pareto efficient; if the choice increases the benefits of the parties more than it decreases third parties' benefits, it will be Kaldor-Hicks efficient.[16] For governments, party autonomy is also a way to observe how users of their services vote with their feet. This would give them information as to what certain services users want, and where, and facilitate the allocation of their resources.[17] Furthermore, some states try to attract users of the legal system, which would make them enter into a competition with other states.[18] Competition between states or jurisdictions might lead eventually to innovation and improvement of the services they offer.[19] This, however, does not mean that party autonomy brings only benefits; as with many activities, it can create externalities that need to be mitigated.[20] If the externalities created are internalised by the parties, they will tend to make efficient use of their party autonomy: for example, by choosing a jurisdiction that is costly, the parties will suffer from the high costs, in which case they will either try to reduce costs or make a better—more efficient—choice of court. The problems start in the event that externalities are not internalised, resulting in the costs being dumped to third parties, and in the state most probably having to step in to mitigate the problem.[21] Therefore, while supporting party autonomy, governments should try to take into account the possible externalities resulting from this autonomy, while parties should consider the externalities created by their own actions.

When choosing a forum for the resolution of disputes, parties are not simply selecting a location they might want to visit as tourists. Indirectly, they are also

[15] Rühl 2007, Choice of Law and Choice of Forum in the European Union: Recent Developments. Social Science Research Network, p. 4, http://papers.ssrn.com/sol3/papers.cfm?abstract_id=1604615. Accessed 6 October 2016; Efficiency of states is still debatable, see Michaels 2008, p. 87, 102.

[16] Rühl 2007, Choice of Law and Choice of Forum in the European Union: Recent Developments. Social Science Research Network, p. 5, http://papers.ssrn.com/sol3/papers.cfm?abstract_id=1604615. Accessed 6 October 2016.

[17] This is also the essence of Tiebout's theory (Tiebout 1956). For a critical discussion on the role of the state as a rational actor that tries to maximise efficiency, see also Michaels 2008, p. 82.

[18] As Peters points out, party autonomy is one of the conditions for the existence of competition involving jurisdictions. Peters 2014, p. 57; Kramer 2014, no. 41.

[19] Michaels 2008, p. 80, claims that the main purpose of party autonomy is to dismiss ineffective laws.

[20] Michaels 2008, p. 87.

[21] Michaels suggests that party autonomy is desirable only in the event that it does not create transaction costs for third parties. It can be said that a Kaldor-Hicks efficiency is still desirable—or, in other words, if the costs to the other party are less than the costs of the parties expressing the party autonomy. See Michaels 2008, p. 87.

choosing the procedure that will be applied to solve the conflict—whether in court or in an ADR venue. It is obvious that procedure has a tremendous impact on the outcome of the process. Therefore, expressing party autonomy by making a choice of court is extremely important.[22] This choice allows parties to choose not only from among state courts, but also from among those courts and private dispute resolution mechanisms. Thus, parties can 'escape' from government-organised conflict resolution and choose more efficient[23] mechanisms. It is this freedom that creates the basis for the functioning and organisation of arbitration, mediation, and other forms of private dispute resolution mechanisms. Furthermore, the existence of such mechanisms can have a positive and a twofold impact on governments: firstly, it releases the pressure on state courts, which in some cases face an enormous workload; secondly, it creates a forum—or fora—that is competitive with the state court, which might spur their reforms and development.

Party autonomy is instrumental in different fields of law, although in some areas—including antitrust law and environmental law, where public interest issues are involved—it is limited or non-existent.[24] Party autonomy relates to the principle of personal private autonomy, which is the right of a person to decide his/her own future and the modalities to pursue it, with or without limited interference from the state. It is an expression of private autonomy, which gives parties the right to choose their legal rights and obligations,[25] and it enhances legal certainty in situations where multiple options are available.[26] Nevertheless, party autonomy should not be used as a means of polluting legal certainty or threatening the defences of the weaker parties, or as a way of overriding other rights.[27] In other words, it is necessary to strike a balance between parties' autonomy and other rights.

2.2.2 *Party Autonomy in Private International Law*

In private international law, party autonomy may be considered one of the greatest achievements of the 20th century.[28] Even though it is accepted in many jurisdictions, party autonomy is more widely accepted in Europe and North America,

---

[22] In many cases, parties make a choice of law, and in doing so they follow the choice of court. It is still not clear how often this happens, but it is understandable why it might.

[23] Apart from efficiency, 'escaping' can also be justified by the parties' desire to find mechanisms of a better quality or that are more neutral than those offered by the government.

[24] Trachtman 1993, pp. 60–61; Symeonides 2013, p. 875–876.

[25] Sieger 2011, p. 197.

[26] Rühl 2007, Choice of Law and Choice of Forum in the European Union: Recent Developments.Social Science Research Network, p. 4, http://papers.ssrn.com/sol3/papers.cfm?abstract_id=1604615. Accessed 6 October 2016; Eidenmüller 2011, p. 710.

[27] Magnus 2012, p. 91.

[28] Brand 2014, p. 375.

compared to, in particular, Latin America.[29] In Europe, parties' autonomy in the choice of court had been accepted long before the Brussels I Regulation[30] or its predecessor the Brussels Convention.[31] However, the Brussels Convention has been celebrated as the first step towards formalising party autonomy at the European level. Enlightened by the lessons learned from the Brussels Convention, the Regulation did a better job of framing the principle of party autonomy in its Article 23, while party autonomy has been strengthened further under Article 25 of the new Brussels Ibis Regulation.[32] In fact, party autonomy can be regarded as one of the founding principles of the Brussels Ibis Regulation, which is also evidenced by the Regulation's recitals, which underline the importance of parties' autonomy.[33] One might even consider Article 25 on choice of court to be the default rule for the Brussels Ibis Regulation,[34] in which case the other provisions can be considered exceptions to the main rule.[35] These exceptions are stated carefully in the Regulation in order to avoid further limitations to party autonomy by courts or even the parties themselves.[36] The limitations to, or the exclusion of, party autonomy are aimed primarily at protecting weaker parties and at avoiding externalities for third parties. Furthermore, governments can limit party autonomy to protect public order,[37] as is also embodied in Article 24 of the Brussels Ibis Regulation. The possibility of limiting party autonomy in the interest of weaker parties, and the general principle that parties can dispose their rights, indicates a tension between public and private law.[38] Unless the legislator provides rules to resolve this tension, it is discharged to the courts, which should find the

---

[29] Symeonides 2013, p. 876; Beaton 2012, p. 268.

[30] Council Regulation (EC) No 44/2001 of 22 December 2000 on jurisdiction and the recognition and enforcement of judgments in civil and commercial matters, OJ L 12, 16.1.2001, pp. 1–23.

[31] Convention on jurisdiction and the enforcement of judgments in civil and commercial matters (Consolidated version)—1968 Brussels Convention OJ C 189, 28.7.1990, pp. 2–24.

[32] Regulation (EU) No 1215/2012 of the European Parliament and of the Council of 12 December 2012 on jurisdiction and the recognition and enforcement of judgments in civil and commercial matters, OJ L 351, 20.12.2012, pp. 1–32.

[33] Recitals 14, 15, and 19 affirm exactly this. Despite some restrictions, party autonomy should be respected. Nielsen 2013, p. 513.

[34] There are two opposing views: the private law view considers party autonomy to be the default position, which can be derogated in the event of certain conditions, while the international law view considers the objective determination of the court to be the default position, and party autonomy to be an exception to the rule (Michaels 2008, p. 95).

[35] Magnus 2012, p. 84; Brand 2014, p. 375.

[36] Ferrero 2014, Le clausole di elezione di foro e le convenzioni arbitrali "unilaterali". Recenti sviluppi nel panorama internazionale e spunti di riflessione nel diritto italiano. BusinessJus. http://www.businessjus.com/le-clausole-di-elezione-di-foro-e-le-convenzioni-arbitrali-unilaterali/. Accessed 6 October 2016; Zimmermann 2006, p. 85; Gottschalk 2007, p. 196.

[37] Brand 2014, pp. 378–379; for the law and economic perspective of this, see Beaulier 2005, p. 183.

[38] Michaels 2008, p. 74.

appropriate balance between party autonomy, the respect regarding other rights, and public order.[39]

At the global level, a true landmark for party autonomy and the enforcement of choice of court agreements was the entry into force of the Hague Convention on Choice of Court Agreements in Mexico and the EU Member States, with the exception of Denmark, on 1 October 2015.[40] Meanwhile, the Convention has also entered into force for Singapore (1 October 2016). It was already signed by the US (in 2009) and recently by Ukraine (in 2016).[41] One of the reasons for the adoption of the Convention by the EU, as is also mentioned in the Council's decision to sign the Convention, is the fact that the Convention can serve as an important tool in furthering and promoting party autonomy regarding the choice of court for international commercial contracts.

The freedom given to parties by private international law instruments has its dark side as well. While providing the freedom to choose the court, these legal instruments presume a certain fair-play between the parties: namely, that parties will select the court that best suits their combined interest. As has been rightly pointed out, there is always the risk of an information asymmetry,[42] and one of the parties might possess more bargaining power.[43] Moreover, party autonomy can also be disrupted by litigation tactics on the part of one of the parties, resulting in negative expressions of forum shopping, and eventually undermining party autonomy. One such notorious instance is the *Gasser* case,[44] in which Gasser, an Austrian company, and MISAT, an Italian company, had chosen the Austrian courts in their contract. When a conflict emerged, MISAT filed a case in an Italian court for a declaratory judgement before Gasser brought its claim for the payment of invoices in the Austrian court on the basis of the choice of court agreement. The Court of Justice decided that a court seized second, even if chosen in the choice of court agreement, must stay proceedings until the first seized court has declared that it has no jurisdiction. This strict lis pendens rule causes the party autonomy to be blocked or frozen. Such tactics involving a rush to the court to frustrate

[39] Strong 2014, p. 1060. Article 24 of the Brussels Ibis Regulation provides an exhaustive list of cases where the parties' autonomy has been restricted for public interest reasons. In a different fashion, Article 6(c) of the Hague Convention allows the courts more discretion to dismiss a choice of court by the parties. This discretion should be justified by a manifested injustice or be manifestly contrary to the public policy of the State of the court seized.

[40] Council Decision 2009/397/EC of 26 February 2009 on the signing on behalf of the European Community of the Convention on Choice of Court Agreements, OJ 2009, L 133/13.

[41] Status available at http://www.hcch.net/index_en.php?act=conventions.status2&cid=98. Accessed 6 October 2016.

[42] Dammann and Hansmann 2008, pp. 15–18.

[43] Basedow 2013, pp. 20–21.

[44] ECJ 9 December 2003, Case C-116/02, ECR 2003 I-12693 (*Erich Gasser GmbH v MISAT Srl*).

proceedings have been infamously referred to as 'Italian torpedo', and have been justly criticised as being abusive and hampering justice and trade.[45] This case shows as well that the principle of party autonomy can be overridden by other principles, such as mutual trust within the EU. Fortunately, in the Brussels Ibis Regulation, this 'gap' in the system has been closed.[46]

Parties that have the possibility of choosing a court will select the one that best serves their interests. Governments that try to attract parties to their jurisdictions tend to offer procedural advantages to parties, which can become enormous assets for the outcome of the case. Lenient procedures and application of the law can benefit litigating parties, but can also result in a deterioration of the procedures and courts. Relaxing legal provisions and protection drags governments into a race-to-the-bottom,[47] as a consequence of which, weaker parties lose their legal and procedural protections, and become vulnerable with regard to their stronger opponents. Ironically, the race-to-the-bottom starts as a result of the parties' autonomy, which enables them to search for more lenient rules. Lenient laws and procedures, which with their superior advantages can distort or neutralise the weaker parties' autonomy, favour few parties. However, some scholars consider the prospects of a race-to-the-bottom as not very likely.[48] In a diametrically opposed scenario, party autonomy and governments that try to attract litigating parties would end up creating a race-to-the-top, which would presuppose higher standards, better procedures, better courts, and a more attractive look for the courts. The prospect of a race-to-the-top might be beneficial for weaker parties, and might better protect the expression of party autonomy. Nevertheless, the discussion with regard to race-to-the-bottom or race-to-the-top remains theoretical, as little or no empirical evidence of their existence has been found.[49]

2.2.3 Empirical Data on Choice of Court

That party autonomy is also exercised in practice is supported by a number of empirical studies. Remarkably, a survey conducted by a group of researchers at Oxford University[50] found that the percentage of respondents that considered the choice of court 'very important' was higher than that regarding choice of law. The results of the survey demonstrate that 61 % of the respondents considered the

---

[45] Fentiman 2007, pp. 489, 495.

[46] See further Sect. 3.3.

[47] Visscher 2012, p. 80; Wagner 2013, pp. 374–375.

[48] Kramer and Van Rhee 2012, pp. 5–6, while in disagreement with Visscher that a race-to-the-bottom can be stopped or checked through the harmonisation of civil procedure, consider that a race-to-the-bottom in the EU can be prevented by existing procedural standards.

[49] Visscher 2012, p. 81.

[50] Available at http://www.law.ox.ac.uk/themes/iecl/ocjsurvey.shtml. Accessed 31 August 2015.

choice of court to be 'very important', while 48 % responded that they had 'often' opted for a foreign court. Another survey, conducted by researchers at the University of Basel, found that parties in commercial contracts considered party autonomy to be the third most important factor when choosing the substantive law to govern their contract.[51] Respondents considered only factors connected to legal certainty to be more important than party autonomy. Practices of restricting party autonomy were, among others, considered to be reasons for avoiding jurisdictions that practised them.[52] Another study, conducted by the consultancy firm PWC and the Queen Mary University in London in 2013[53], found that the choice of forum option was applied often. In fact, disputes that could not be resolved amicably were referred equally to arbitration and litigation, with 47 % each. The remaining cases were referred to 'expert determination/adjudication'. In other words, parties in approximately half of the cases made a choice of court, and probably even more did so if one were to discount the cases in which a choice of court was not possible.

While data from surveys show that the business sector is highly appreciative of party autonomy, the reasons for choosing one court over another remain unclear. The survey conducted by the Oxford researchers contained some questions related to the choice of court.[54] As mentioned above, respondents valued the possibility of choosing a court for their disputes. When asked about their preferred court, England (17 %), Italy (12 %), Germany (10 %), and Switzerland (10 %) were among the top choices.[55] If these answers were controlled for the home country of the respondents, Switzerland (19 %), England (14 %), France (13 %), and Germany (10 %) were the most preferred. As can be seen, there is a difference between the two results, which speaks of a home bias for certain counties like England, Italy, the Netherlands, Spain, and Poland.[56] Jurisdictions like Switzerland and France have a better result by removing the home bias, while the percentage for Germany remains the same. These results suggest that the home bias is not spread uniformly, and some jurisdictions fare better without it. Asked about the factors taken into account when making a choice of court, respondents considered 'quality of judges and courts', 'fairness of the outcome', 'corruption',[57] and 'predictability of the outcome' to be the top four. The same factors

[51] With 46.7 % of the respondents, party autonomy came third after 'legal rules that were easy to ascertain' (68.72 %) and 'body of case law that facilitates interpretation of legal rules' (53.74 %). Moser 2015, p. 43.

[52] Moser 2015, pp. 46–47.

[53] International Arbitration Survey 2013: Corporate choices in International Arbitration, available at http://www.pwc.com/arbitrationstudy. Accessed 31 August 2015.

[54] The survey conducted by Vogenauer and Weatherill did not contain questions related to choice of court or choice of forum.

[55] Arbitration was chosen by 16 % of the respondents; however, it is not included in this analysis because it is not a state-organised court.

[56] Not shown here; see question 30 and 30.1 of the survey, footnote 50.

[57] Or rather 'lack of corruption'.

were considered the most important in instances of trying to avoid a specific court. Apparently, the factors taken into consideration are consistent for choosing and avoiding courts, but the survey does not show whether both parties are well informed. The question is whether parties do in fact consider all the options. Do they have the means and the tools to quantify or to assess the relevant factors to make a choice of court? Are judges in Switzerland less corrupt than their colleagues in the Netherlands, Sweden, or Germany? Is the quality of judges higher in England than in Germany or Italy? The same questions can be asked about all other factors that some parties take into account. By analysing all known empirical researches on choice of forum, Vogenauer concludes that parties are heavily influenced by 'familiarity', 'neutrality', and 'image' of the forum.[58] These are not primarily legal or true qualitative considerations, but are related to market conformity (image and familiarity) and perceived quality (neutrality and image). Clearly showing his disappointment in these findings, Durand-Barthez considered the choice of court in Europe to be afflicted by psychological factors rather than purely technical ones.[59] Indeed, the fact that these considerations seem to outweigh the intrinsic quality of the court system as such is somewhat disenchanting.[60] It might be disappointing for lawmakers and governments that, on the face of it, factors other than legal ones can influence—even dominate—a party's choice. Attempts by governments to attract parties might be futile, considering the cold reaction on the part of lawyers. Scholars that cherish competition of jurisdictions as an incentive to improve the quality and efficiency of courts must comfort themselves with the thought that this situation might change one day. Hope is always the last thing to perish, and we would like to think that a more active role on the part of competing governments might succeed in changing the attitude of lawyers and corrode the primacy that English courts enjoy in the choice of court.

2.3 Choice of Forum in the Brussels Ibis Regulation

2.3.1 The Brussels Regime: Development and Shortcomings

The Brussels regime—from the Brussels Convention to the Brussels I Regulation[61] and now the Brussels Ibis Regulation—has secured the validity and enforcement of choice of court agreements. The choice of court provision, according to the Court of Justice, is based on the independent will of the parties in deciding which courts are to have jurisdiction for a dispute that comes under the scope

[58] Vogenauer 2013, pp. 256–263.

[59] Durand-Barthez 2012.

[60] Kramer 2014, no. 31.

[61] Along with the Lugano Convention of 1988 and 2007.

of the Brussels regime.[62] The forum selection embodies party autonomy, and aims at ensuring legal certainty as to which court will have jurisdiction in the event of a dispute. In the following versions, amendments have been made to make the formal requirements more flexible and to adapt these to commercial practice. While the original version of the Convention of 1968 only allowed a choice of court that was agreed or evidenced in writing, the 1978 Accession Convention incorporated the conformity with international trade uses (e.g. a reference to standard branch conditions), and with the 1989 Accession Convention, the form that accords with parties' practices.[63] In addition, the Brussels I Regulation equalled communication by electronic means that provide a durable record to a written agreement.

From the Heidelberg report, evaluating the Brussels I Regulation, it is clear that the provision on choice of court agreements generally functions well. Several persisting problems in the application in the Member States were identified,[64] most of which were picked up in the Green Paper[65] and in the following Commission proposal,[66] and have been tackled in the Brussels Ibis Regulation.[67]

A general issue concerned the functioning of the Brussels I Regulation in the international legal order, in particular the scope of the rules, including the choice of court provision, vis-à-vis third country parties. Connected to this is the relation to the Hague Choice of Court Convention that was signed by the European Union in 2009, since this Convention contains rules that are not in line with the scheme of the Brussels I Regulation. Another shortcoming of the Brussels I Regulation was that it did not resolve the substantive validity of choice of court agreements. While the formal validity has been exhaustively regulated,[68] and has been further crystalised by a series of rulings of the Court of Justice, a uniform rule regarding the substantive validity was lacking. The most pressing issue that was brought somewhat excruciatingly to the surface by the *Gasser* ruling of the Court of Justice concerned the strict application of the lis pendens rule.[69] The priority of this rule enabled a party to frustrate the effectiveness of the choice of court agreement by bringing the case elsewhere by way of delaying tactics, generally referred to as torpedo actions.

The new rules on choice of court and lis pendens in the Brussels Ibis Regulation will be discussed briefly in the following subsections.

---

62 ECJ 9 November 1978, Case 23/8, ECR 1978 2133 (*Nikolaus Meeth v Glacetal*).

63 See also Garcimartin 2015, no. 9.03, pp. 278–279.

64 Hess et al. 2007, no. 374–397.

65 See footnote 1.

66 See extensively on the Commission proposal Magnus 2012, 83–102.

67 For a discussion of the new choice of court provision, see *inter alia* Hartley 2013, pp. 309–316.

68 See Article 23(1) Brussels I Regulation, now included in Article 25(1) Brussels Ibis Regulation.

69 ECJ 9 December 2003, Case C-116/02, ECR 2003 I-14693 (*Erich Gasser GmbH v MISAT Srl*).

2.3.2 Extended Scope, Substantive Validity Rule, and Severability Clause

The scope of the jurisdiction rules including that of the choice of court provision was discussed intensively during the negotiations on Brussels I. The Commission's proposal to extend the scope of the other jurisdiction rules to third country defendants[70] was not generally adopted,[71] but the proposal to widen the territorial reach of the provision on choice of court agreements was. Article 25 Brussels Ibis no longer requires that one of the parties be domiciled in an EU Member State; it applies to choice of court agreements in favour of the courts of a Member State regardless of the domicile of the parties.[72] This extension of the scope of applicability of this provision is to be welcomed, as it now covers all instances in which parties have selected the courts of an EU Member State.[73] However, the choice of court for a third State court is still not regulated by Brussels Ibis. In principle, these continue to be governed by the national law of the Member States, subject to the applicability of the Lugano Convention, the Hague Choice of Court Convention, or another (bilateral) convention.[74] As party autonomy is one of the primary objectives of the Brussels regime, a Member State seized notwithstanding a choice of court in favour of a third court cannot ignore such a choice, thereby limiting party autonomy. As the Court of Justice made clear, a court seized should in such a case assess the validity of the clause according to the applicable law, including the conflict of law rules.[75] A certain reflexive effect of the choice of court provision cannot be denied.[76] As Garcimartin has rightfully assumed, if a choice in favour of a non-EU Member State were to lead to the non-application of other jurisdiction rules of the Regulation, the choice should satisfy the formal requirements of Article 25(1) and not be contrary to the protective and exclusive jurisdiction as referred to in Article 25(4) Brussels Ibis Regulation.[77]

A second adjustment is the introduction of a provision on the substantive validity of a choice of court agreement. Article 25(1) refers to the law of the Member State of the chosen court. The Commission aimed at introducing a harmonised conflict-of-law rule, since there was no uniformity as to the law to be applied to

---

[70] Proposal for a Regulation of the European Parliament and of the Council on judgments in civil and commercial matters, COM(2010) 748, p. 8 and Article 4.

[71] Only in relation to consumer and employment contracts; see Article 18(1) and in a more limited manner, Article 21(2) Brussels Ibis Regulation.

[72] See Article 25(1) Brussels Ibis Regulation.

[73] This is also in line with the scope of the Hague Choice of Court Convention. See Sect. 4.1.

[74] See also ECJ 9 November 2000, Case C-387/98, ECR 2000 I-9337 (*Coreck Maritime v Handelsveem*).

[75] ECJ 9 November 2000, Case C-387/98, ECR 2000 I-9337 (Coreck Maritime v Handelsveem), point 19.

[76] See *inter alia* Stone 2014, p. 185, referring to the 'implied reflexive effect' of this provision.

[77] Garcimartin 2015, no. 9.15 and 9.15, p. 281.

questions of substantive validity. As Recital 20 clarifies, the 'law of the Member State' includes the choice of law provisions of that Member State, which is in line with the Hague Choice of Court Convention.[78] It is submitted that this rule is highly inefficient in the European context, as the Rome I Regulation excludes choice of court agreements from its scope, and consequently there is no uniform conflict of law rule designating the applicable law to the validity of the agreement.[79] This means that Member States will continue to use their own choice of law rules, and will either apply the *lex fori*, the *lex causae*, or a combination of these.[80]

The third amendment to the provision on choice of court is the codification of the severability rule. Article 25(6) provides that the validity of the choice of court agreement cannot be contested solely on the ground that the contract in which the clause is concluded is not valid. This rule is not new, as it affirms the case law of the Court of Justice.[81] It is a well-established principle that aims to avoid a situation in which the invalidity of the main contract invalidates the choice of court agreement, thus creating uncertainties as to the court having jurisdiction. The choice of court agreement should be treated as an independent agreement, as Article 25(6) specifies, and the validity of this agreement should be assessed on its own merits. The same rule is included in the Hague Convention.[82]

2.3.3 Reversing the Lis Pendens Rule: Mutual Trust, Competition, and Efficiency

The most debated and important novelty in the Brussels choice of court regime is the priority that the forum clause has obtained over the lis pendens rules. According to Article 31(2) Brussels Ibis, any court seized other than the one exclusively chosen should stay its proceedings until the chosen court declines jurisdiction. If the chosen court accepts jurisdiction, any other court seized shall decline jurisdiction (Article 31(3) Brussels Ibis). An exception is made for insurance, consumer, and employment contracts where the weaker party is the claimant and the choice is invalid pursuant to Sects. 2.3, 2.4, or 2.5 (Article 31(4) Brussels Ibis).

---

78 Article 5(1) Hague Choice of Court Convention. From the explanatory report, it is clear that 'the law of that State' in this provision includes the choice of law rules; see Hartley and Dogauchi 2007, Explanatory Report on the 2005 Hague Choice of Court Agreements Convention. HCCH Publication, no. 43, www.hcch.net/upload/expl37e.pdf.

79 See Article 1(2)(d) of Regulation (EC) 593/2008 on the law applicable to contractual obligations, *OJ* 2008, L 177/6.

80 Nielsen 2013, 523. See more extensively Garcimartin 2015, no. 9.62–970, pp. 295–298.

81 ECJ 3 July 1997, Case C-269/95, ECR 1997 I-3767 (*Benincasa v Dentalkit*).

82 See Articles 3(d) and 15 Hague Choice of Court Convention.

In the background of this amendment is the practice of torpedo actions that were unsatisfactorily facilitated by the ruling of the Court of Justice in the *Gasser* case, as described above in Sect. 2.2. Relying heavily on mutual trust and on the implied equality of courts—each can rule on its own jurisdiction—the Court of Justice upheld the 'first seized' rule despite the fact that a party willingly seized a court other than the one selected, thereby freezing the jurisdiction of the chosen court. The fact that it might take years for the adjudicated Italian court to decide on the question of jurisdiction before it assumedly declines jurisdiction, in view of the choice of court agreement in favour of the Austrian court, did not change this. The Court ruled that the lis pendens provision could not be derogated from, not even when the duration in the court first seized was excessively long. The 'competition' between courts for international commercial disputes takes a negative course in these types of situations. A party can wilfully address a slow court, with the intention of blocking the jurisdiction of the mutually chosen court for a long period of time in order to frustrate effective dispute resolution or to force a settlement.[83]

This ruling has rightfully been heavily criticised, and has urged the Commission to more effectively protect autonomy.[84] Several options were put forward, including improving the communication between courts in the case of lis pendens, imposing a time limit on giving a decision on jurisdiction, or granting a right to damage in the case of violation of a choice of court agreement.[85] The preferred option, however, was to make an exception to the lis pendens rule, and thus give priority to the chosen court. This rule is also in line with the Hague Choice of Court Convention.[86] Recital 22 clarifies that this exception to the lis pendens rule is intended to enhance the effectiveness of exclusive choice of court agreements, and to avoid abusive litigation tactics. The chosen court is given priority to decide on the validity of the choice of court agreement, and the non-chosen court that was seized first must stay the proceedings. Giving priority to the chosen court rather than the court first seized is to be welcomed, as it reinforces party autonomy and contributes to a more efficient dispute resolution.

2.4 The Hague Choice of Court Convention

2.4.1 A Long Way Down the Road

The Hague Choice of Court Convention is the result of a long and bumpy process of negotiations started on the initiative of the United States in 1992, on what was

[83] Garcimartin 2015, no. 11.42, p. 337.

[84] See *inter alia* Hartley 2005, pp. 322–335; Dickinson 2010, pp. 295–296.

[85] Green Paper, pp. 4–5.

[86] See Article 5(2) Hague Choice of Court Convention.

intended to result in a 'judgment convention'.[87] As is well known, a 1999 draft of the mixed convention, including rules on recognition and enforcement coupled with a white, grey, and black list of jurisdiction grounds, raised substantial objections from the side of the US and a number of other countries. These objections concerned both the format of the draft convention, which resembled too greatly the double treaty format of the Brussels regime, as well as the content of many of the proposed jurisdiction rules to guide the enforcement.[88] The project was eventually downsized to a framework on choice of court agreements for which, thanks to the exhaustive diplomatic efforts of the Permanent Bureau of the Hague Conference, common ground could be found. The Convention was finally adopted on 30 June 2005.

It then took ten more years for the Convention to become applicable after the two required ratifications had been obtained, from Mexico in 2007, and eventually the European Union in 2015.[89] Since 1 October 2015, the Hague Choice of Court Convention applies in Mexico and the EU Member States (with the exception of Denmark), and since 1 October 2016 in Singapore, to exclusive choice of court agreements that are concluded after this date.[90] The substantive scope is more limited than that of the Brussels Ibis Regulation. In its Article 2, it excludes consumer contracts and a number of other contracts, including transport contracts, specific maritime claims, anti-trust, and nuclear liability, as well as most types of claims based on tort or delict (personal injury, damage to tangible property, intellectual property infringements). Contrary to the Brussels Ibis Regulation, the Hague Convention applies only to exclusive choice of court agreements.[91] For the application, it is required that the chosen court be that of a State that is a party to this Convention.[92]

[87] Baumgartner 2002, pp. 219–224; Hess 2005, pp. 263–269; Brand 2003, pp. 71–80.

[88] Letter regarding Preliminary Draft Hague Convention on Jurisdiction and the Enforcement of Civil Judgments, Jeffrey D Kovar, US Department of State Assistant Legal Adviser for Private International Law, to J.H.A. van Loon, Secretary General, Hague Conference on Private International Law, 22 February 2000, available at http://www.cptech.org/ecom/hague/kovar2loon22022000.pdf. Accessed 31 August 2015. See also Schulz 2006, pp. 244–246.

[89] See Articles 27 and 31 Hague Choice of Court Convention. The EU had already signed the Convention in 2009, but the ratification was postponed primarily because of the ongoing recast of the Brussels I Regulation and the need to align the rules of these instruments.

[90] Article 16 Hague Choice of Court Convention provides that the Convention applies to choice of court agreements concluded after the date of entry into force in that State, and shall not apply to proceedings instituted before its entry into force in the State of the court seized.

[91] Articles 1(1) and 3(a) Hague Choice of Court Convention.

[92] As is clear from 3(b) Hague Choice of Court Convention. This rule coincides with the extended scope of Article 25 Brussels I-bis; see Sect. 3.2.

2.4.2 Regulatory Framework

The basic rules of the Hague Choice of Court Convention are straightforward:[93] firstly, the choice of court must be an exclusive one within the meaning of Article 3; secondly, it must be formally valid. According to Article 3 of the Convention, a choice of court is formally valid if it was made in writing or by any other means of communication that renders information accessible so as to be usable for subsequent reference. This makes the scope of this Convention narrower than that of Article 25 of the Brussels Ibis Regulation, which extends to non-exclusive choice of court agreements. Moreover, the formal requirements are stricter, since the reference to parties' practice and trade usages is not included.

The jurisdictional part includes two key rules, the first being Article 5 of the Convention, which is aimed at the chosen court. According to this provision, the chosen court must assume jurisdiction in relation to an exclusive choice of court agreement that is formally valid pursuant to Article 3, unless the agreement is null and void under the law of that State. The explanatory Hartley/Dogauchi report clarifies that this includes the choice of law provisions of that State.[94] As discussed in Sect. 3.2, the Brussels Ibis Regulation includes a similar rule on the substantive validity. Since the Convention does not extend to consumer contracts and excludes several other types of disputes, including the ones for which the Brussels Ibis Regulation contains exclusive jurisdiction rules, there are no further exceptions to this rule. Article 5(2) explicitly rules out lis pendens and forum non conveniens as grounds to refuse jurisdiction.[95] The second key rule, Article 6 of the Convention, mirrors this provision, and provides that all courts other than the one chosen must suspend or dismiss proceedings. There are five exceptions to this, and they pertain to the following: invalidity of the choice of court agreement; incapacity to conclude the agreement; manifestation of injustice or public policy; exceptional reasons for which the agreement cannot reasonably be performed; and situations in which the chosen court has decided not to hear the case.

The jurisdiction section of the Convention is complemented by Article 7 concerning interim measures of protection. These are excluded from the scope of the Convention, and for this reason the Convention does not prohibit the granting of such measures by a court other than the one exclusively chosen.[96]

---

[93] See *inter alia* Hartley 2013, pp. 209–216; Schulz 2006, pp. 250–265; Kruger 2006, pp. 448–452; Kramer 2006a, pp. 110–116; Rühl 2005, pp. 412–415.

[94] Hartley and Dogauchi 2007, Explanatory Report on the 2005 Hague Choice of Court Agreements Convention. HCCH Publication, no. 43, www.hcch.net/upload/expl37e.pdf.

[95] Article 19 Hague Choice of Court Convention, however, does allow a State to make a declaration stating that it can refuse to accept jurisdiction if, with the exception of the location of the chosen court, there is no connection between that State and the parties or the dispute.

[96] Provisional and protective measures are included in the Brussels Ibis Regulation, but are largely in effect since a choice of court agreement does not prohibit another court from granting a provisional or protective measure provided that it can derive jurisdiction from Article 35 as interpreted in ECJ 17 November 1998, Case C-391/95, ECR 1998, I-7091.

A tremendous achievement reached by the Hague Choice of Court Convention is that judgments given by the court that was designated in an exclusive choice of court agreement will be recognised and enforced, in accordance with Article 8 *ff*. Inherent to the global nature of the Convention, the rules are more restrictive than those of the Brussels Ibis Regulation, but it is a big step forward, since this is the first general Convention to establish a worldwide system of recognition and enforcement for judgments.[97]

2.4.3 Interaction with the Brussels Ibis Regulation

During the negotiations on the Hague Choice of Court Convention the relationship with the other international instruments—and in particular the (then) Brussels I Regulation—was an important concern. The explanatory Hartley/Dogauchi report even designates it as 'one of the most difficult ones'.[98] This might in part account for the cryptic formulation of Article 26(6) of the Hague Choice of Court Convention. Priority is given to the Convention, where one party is resident in an EU Member State or in a third State that is not a member of the Hague Convention, and the other in a non-EU State that is a party to the Hague Convention, even if the parties designate the courts of an EU Member State. The Brussels Ibis Regulation remains applicable when none of the parties is resident in a State that is a party to the Hague Convention (provided they have chosen one of the Member State courts pursuant to Article 25 Brussels Ibis).

As the rules of the Brussels regime are now aligned largely with those of the Hague Choice of Court Convention, the demarcation between these two international instruments has become less of an issue. They are mainly communicating vessels that in a similar manner secure party autonomy and contribute to the efficiency of international commercial litigation.

2.5 Concluding Remarks

Party autonomy is a key principle in private international law, and also draws support and inspiration from other disciplines. Psychologically and sociologically, party autonomy has been considered an expression of the individuals' freedoms.

---

[97] In 2011, a renewed Judgment Project is undertaken by the Hague Conference on Private International Law, following earlier attempts to establish a worldwide judgement convention. See http://www.hcch.net/index_en.php?act=text.display&tid=149. Accessed 31 August 2015. On the developments, see Beaumont 2014, pp. 532–539.

[98] Hartley and Dogauchi 2007, Explanatory Report on the 2005 Hague Choice of Court Agreements Convention. HCCH Publication, no. 25, www.hcch.net/upload/expl37e.pdf, See also Pertegás 2010, pp. 22–23.

Law and economics considers party autonomy to be an important factor in improving the efficiency of laws and institutions, in decreasing the costs relating to transitions, and in the optimal allocation of resources. On the negative side, party autonomy can create externalities that might increase costs for society or third parties. Furthermore, the position of weaker parties might be in danger of potential abuse by parties whose negotiating power is stronger.

In the EU, party autonomy is considered important in furthering cross-border trade and facilitating the internal market, and it is a cornerstone of the Brussels Ibis Regulation. On the global level, the choice of court has found recognition with the establishment and the recent entry into force of The Hague Choice of Court Convention. It is a breakthrough towards a worldwide enforceability of choice of court agreements to the benefit of international commerce. It is hoped that the US and Ukraine will soon ratify the Convention; a number of other countries have already indicated their interest in its possible ratification.[99]

It must be noted that party autonomy also has its downsides, as it assumes an equal bargaining power that is often lacking in practice. In the Brussels regime, insofar as it concerns recognised weaker parties (insurance, consumer and employment contracts), this has been tackled by offering protection against imposed choice of court clauses. Moreover, the Brussels I Regulation with its strict lis pendens rule opened the door to litigation tactics torpedoing the effectiveness of choice of court agreements and litigation. It is certainly an improvement that the Brussels Ibis Regulation the risk of abusive litigation has been mitigated by reversing the lis pendens rule. As is the case in the Hague Choice of Court Convention, choice of court now takes priority over the first seized rule, giving way to the chosen court.

The new Brussels regime on choice of court and its extended territorial scope coupled with the Hague Choice of Court Convention will strengthen the international effectiveness of choice of court agreements. This increases legal certainly, and paves the way for a healthy competition between jurisdictions for the benefit of commercial parties seeking the optimal court in terms of, among other things, costs, reliability, quality, and applicable law. At the same time, the increased international enforceability of choice of court agreements makes court litigation a more viable alternative for parties that do not wish to opt for arbitration.[100]

Empirical evidence shows that party autonomy is in fact highly regarded in commercial practice, and a choice of court (choice of dispute resolution) clause is present in almost every major commercial contract. As suggested by several surveys, in making a choice of court, parties consider a number of legal and practical factors to be the most important. However, the significance given to these factors does not explain fully why some jurisdictions (with special regard to England) are more attractive compared to others. Some scholars explain this by pointing out that parties in fact make their choice of court based primarily on market

[99] Pertegás 2015, p. 374. These include Australia, New Zealand, the People's Republic of China, and Serbia.

[100] See also Schulz 2006, pp. 267–268; Kramer 2006b, pp. 171–172.

conformity and perceived quality. The weight of these factors rather than the high quality of the legal rules might be disappointing, and are difficult to influence by countries. We consider that optimism should prevail, and academics should further their research into the factors that influence the choice of court. Ultimately, true party autonomy can be developed only by way of a better understanding of the process pertaining to choice of court and of the factors that influence it.

References

Alpa G (2006) Harmonisation of and codification in european contract law. In: Vogenauer S, Weatherill S (eds) The harmonisation of European contract law: implications for European private laws, business and legal practice. Hart Publishing, Oxford, pp 149–170

Basedow J (2013) Exclusive choice-of-court agreements as a derogation from imperative norms. In: Lindskoug P, Manusbach U, Millqvist G et al (eds) Essays in honour of Michael Bogdan. Juristförlaget, Lund, pp 15–31

Baumgartner SP (2002) The proposed hague convention on jurisdiction and foreign judgments: where we are and the road ahead. Eur J Law Reform 4:219–243

Beaton P (2012) Globalisation and Scottish law. In: Kramer XE, van Rhee CH (eds) Civil litigation in a globalising world. T.M.C Asser Press, The Hague, pp 263–276

Beaulier S (2005) Polycentrism and power: a reply to Warren Samuels. In: Stringham E (ed) Anarchy, state and public choice. Edward Elgar, Cheltenham, pp 178–190

Beaumont P (2014) The revived judgments project in The Hague. Ned Int Privaat Recht 4:532–539

Brand RA (2003) Concepts consensus and the status quo zone: getting to "yes" on a hague jurisdiction and judgments convention. In: Carmody C, Iwasawa Y, Rhodes S (eds) Trilateral perspectives on international legal issues: conflict and coherence. American Society of International Law, Baltimore, MD, pp 71–108

Brand RA (2014) The evolving private international law/substantive law overlap in the European Union. In: Mankowski P, Wurmnest W (eds) Festschrift für Ulrich Magnus zum 70. Sellier European Law Publishers, München, Geburtstag, pp 371–383

Dammann J, Hansmann H (2008) Globalizing commercial litigation. Cornell Law Rev 94(1):1–72

Dickinson A (2010) Surveying the proposed Brussels I bis regulation: solid foundations but renovation needed. In: Bonomi A, Romano GP (eds) Yearbook of private international law, vol XII. Sellier European Law Publishers, München, pp 247–310

Durand-Barthez P (2012) The "governing law" clause: legal and economic consequences of the choice of law in international contracts. Int Bus Law J—Revue de Droit des Affaires Int 5:505–518

Eidenmüller H (2011) The transnational law market, regulatory competition, and transnational corporations. Indian J Global Legal Stud 18(2):707–749

Evro L (2014) Nordic court culture in progress: historical and futuristic perspectives. In: Ervo L, Nylund A (eds) The future of civil litigation. Springer International Publishing, Switzerland, pp 383–408

Fentiman R (2007) Lis pendens–related actions. In: Magnus U, Mankowski P (eds) Brussels I Regulation, vol 1. Sellier. European Law Publishers, München, pp 475–522

Garcimartin P (2015) Prorogation of jurisdiction. In: Dickinson A, Lein E (eds) The Brussels I regulation recast. Oxford University Press, Oxford, Arts, pp 25–26

Gottschalk E (2007) The law applicable to intellectual property rights: is the Lex Loci protection is a pertinent choice-of-law approach? In: Gottschalk E, Michaels R, Rühl G et al (eds) Conflict of laws in a globalized world. Cambridge University Press, Cambridge, pp 184–219

Hartley T (2005) Choice-of-courts agreements, lis pendens, human rights and the realities of international business: reflections on the Gasser case. In: Jobard-Bachellier M, Mayer P (eds) Le droit international privé: esprit et méthodes: mélanges en l'honneur de Paul Lagarde. Dalloz, Paris, pp 383–392

Hartley T (2013) Choice-of-court agreements and the new Brussels I regulation. Law Q Rev 129:309–317

Hess B (2005) The draft hague convention on choice of court agreements, external competencies of the European Union and recent case law of the european court of justice. In: Nuyts A, Watté N (eds) International civil litigation in Europe and relations with third states, Bruylant, Brussels, pp 263–284

Hess B, Pfeiffer T, Schlosser P (2007) Report on the application of regulation Brussels I in the member states. CF Müller, Heidelberg

Kramer XE (2006a) Het nieuwe Haags Forumkeuzeverdrag: Een welkom compromis met vallen en opstaan. Nederlands Internationaal Privaatrecht 24:109–118

Kramer XE (2006b) De forumkeuze als betrouwbaar alternatief voor het arbitraal beding in de internationale handelspraktijk? Het nieuwe Haags Forumkeuzeverdrag. Nederlands Tijdschrift voor Handelsrecht 5:165–172

Kramer XE (2014) Competitie in de Europese civiele rechtsruimte: een spanningsveld in de grensoverschrijdende geschillenbeslechting? Tijdschrift voor Privaatrecht 51(4):1745–1806

Kramer XE, van Rhee CH (2012) Civil litigation in a globalising world: an introduction. In: Kramer XE, van Rhee CH (eds) Civil litigation in a globalising world. T.M.C Asser Press, The Hague, pp 1–16

Kruger T (2006) The 20th session of the hague conference: a new choice of court convention and the issue of EC membership. Int Comp Law Q 55(2):447–456

Low G (2013) A psychology of choice of laws. Eur Bus Law Rev 24(3):363–387

Magnus U (2012) Choice of court agreements in the review proposal for the Brussels I regulation. In: Lein E (ed) The Brussels I review proposal uncovered. The british institute of international and comparative law, London, pp 83–102

Michaels R (2008) Economics of law as choice of law. Law Contemp Probl 71(3):73–105

Moser LGM (2015) Parties' preferences in international sales contracts: an empirical analysis of the choice of law. Uniform Law Rev 20:19–55

Nielsen PA (2013) The new Brussels I regulation. Common Market Law Rev 50(2):503–528

Pertegás M (2010) The Brussels I regulation and the Hague convention on choice of court agreements. ERA Forum 11:19–27

Pertegás M (2015) Feeling the heat of disputes and finding the shade of forum selection. Nederlands Internationaal Privaatrecht: 374–375

Peters A (2014) The competition between legal orders. Int Law Res 3(1):45–65

Rammeloo S (2003) The long and winding road towards freedom of establishment for legal persons in Europe. Maastricht J Eur Comp Law 10(2):169–197

Rühl G (2005) Das Haager Übereinkommen über die Vereinbarung gerichtlicher Zuständigkeiten: Rückschritt oder Fortschritt? Praxis des Internationalen Privat- und Verfahrensrechts 25:410–415

Rühl G (2007) Party autonomy in the private international law of contracts: transatlantic convergence and economic efficiency. In: Gottschalk E, Michaels R, Rühl G et al (eds) Conflict of laws in a globalized world. Cambridge University Press, Cambridge, pp 153–183

Salecl R (2009) Society of choice. Differences 20(1):157–180

Salecl R (2012) Violence as a response to the ideology of choice. Cardozo Law Rev 33(6):2275–2288

Schulz A (2006) The Hague convention of 30 June 2005 on choice of court agreements. J Private Int Law 2(2):243–269

Schwartz B (2000) Self-determination: the tyranny of freedom. Am Psychol 55(1):79–88

Sieger LE (2011) Civil rights. In: Chatterjee DK (ed) Encyclopedia of global justice. Springer Science+Business Media, Dordrecht, pp 137–140

Smits J (1998) A european private law as a mixed legal system. Maastricht J Eur Comp Law 5:328–340
Stone P (2014) EU private international law. Edward Elgar Publishing, Cheltenham
Strong S (2014) Limits of procedural choice of law. Brooklyn J Int Law 39:1027–1121
Symeonides SC (2013) The Hague principles on choice of law for international contracts: some preliminary comments. Am J Comp Law 61(4):873–899
Thiele C (2007) The Hague convention on choice-of-court agreements: was it worth the effort? In: Gottschalk E, Michaels R, Rühl G et al (eds) Conflict of laws in a globalized world. Cambridge University Press, Cambridge, pp 63–88
Tiebout CM (1956) A pure theory of local expenditures. J Polit Econ 64(5):416–424
Trachtman JP (1993) International regulatory competition, externalization, and jurisdiction. Harvard Int Law J 34(1):47–104
Visscher L (2012) A law and economics view on harmonisation of procedural law. In: Kramer XE, van Rhee CH (eds) Civil litigation in a globalising world. T.M.C. Asser Press, The Hague, pp 65–91
Vogenauer S (2013) Regulatory competition through choice of contract law and choice of forum in Europe: theory and evidence. In: Eidenmüller H (ed) Regulatory competition in contract law and dispute resolution. Verlag C.H. Beck and Hart Publishing, München, Oxford, pp 227–286
Vogenauer S, Weatherill S (2006) The European community's competence to pursue the harmonisation of contract law—an empirical contribution to the debate. In: Vogenauer S, Weatherill S (eds) Studies of the Oxford Institute of European and comparative law. Hart Publishing, Oxford/Portland Oregon, pp 105–148
Wagner G (2013) Dispute resolution as a product: competition between civil justice systems. In: Eidenmüller H (ed) Regulatory competition in contract law and dispute resolution. C.H. Beck, Nomos Verlagsgesellschaft, and Hart Publishing, München, Baden-Baden, Oxford, pp 347–422
Wauschkuhn JL (2014) Babel of international litigation: court language as leverage to attract international commercial disputes. Ned Int Privaatrecht (3):343–350
Weller M (2015) Mutual trust: in search of the future of European Union private international law. J Private Int Law 11(1):64–102
Zimmer D (2000) Private international law of business organisations. Eur Bus Org Law Rev 1(3):585–599
Zimmermann R (2006) Contract law reform: the German experience. In: Vogenauer S, Weatherill S (eds) The harmonisation of european contract law: implications for european private laws, business and legal practice. Hart Publishing, Oxford, pp 71–88

Chapter 3
Procedural Position of a 'Weaker Party' in the Regulation Brussels Ibis

Vesna Lazić

Abstract This contribution discusses the changes introduced by the revised Regulation regarding cross-border disputes involving a policyholder, the insured or a beneficiary under the insurance agreements, a consumer or an employee. It addresses most important amendments particularly those relating to expanding the Regulation's scope of application *ratione personae*, adjustments of the rule on tacit prorogation and on the revised rules on enforcement that have bearing on disputes involving parties with a weaker bargaining position.

Keywords Regulation Brussel Ibis · Weaker parties · Consumer disputes · Insurance contracts · Individual contracts of employment · Jurisdiction · Recognition and enforcement of judgements · *Lis pendens* · Choice of court agreements

---

Procedural Position of a 'Weaker Party' in the Regulation Brussels Ibis is a revised version of an earlier publication: Lazić (2014) Procedural Justice for 'Weaker Parties' in Cross-Border Litigation under the EU Regulatory Scheme. Utrecht Law Review 10(4) pp. 100–117. doi:http://doi.org/10.18352/ulr.293.

V. Lazić (✉)
T.M.C. Asser Institute, The Hague, The Netherlands
e-mail: V.Lazic@asser.nl

V. Lazić
Utrecht University, Utrecht, The Netherlands

V. Lazić
University of Rijeka, Rijeka, Croatia

V. Lazić and S. Stuij (eds.), *Brussels Ibis Regulation*, Short Studies in Private International Law, DOI 10.1007/978-94-6265-147-0_3

Contents

3.1 Introduction

The jurisdictional and enforcement regime of the Brussels I Regulation[1] contain provisions the purpose of which is to minimise the imbalance and to restore the bargaining position of 'weaker' parties in commercial legal relationships. These provisions intend to ensure that any advantage presumed or achieved by a contracting party with a dominant bargaining position will remain without legal entitlement and effect. Consequently, certain rights obtained in such legal transactions will be unenforceable against a 'weaker party'. To this end rules on jurisdiction and enforcement are adjusted so as to enhance the position of a weaker party in proceedings before national courts. The provisions aiming at protecting a weaker party relate to disputes arising under insurance contracts, and consumer and labour disputes.[2]

Additionally, a prorogation of jurisdiction is only valid to the extent that it complies with the special rules provided for weaker party disputes. Consequently, the courts in the EU Member States can establish jurisdiction against a weaker party defendant only on the basis of the Regulation. The applicability of national rules on jurisdiction is thereby excluded. In other words, such defendants are 'protected' against national rules on jurisdiction in EU Member States including exorbitant jurisdictional grounds.

The revised Regulation[3] further enhances the level of protection of weaker parties. The present contribution addresses the major changes in that respect.

---

[1] Council Regulation (EC) No. 44/2001 of 22 December 2000 on jurisdiction and the recognition and enforcement of judgments in civil and commercial matters, OJ L 12, 16.2.2001, pp. 1–23 (hereinafter: Regulation Brussels I).

[2] As such these rules prevail over both the general rule in Article 2 and alternative jurisdictional grounds in Articles 5, 6 and 7. See e.g., ECJ Judgment in *FBTO Schadeverzekeringen* of 13 December 2007, Case C–463/06, EU:C:2007:792, para 28. On the other hand, the rules on exclusive jurisdiction have prevalence over the jurisdictional rules in Sections 3, 4 and 5. Among the latter rules themselves, the rules on insurance contracts prevail over the rules on jurisdiction in consumer disputes.

[3] Regulation (EU) No. 1215/2012 of the European Parliament and of The Council of 12 December 2012 on jurisdiction and the recognition and enforcement of judgments in civil and commercial matters (recast), OJ L 351, 20.12.2012, pp. 1–32, it applies from 10 January 2015 (hereinafter: Brussels Ibis Regulation).

3.2 Rules on Jurisdiction in Brussels I Regulation

The provisions aimed at protecting the position of a weaker party in litigation under the Brussels I regime can be summarised as follows:

(a) A weaker party—a policyholder, the insured or a beneficiary, consumer or employee—has a choice to bring proceedings against the other party to a contract either in the court of the Member State in which that other party is domiciled or in which it is more convenient to a weaker party (most likely in the country of its own domicile) or which is otherwise closely related to the dispute.
(b) Conversely, proceedings may be brought against a weaker party to the contract only in the courts of the Member State in which the 'weaker' party is domiciled.
(c) Forum selection clauses in these disputes have limited binding effect against a 'weaker' party. In other words, they may be successfully invoked against a weaker party only if the conditions provided in the relevant provisions of the Regulation are met.[4]

Thus, an insurer domiciled in a Member State may be sued in the Member State of its domicile or in the Member State where the plaintiff is domiciled if an action is brought by a policyholder, the insured or a beneficiary. A co-insurer may be sued in a Member State where proceedings were brought against the leading insurer.[5] With respect to liability insurance or the insurance of immovable property, the insurer may also be sued in the courts of the place where the harmful event occurred.[6] The same holds true 'if movable and immovable property are covered by the same insurance policy and both are adversely affected by the same contingency'.[7] Also, the insurer may be joined in the proceedings initiated by an injured party against an insured if the law of the court where such proceedings are pending so permits. However, it is only the injured party that is to be protected under Article 11(2) of the Brussels I Regulation and not any statutory assignee. A social security institution cannot be considered to be a weaker party deserving protection in the application of the rules on the international jurisdiction of courts. Therefore, an insurer (a statutory assignee) cannot sue the insurer of an injured party before the courts of its Member State when the insurer is located in another Member State.[8]

---

[4] This issue is addressed in a greater detail in Sect. 3.2.2.1, infra.

[5] Article 9(1) Regulation Brussels I.

[6] No definition of 'where the harmful event occurred' can be found in the Recast, but it must be assumed that an interpretation similar to that of Article 7(1)(b)(2) should be applied. See also, Kropholler & von Hein 2011, Article 10 note 1.

[7] Article 10 Brussels I Regulation.

[8] ECJ Judgment in *VorarlbergerGebietskrankenkasse v. WGV-SchwäbischeAllgemeineVersicherungs AG* of 17 September 2009, Case C-347/08, EU:C:2009:561.

On the other hand, the insured, policy holder or beneficiary as a weaker party may be sued only in the courts of the Member State of its domicile. Thus, a weaker party may choose among the possibilities given in Articles 9 and 10 when filing an action against the insurer, whilst it can be sued exclusively in the country of its domicile. The only exception is in the case of direct actions by an injured party against the insurer when the law governing such direct actions provides that the policy holder or the insurer may be joined as a party.[9]

Similarly, when a contract complies with the definition of a 'consumer contract' under Article 15 of the Regulation,[10] a consumer may choose between the *forum rei* and *forum actoris*.[11] Conversely, a consumer may only be sued in the courts of the place where he/she is domiciled (Article 16(2)). As in the case of insurance contracts,[12] the right to bring a counterclaim in the court where the original claim is pending is retained.[13]

Also, an employee may only be sued in the Member State of his/her domicile. The action against an employer may be brought in the courts of the country of its domicile, in the country where the employee habitually carries out or has carried out his work or in the courts where the business which engaged the employee is or was situated, if the employee does not carry out his work in any one country. Accordingly, an employee may choose between the *forum rei* and *forum laboris*—the courts where he habitually carries out his work or the courts of the last place where he carried out his work. If the employee does not habitually carry out his work in any one country, he/she may choose between the courts of the employer's domicile and the courts where the business that engaged the employee is or was situated.[14]

---

[9] Articles 12(1) and 11(3) Brussels I Regulation. See also, Kropholler and von Hein (2011) stating that rhe concept 'matters relating to a contract' must be interpreted broadly in order to include a wide variety of agreements, for example, life insurance policies'.

[10] For more particulars, see Sect. 3.2.1.2 infra.

[11] Article 16(1) Brussels I Regulation. In the CJEU Judgment in *Armin Maletic,Marianne Maletic v. lastminute.com GmbH, TUI Österreich GmbH* of 14 November 2013, Case C–478/12, EU:C:2013:735, the Court stated that Article 16(1) also applies with respect to jurisdiction in proceedings against 'the contracting partner of the operator with which the consumer concluded that contract and which has its registered office in the Member State in which the consumer is domiciled'.

[12] Article 12(2) Brussels I Regulation.

[13] Article 16(3) Brussels I Regulation.

[14] Article 19 Brussels I Regulation reads: 'An employer domiciled in a Member State may be sued:
1. in the courts of the Member State where he is domiciled; or
2. in another Member State:
(a) in the courts for the place where the employee habitually carries out his work or in the courts for the last place where he did so, or
(b) if the employee does not or did not habitually carry out his work in any one country, in the courts for the place where the business which engaged the employee is or was situated.

In applying the Regulation and its predecessor, the 1968 Brussels Convention, the relevant case law of the ECJ illustrates that the criterion 'habitually carries out his work' can also be applied when the work is carried out in the performance of a contract of employment in more than one Member State. According to the relevant case law of the CJEU, it is the place where an employee has established the effective centre of his working activities.[15] In order to identify that place, certain relevant circumstances need to be taken into account, such as where the employee spends most of his working time, 'where he has an office where he organises his activities for his employer and to which he returns after each business trip abroad'.[16] In the absence of an office, it will be the place in which employee carries out the majority of his work.[17] The Court, in its various decisions interpreting jurisdictional grounds, has emphasised the need to guarantee adequate protection to the employee as the weaker of the contracting parties also when the employee carries out his work in more than one contracting state.[18] In other words, such an employee should not be deprived of procedural protection under the Regulation. Only if the effective centre of his working activities cannot be established will the employee have to file the claim against his employer either in the courts of the employer's domicile or the courts where the business that engaged the employee is or was situated. The need to ensure 'more adequate protection for the party who from the socio-economic point of view is regarded as the weaker in the contractual relationship'[19] is reflected not only in private international law instruments that regulate procedural issues, but also in those that unify conflict of law rules.[20]

---

[15] See the CJEU Judgment in *Heiko/Koelzsch* of 15 March 2011, Case C-29/10, EU:C:2011:151.

[16] ECJ Judgment in *Petrus Rutten v. Cross Medical Ltd* of 1 December 1995, Case C-383/95, EU:C:1997:7. See also, ECJ Judgment in *Mulox IBC Ltd v. Hendrick Geels* of 13 July 1991, Case C-125/92, EU:C:1993:306.

[17] CJEU Judgment in *Weber* of 3 April 2014, Case C-37/00, EU:C:2014:12, para 42.

[18] See e.g., ECJ Judgment in *Petrus Rutten v. Cross Medical Ltd* of 1 December 1995, Case C-383/95, EU:C:1997:7, Para. 22; ECJ Judgment in *Giulia Pugliese v. Finmeccanica SpA, Betriebsteil Alenia Aerospazio* of 10 April 2003, Case C-437/00, EU:C:2003:219, para 18.

[19] Giuliano and Lagarde 1980, p. 1.

[20] See e.g., 1980 Convention on the law applicable to contractual obligations, converted into Regulation No. 593/2008 of the European Parliament and of the Council of 17 June 2008 on the law applicable to contractual obligations, OJ L 177, 4.7.2008, pp. 6–16 (Rome I Regulation) in which party autonomy in determining the applicable law is somewhat restricted so as to ensure that the rights and interests of consumers and employees receive maximum protection. With respect to contracts of employment, the objective of the relevant provision of Article 6 of the Convention is to guarantee adequate protection for the employee. Within that context, the ECJ emphasized that the criterion of the country in which the employee 'habitually carries out his work' must be given a broad interpretation. The subsidiary criterion—the place of business through which the employee was engaged—can determine the applicable law only in cases where the court cannot determine the place where the employee habitually carries out his work. See e.g., CJEU Judgment in *Heiko Koelzsch v. Luxembourg of* 15 March 2011, Case C-29/10, EU:C:2011:151, para 44 and CJEU Judgment in *Jan Voogsgeerd v. Navimer SA* of 15 December 2011, Case C-384/10, EU:C:2011:842. For more particulars on the topic, including the commentaries on the relevant case law, see van Hoek 2011, pp. 650–658; Van den Eeckhout 2014, pp. 3–8; Even 2013, pp. 13–24; Laagland 2012, pp. 63–78; Derks 2011, pp. 8–11; Boonstra 2014.

The analysis of the rules on jurisdiction illustrates that the Brussels I Regulation departs, to a certain extent, from the general rule contained in Article 2—domicile of the defendant—in lawsuits against a 'stronger party'.[21] In disputes arising under consumer and insurance contracts, a weaker party is given the possibility to choose between the *forum rei* and *forum actoris* (consumers) and some other fora (the insured). Although following similar lines, a slightly different approach has been adopted in setting out the grounds for jurisdiction in disputes arising from individual employment contracts. A weaker party—an employee—is given the possibility to choose between fora closely related to the individual contract of employment. In particular, he/she can file the claim in the courts where he/she habitually carries out his/her work. However, differently from insurance and consumer contracts, the choice does not expressly include the *forum actoris*, even though in practice the place where an employee habitually carries out his work and his domicile will most frequently be in the same country. Outside the context of 'weaker party disputes', the domicile of the plaintiff, as well as the nationality of a claimant, is generally considered to be an exorbitant jurisdictional ground—i.e., a criterion that, according to internationally accepted standards, does not justify assuming jurisdiction against a defendant domiciled abroad.

3.2.1 Brussels Ibis Regulation—Consequences for Weaker Party Disputes

The Brussels Ibis Regulation applies as of 10 January 2015. It introduces changes in a number of areas.[22] Among the changes which are relevant to the issues discussed in the present contribution, extending the territorial (or formal/ratione personae) scope of application in disputes involving weaker parties has to be mentioned. Besides, a number of new provisions are inserted either to ensure a greater degree of protection for weaker parties or to clarify the existing regulatory scheme aimed at the protection of such parties.

3.2.1.1 Scope of Application Ratione Peronae

In the Commission's Proposal the universal application of jurisdictional rules and their extension to disputes involving third party defendants was suggested.[23]

---

[21] The domicile of the defendant is the main rule under the Regulation and is a generally accepted standard for international jurisdiction (*actor sequitur forum rei*).

[22] The amendments relate to the provisional measures, the *lis pendens* rule and choice of court clauses, expanding the territorial scope of application, and some new provisions intended to ensure a further protection of weaker parties. With respect to the enforcement of judgments, the exequatur is no longer required, but the public policy exception has been retained among the grounds for refusing recognition and enforcement.

[23] For detailed comments on the proposal for universal jurisdiction, see Weber 2011, pp. 620 et seq.

The so-called 'universal scope' would result in the abolition of the dual regime of jurisdictional rules in cross-border cases within the European Union. Consequently, no exorbitant jurisdictional grounds could be relied upon in cases involving defendants from outside the European Union. The idea of universal application has not been accepted in the Recast Regulation. Yet its territorial (personal or formal) scope of application has been somewhat extended. In principle, the Regulation still applies only if the defendant is domiciled in an EU Member State. The exceptions in cases of choice of court agreements and exclusive jurisdiction have been retained. The scope of application in cases of prorogation of jurisdiction has thereby been expanded even further, so that the domicile of the parties has become irrelevant. Consequently, the provision of Article 25 (the current Article 23 of Regulation 44/2001) will apply in all cases where the jurisdiction of a court in an EU Member State has been agreed upon.[24] Choice of court agreements providing for the jurisdiction of a court of a third state will still be governed by national rules.

Additionally, the personal scope is expanded in the Recast Regulation so as to include certain 'weaker' party disputes, notably consumer and labour law disputes. The provision of Article 6(1) of the Recast Regulation (the current Article 4 of the Brussels I Regulation) reads as follows:

> 1. If the defendant is not domiciled in a Member State, the jurisdiction of the courts of each Member State shall, subject to Articles 18(1), 21(2) and Articles 24 and 25, be determined by the law of that Member State.

The reference to Articles 24 and 25 relates to exclusive jurisdiction and a prorogation of jurisdiction respectively (the current Articles 22 and 23). The provisions of Articles 18 and 21 relate to disputes involving consumers and employees.

Thus, a court in a Member State may establish its jurisdiction on the basis of the jurisdictional rules of Brussels Ibis Regulation in all disputes involving a consumer or an employee regardless of the domicile of the other party. The provision of Article 6(1) refers only to consumer (Article 1(1)) and labour disputes (Article 21(2)), but there is no reference to insurance contracts. Consequently, the jurisdictional rules contained in Sect. 3.3 relating to insurance contracts only apply if a defendant is domiciled in an EU Member State.[25] The relevant provisions on jurisdiction in

---

[24] Under Article 25 of Brussels Ibis Regulation it is no longer required that one of the parties to the agreement on jurisdiction is domiciled in an EU Member State. Under the current regime of Article 23 of Brussels I, for its applicability it is required that a court of an EU Member State is agreed upon and that one of the parties is domiciled in a Member State. Under the revised Article 25 it applies to prorogation clauses providing for the jurisdiction of a court in a Member State regardless of the domicile of the parties.

[25] For more particulars on the territorial scope of application of the Recast Regulation, see Lazić in Bodiroga-Vukobrat et al. 2013, pp. 184–188.

Article 18[26] relating to consumer contracts (Article 16 of the Brussels I Regulation) and Article 21[27] relating to contracts of employment (Article 19 of the Brussels I Regulation) have been adjusted so as to reflect the changes introduced to the territorial scope of application in Article 6 of the Recast. Accordingly, the new regulatory scheme further enhances the protection of consumers and employees. In particular, such 'weaker parties' may rely on the rules on international jurisdiction in disputes against professionals and employees domiciled outside the European Union. On the other hand, the Regulation continues to apply only to claims against consumers and employees domiciled in the EU Member States. Such a conclusion follows from the fact that Article 6 refers only to Article 18 para 1[28] and Article 21 para 2 respectively.

3.2.1.2 Revised Provision on Tacit Prorogation

Besides the scope of application and relevant rules on jurisdiction in disputes involving consumers and employees, there is a further amendment to the provision on the tacit prorogation of jurisdiction. It has been amended so as to better accommodate the interests of 'weaker' parties. Under the current regime of Brussels I, if a defendant enters an appearance, a court in an EU Member State in principle does not examine *ex officio* whether or not it has jurisdiction under the Regulation. The exception is an obligation to examine whether a court in another state has exclusive

---

[26] Article 18 of Brussels Ibis Regulation reads as follows:
'1. A consumer may bring proceedings against the other party to a contract either in the courts of the Member State in which that party is domiciled or, *regardless of the domicile of the other party*, in the courts for the place where the consumer is domiciled.
2. Proceedings may be brought against a consumer by the other party to the contract only in the courts of the Member State in which the consumer is domiciled.
3. This Article shall not affect the right to bring a counter-claim in the court in which, in accordance with this Section, the original claim is pending.' (emphasis added).

[27] Article 21(1) of Brussels Ibis Regulation reads as follows:
'1. An employer domiciled in a Member State may be sued:
(a) In the courts of the Member State in which he is domiciled; or
(b) In another Member State:
(i) in the courts for the place where or from where the employee habitually carries out his work or in the courts for the last place where he did so, or
(ii) if the employee does not or did not habitually carry out his work in any one country, in the courts for the place where the business which engaged the employee is or was situated.
2. An employer not domiciled in a Member State may be sued in a court of a Member State in accordance with point (b) of paragraph 1.' (emphasis added).

[28] Article 18(1) determines jurisdiction when a professional is the defendant, see the text supra note 51.

jurisdiction according to Article 22. This follows from the current text of Article 24 of Brussels I which relates to tacit prorogation,[29] as well as from Article 25.[30]

The jurisdictional rules in disputes involving weaker parties are not mentioned in Article 24 of Brussels I Regulation. Yet a violation of the jurisdictional grounds in disputes arising out of insurance contracts and consumer disputes, as well as the rules on exclusive jurisdiction, presents a valid ground to refuse the enforcement of the judgment under Article 35(1) of the Brussels I Regulation. Considering that the provision on tacit prorogation in Article 24 of Brussels I Regulation does not refer to disputes involving weaker parties, the CJEU has held that the court seised could validly assume jurisdiction in such disputes if a weaker party enters an appearance without contesting jurisdiction.[31] It reasoned, inter alia, that 'although in the fields concerned by Sections 3 to 5 of Chap. II of that regulation the aim of the rules on jurisdiction is to offer the weaker party stronger protection (…), the jurisdiction determined by those sections cannot be imposed on that party'.[32] One could expect that a weaker party should be put in a position to be fully aware of the effects of submitting his/her defence as to the substance and that the court seised should therefore determine *ex officio* what is the intention of entering an appearance. However, the Court held that '[s]uch an obligation could not be imposed other than by the introduction into Brussels I Regulation of an express rule to that effect'.[33]

Thereby the protection intended to be ensured in Article 35(1) is somewhat undermined, as the 'violation' of the jurisdictional rules referred to therein would not qualify as a ground for refusing the enforcement of the judgment even if a weaker party was unaware of the protection of its procedural position provided

[29] Article 24 of Brussels I Regulation reads as follows:
'Apart from jurisdiction derived from other provisions of this Regulation, a court of a Member State before which a defendant enters an appearance shall have jurisdiction. This rule shall not apply where appearance was entered to contest the jurisdiction, or where another court has exclusive jurisdiction by virtue of Article 22.'

[30] Where a court of a Member State is seised of a claim which is principally concerned with a matter over which the courts of another Member State have exclusive jurisdiction by virtue of Article 22, it shall declare of its own motion that it has no jurisdiction.

[31] See CJEU Judgment in *Česká podnikatelská pojišťovna as, Vienna Insurance Group v. Michal Bilas* of 20 May 2010, Case C-111/09, EU:C:2013:165, where the Court held that 'Article 24 (…) must be interpreted as meaning that the court seised, where the rules in Section 3 of Chap. 2 of that regulation were not complied with, must declare itself to have jurisdiction where the defendant enters an appearance and does not contest that court's jurisdiction, since entering an appearance in that way amounts to a tacit prorogation of jurisdiction.'.

[32] Ibid., para 30. Majority took the view that the holding expressed in this judgement was not only valid for insurance contracts, but would also apply to consumer contracts and individual contracts of employment. See, e.g., Magnus et al. (2016a, b) Article 26, p. 678, para 24.

[33] Ibid. With respect to a dispute against consumers, when interpreting the Consumer Directive, the ECJ on various occasions held that that the courts were to examine *ex officio* whether a dispute settlement clause, including forum-selection clauses, had to be considered as unfair contractual terms. See e.g., the ECJ Judgment in *Pannon GSM Zrt.* of 4 June 2009, Case C-243/08, EU:C:2009:350. For more particulars, see Sect. 2.2.3, infra.

under the Regulation. The newly introduced provision in Article 26(2) of the Recast Regulation remedies such a result and improves the positions of weaker parties. It reads as follows:

> In matters referred to in Sections 3, 4 and 5 (…) where the policyholder, the insured, the injured party of a beneficiary of the insurance contract, the consumer or the employee is the defendant, the court, before assuming jurisdiction under paragraph 1, shall ensure that the defendant is informed of his right to contest the jurisdiction and of the consequences of entering or not entering an appearance.

Thus, the court seised is under an obligation to inform a 'weaker' party defendant i.e., a policy holder/an insured/injured party/a beneficiary of the insurance contract, a consumer or an employee of the consequences of entering an appearance. Such additional protection for a weaker party is to be met with approval.[34]

The provision of Article 24 of Brussels I Regulation has remained unchanged and is contained in Article 26(1) of the Brussels Ibis Regulation. In accordance with para 1 of this provision, a weaker party will be 'protected' as any other party domiciled in a one Member State sued in a court of another Member State but does not enter an appearance. In such a case, the court seised is required to declare *ex officio* its lack of competence if it cannot establish its jurisdiction based on the provisions of the Regulation. When a defendant does enter an appearance the court seised is only required to examine jurisdiction on its own motion when the courts of another Member State have exclusive jurisdiction under the Regulation. As already explained, according to the new regulatory scheme of Brussels Ibis Regulation, the court will have to warn a weaker party about the need to contest jurisdiction and the consequences of its failure to do so. A failure to inform a weaker party under Article 26(2) should present a reason to refuse the enforcement of a judgment according to Article 45 Regulation Brussels Ibis.[35]

The further amendments affecting the regulatory scheme on the prorogation of jurisdiction are discussed infra Sect. 3.2.1.3.

3.2.1.3 Limited Binding Nature of Choice of Court Agreements Under the Brussels Ibis Regulation

The idea of limiting the effectiveness of choice of court agreements has been retained in the revised Regulation. In fact, no changes have been introduced

[34] See also, Hays 2013, p. 4; Lazić 2013a, b, p. 12.

[35] *Contra*, Magnus et al. (2016a, b), p. 682, para 35, refereing to Nuyts, La refonte du règlement Bruxelles I, RCDIP 2013, 1, 60. The author, however, gives no reason or argumentation in support of such a view. Others merely conclude that Article 26(2) neither expressly no impliedly provides which consequences follow from a breach of the obligation by a court to inform a weaker party of the right to contest jurisdiction, but offer no suggestion on how to interpret and apply the changes introduced. Magnus et al. (2016a, b) Article 19, para 49.

regarding the provisions specifically regulating the validity of forum-selection clauses with respect to weaker party disputes. Yet some alterations to the general provision on prorogation of jurisdiction in Article 25 (ex Article 23 of the Regulation Brussels I), as well as changes to the *lis alibi pendens* rule in Article 29 (ex Article 27) may have some bearing on the regulation of forum-selection clauses in disputes involving weaker parties. The analysis of the changes introduced is preceded by an outline of the regulatory scheme under the Brussels I Regulation.

Choice of Court Agreements Under the Brussels I Regulation

Prorogation of jurisdiction is dealt with in Article 23 of the Brussels I Regulation. In particular, the definition of the 'written form requirement' is provided in paras 1 and 2. The issue of substantive validity is to be determined on the basis of the applicable national law. In accordance with Article 23(5), a jurisdiction agreement concluded in violation of the provisions of Articles 13, 17 and 21 will have no legal force. These provisions define the conditions for the validity of prorogation agreements in insurance, consumer and labour law disputes respectively. In the same vein, no effect will be given to agreements purporting to exclude the jurisdiction of the courts having exclusive jurisdiction under Article 22.[36]

Only an insured person, a consumer and an employee are protected by the rules restricting the effectiveness of jurisdiction agreements. No other category of 'weaker parties' is protected by the provision on the prorogation of jurisdiction under the Regulation, even though some other parties such as commercial agents, distributors and franchisees also have a weaker bargaining position.[37] The same was true of claims arising out of maintenance which had been within the substantive scope of application of Brussels I before the Maintenance Regulation came into force. The latter permits the prorogation of jurisdiction in Article 4, but only in favour of the courts in a Member State which either has a close connection with the parties and their relationship[38] or the courts which are otherwise competent to hear certain closely related disputes.[39]

[36] Some authors have argued that such an agreement will be invalid as far as international jurisdiction is concerned, but may still be valid as an agreement on local jurisdiction within a Member State, if such agreements would be valid and permitted under the relevant national law. See Magnus and Mankowski 2012, p. 497.

[37] Compare ibid., referring to a principal-agent relationship.

[38] The courts in a Member State of the habitual residence or nationality of either party, Article 4(1)(a) and (b).

[39] According to Article 4(1)(c), in disputes concerning maintenance obligations between spouses or former spouses the parties may agree on the jurisdiction of the court which has jurisdiction in matrimonial matters or the court in a Member State of their last common habitual residence for a period of at least one year. Besides, according to Article 4(3) of the Maintenance Regulation the provision on the choice of court agreements 'shall not apply in a dispute relating to a maintenance obligation towards a child under the age of 18'.

The special regime on the restricted effectiveness of prorogation agreements in disputes involving insured persons, consumers and employees can be summarised as follows:

(a) Jurisdiction agreements entered into after a dispute(s) has arisen may successfully be relied upon by both parties. Thus, there are no restrictions on the biding nature and enforceability of such agreements in disputes relating to insurance, consumer and individual contracts of employment.[40]
(b) Prorogation of jurisdiction stipulated before a dispute has arisen may successfully be invoked by a weaker party if it gives the possibility to a weaker party to sue in courts other than those indicated in the relevant Sections 3, 4 and 5.[41] However, against a weaker party such an agreement either cannot be enforced at all[42] or has biding effect only if the parties have agreed on the jurisdiction of courts in a particular Member State connected to the dispute as determined under the relevant provisions of the Regulation.[43]

Thus, an agreement on jurisdiction entered into after a dispute has arisen is enforceable against both an employee and an employer. An agreement on jurisdiction entered into before a dispute has arisen may be relied upon by an employee, when such an agreement allows the employee to sue in courts other than the courts specified in Section 5. However, it cannot be successfully invoked against him.[44]

In a similar vein, choice of court agreements involving consumers entered into after a dispute has arisen are binding upon both parties (Article 17(1) Brussels I Regulation). Jurisdictional clauses entered into before a dispute has arisen are binding if relied upon by a consumer, allowing the consumer to bring proceedings in courts other than those specified in Section 4 (Article 17(2) of the Brussels I Regulation).[45] Both parties may successfully invoke an agreement which provides for the jurisdiction of courts in the EU Member State of their common domicile or habitual residence at the moment of contracting, if such an agreement is permitted under the law of that Member State.[46] Thus, when the parties (or one of them) change their domicile or habitual residence from the moment of the conclusion of the contract, a forum-selection clause providing for the jurisdiction of the courts of

---

40 Articles 13(1), 17(1) and 21(1) of Brussels I Regulation.

41 Articles 13(2), 17(2) and 21(2) of Brussels I Regulation.

42 This is the case relating to individual contracts of employment.

43 Articles 13(3)–(5) and 17(3) of the Brussels I Regulation.

44 Article 21 of the Brussels I Regulation.

45 Article 17(2) of the Brussels I Regulation provides that such a clause is enforceable if it allows the consumer to bring proceedings in courts other than those indicated in this Section.

46 Article 17(3) of the Brussels I Regulation provides that provisions on jurisdiction under that Section may only be departed from by an agreement 'which is entered into by the consumer and the other party to the contract, both of whom are at the time of conclusion of the contract domiciled or habitually resident in the same Member State, and which confers jurisdiction on the courts of that Member State, provided that such an agreement is not contrary to the law of that Member State'.

the parties' common domicile or habitual residence may be successfully invoked against a consumer, subject to the condition that such a choice is permitted under the law of the Member State of the chosen court.

As to matters relating to insurance, jurisdiction agreements entered into before a dispute(s) has arisen is binding upon an insurer if it permits an insured to institute proceedings in courts other than those mentioned in Sect. 3.3. Against the ensured such an agreement will be binding under the conditions provided for in Article 13(3)–(5). Thus, it will be enforceable against a weaker party if it provides for the jurisdiction of the courts in the Member State of the parties' common domicile or habitual residence even though a harmful event occurred abroad, if such an agreement is not contrary to the law of that state.[47] Also, such an agreement will be enforceable in cases of compulsory insurance or insurance related to immovable property in a Member State against a policy holder who is not domiciled in a Member State or if a contract of insurance covers one or more risks set out in the Regulation.[48] Just as in the case of employment and consumer contracts, choice of court agreements entered into after a dispute has arisen will be binding against both parties.

Choice of Court Agreements in Brussels Ibis Regulation

The provisions relating to choice of court agreements in insurance, consumer and labour law contracts have remained unchanged in Brussels Ibis Regulation. Yet it introduces a number of amendments to the prorogation of jurisdiction in Article 25 (Article 23 of Brussels I). First of all, the applicability of this provision is extended so that it is no longer required that one of the parties to the agreement on jurisdiction is domiciled in an EU Member State. Under the current regime of Brussels I, for Article 23 to apply it is required that a court of an EU Member State is agreed upon and that one of the parties is domiciled in a Member State. Under the revised Article 25, it applies to prorogation clauses providing for the jurisdiction of a court in a Member State regardless of the domicile of the parties. Forum-selection agreements providing for the jurisdiction of a court of a third state are accordingly governed by national rules. As to 'weaker party' disputes, expanding the scope of application with respect to choice of court agreement will have consequences regarding insurance contracts and to some extent with respect to individual employment and consumer contracts, even though the personal scope of application is extended in Brussels Ibis Regulation as already explained.[49]

---

[47] Such an agreement confers jurisdiction on the courts in a Member State which is closely connected with both parties. See also, Kropholler and von Hein 2011, Article 13, nos. 3 and 4.

[48] Articles 13(3)–(5) and 14 of the Brussels I Regulation. For more particulars on jurisdiction in insurance contracts, see Vassilakakis 2014, pp. 1079 et seq.

[49] See Sect. 3.2.2, supra.

Another amendment is a conflict of law rule for the substantive validity of prorogation agreements. According to the newly introduced rule, the law of the Member State of the chosen court will govern the substantive validity of such agreements.[50] The relevant decisions of the ECJ illustrate that the same law will also apply with respect to the interpretation of the choice of court agreement, its renewal or succession into a forum-selection agreement.[51] Recital (20) of Brussels Ibis Regulation clearly states that the reference to the law of the Member State of the chosen court includes the conflict of law rules of that state. Such a solution under Brussels Ibis Regulation is a major shortcoming of the newly introduced rule on the choice of law for the substantive validity of prorogation agreements. This provision does not present a true uniform private international law rule. Instead, it merely refers to the national conflict of law rules of the Member State whose court has been chosen. Consequently, there is no uniform conflict of law rule within the EU for the law applicable to the substantive validity of jurisdiction agreements.[52] This provision will also apply to the prorogation of jurisdiction in weaker party disputes.

The most important change is the revision of the *lis pendens* rule so as to depart from the 'priority rule' expressed in Article 27 of the Brussels I Regulation. According to this provision, the court of a Member State seised of a matter involving the same cause of action and between the same parties shall of its own motion stay its proceeding until the court first seised has established its jurisdiction. With a view of enhancing the efficiency of choice of court agreements and combating 'torpedo actions',[53] Brussels Ibis Regulation provides for an exception to this rule when there is a prorogation of jurisdiction. In such a case, any court seised other than the court designated in an exclusive choice of court agreement shall stay the

[50] Article 25(1) provides that a court or the courts of a Member State designated by an agreement between the parties shall have jurisdiction 'unless the agreement is null and void as to its substantive validity under the law of that Member State'.

[51] Under Article 23 of the Brussels I Regulation these issues are to be dealt with in accordance with the national substantive law determined by national conflict of law rules. See e.g., the ECJ Judgment in *Benincasa* of 3 July 1997, Case C-269/95, EU:C:1997:337, para 31; ECJ Judgment in *Iveco Fiat* of 11 November 1986, Case C-313/85, EU:C:1986:423, paras 7–8; ECJ Judgment in *Coreck Maritime* of 9 November 2000, Case C-387/98, EU:C:2000:606, para 24.

[52] On the criticism relating to the provision on the substantive validity of forum-selection clauses, see Lazić 2013a, b, p. 16. With respect to comments on the Proposal, see Heinze 2011, p. 8, electronic copy available at http://ssrn.com/abstract=1804111 (last visited 8 October 2014); Camilleri 2011, p. 298. But see Beaumont and Yüksel, in Boele-Woelki et al. (eds.) 2010, pp. 563–577. At pp. 575–577, in their comments to the Proposal the authors favour the solutions in both the 2005 Hague Convention and the changes suggested to be introduced in Article 23, including *renvoi*.

[53] 'Torpedo actions' or the 'Italian torpedo' refers to actions instituted before a non-chosen court in order to postpone filing an action before the court designated in a forum-selection clause. In accordance with the current priority rule in Article 27, the latter must stay its proceedings until the court first seised has decided on its jurisdiction. For more particulars, see Lazić 2013a, b, pp. 5–27.

proceedings until the court seised on the basis of the agreement declares its lack of jurisdiction.[54] Accordingly, the designated court will have priority 'to decide on the validity of the agreement and on the extent to which the agreement applies to the dispute pending before it',[55] even if a court of another Member State has been seised first. The court chosen in the agreement can proceed regardless of whether or not the non-designated court has decided to stay proceedings.

However, the rule on the priority of the chosen court is deviated from in some, but not in all cases involving 'weaker parties'. Thus, Article 31(4) of Brussels Ibis Regulation provides that the priority rule in favour of the chosen court does not apply when a 'weaker party' is a claimant and the choice of court agreement is invalid under the provisions of the Regulation. Such wording implies that the new 'priority rule' does not apply when a prorogation clause is invoked by an insurer, an employer or a professional. Conversely, if a forum-selection clause is invoked by a weaker party, then a court before which a 'stronger party' has initiated proceedings will be bound by a new 'priority in favour of the chosen court' rule. Accordingly, the provision of Article 31(4) implies no changes with respect to weaker party disputes. It merely ensures that the new rule will not affect the jurisdictional rules of the Regulation intended to protect the procedural position of a weaker party, including those on the prorogation of jurisdiction. Thus, the court seised of a matter by a 'weaker party', and not the chosen court, will be competent to rule whether a forum-selection clause is valid and enforceable under the Regulation.

The possibility to determine the jurisdiction of a court by an agreement between the persons involved in a dispute may be restricted in other private international law instruments to an even greater extent. This is the case with respect to disputes concerning maintenance obligations, and even more so in matters of inheritance and family law. Thus, the possibility to choose a competent court is limited in different ways in the Maintenance Regulation.[56] First, it is limited by the requirement of a 'link' between the dispute, the parties and the chosen court (Article 4(1)(a) ad (b)). Besides, there is no possibility to choose the competent court in disputes relating to maintenance obligations towards minors.[57] These legal sources remain outside the scope of the present contribution and accordingly are not further discussed.

---

[54] Article 31(2) of Brussels Ibis Regulation.

[55] Recital (22) of Brussels Ibis Regulation.

[56] Council Regulation (EC) No. 4/2009, supra note 5.

[57] In Regulation (EU) No. 650/2012, there is a rather exceptional possibility for the parties in the matter of succession to agree on jurisdiction: if the deceased has made a choice for the applicable law all the parties in the succession can agree that the courts in this country would be competent to rule on all matters in succession. Although it should generally be distinguished from the prorogation of jurisdiction in civil and commercial matters, the regulatory scheme of Council Regulation (EC) No. 2201/2003, Article 12 also provides for a limited possibility to deviate from the jurisdictional rules in matters of parental responsibility.

Relevance of Other EU Legal Sources and the Case Law of the CJEU for the Limited Binding Nature of Choice of Court Agreements

The procedural position of a weaker party is not only protected in EU private international law instruments. Other legal sources, such as directives, may indirectly serve the same purpose even though they are primarily aimed at the approximation of substantive law. This is particularly so as far as Council Directive 93/13/EEC of 5 April 1993 on unfair terms in consumer contracts is concerned. In order to protect the procedural position of a weaker party, the effectiveness of dispute resolution clauses—a prorogation of jurisdiction entered into before a dispute has arisen[58]—may be further restricted. The main reason is that such agreements in transactions involving 'weak parties' are in principle not freely negotiated. Usually they are part of the general terms and conditions or rather standard contracts drafted by business parties which consumers automatically adhere to. A weaker party—a consumer—is left with no choice but to accept such a clause if he/she wishes to enter into a particular legal transaction ('take it or leave it'). The same holds true for employees and insurance policy holders or beneficiaries under contracts of insurance.

When interpreting Directive 93/13/EEC, the CJEU firmly supports the protection of the procedural position of a consumer.[59] Thus, the Court has held that the national courts of the Member States have the power and obligation to examine of their own motion the unfairness of a contractual term conferring jurisdiction on the courts within the meaning of Article 3(1) of the Directive.[60] In its decision of 4 June 2009 (*Pannon GSM Zrt. V. Erzsébet Sustikné Győrfi*) the Court held, inter alia, that 'Article 6(1) of Council Directive 93/13/EEC of 5 April 1993, on unfair terms in consumer contracts, must be interpreted as meaning that an unfair contract term is not binding on the consumer, and it is not necessary, in that regard, for that consumer to have successfully contested the validity of such a term beforehand.' More importantly, the Court has held that a national court is 'required to examine, of its own motion, the unfairness of a contractual term'. Where such a term has been found to be unfair, the national court must not apply it. The same duty exists when the national court ascertains its own territorial jurisdiction.

When determining whether a contractual term is to be categorised as unfair within the meaning of Article 3(1) of Directive 93/13 it has held that a contractual term which was drafted in advance by a professional and was not subject to individual negotiations conferring jurisdiction on a court of the professional's

---

[58] The same holds true for arbitration clauses.

[59] For the debate on the case law of the ECJ and whether the ECJ in interpreting these Directives overemphasises consumer interests, see Trstenjak and Beysen 2011, pp. 95–124.

[60] ECJ Judgment in *Pannon GSM Zrt. V. Erzsébet Sustikné Győrfi* of June 2009, Case C-243/08, EU:C:2009:350; see also the ECJ Judgment in the joined cases *Océano Grupo Editorial and Salvat Editores* of 27 June 2000, Cases C-240/98 to C-244/98, EU:C:2000:346, paras 21–24.

principal place of business satisfies the criteria to be qualified as unfair for the purposes of the application of the Directive.[61]

3.3 Procedural Position of a Weaker Party—Rules on the Recognition and Enforcement of Judgments

In principle, when deciding on the recognition and enforcement of a judgment rendered by a court of an EU Member State, the courts are not permitted to examine whether or not jurisdiction was properly ascertained. Yet, in exceptional circumstances it is possible to review a decision as to jurisdiction even though such a possibility is very much restricted.[62] The jurisdiction may be the subject of a review pursuant to Article 35 of the Brussels I Regulation, with respect to exclusive jurisdiction, jurisdiction in insurance and consumer disputes and Article 72. If a court violates these rules the judgment rendered may be refused recognition and enforcement in another Member State.

It should be noted that Section 5 relating to disputes arising out of employment contracts are not mentioned. The rationale behind this is that it would be contrary to the interest of an employee considering that the employee is the claimant in the vast majority of cases.[63] Yet, employees are treated differently and less favourably than consumers and insured/policy holders. As rightly emphasised in the literature, it 'generates a split between the rules on jurisdiction on the one hand and the rules on recognition on the other hand'.[64]

The changes introduced in this respect in Brussels Ibis Regulation should be met with approval as they enhance the level of protection for weaker parties. The

---

[61] ECJ Judgment in the joined cases *Océano Grupo Editorial and Salvat Editores* of 27 June 2000, C-240/98 to C-244/98, EU:C:2000:346, paras 21–24. The same line of reasoning may be applied with regard to arbitration agreements. In Article 3(3) of the Directive reference is made to the Annex which provides for an indicative and non-exhaustive list of the terms which may be regarded as unfair. The Annex expressly refers to arbitration agreements as follows: '(q) excluding or hindering the consumer's right to take legal action or exercise any other legal remedy, particularly by requiring the consumer to take disputes exclusively to arbitration not covered by legal provisions, unduly restricting the evidence available to him or imposing on him a burden of proof which, according to the applicable law, should lie with another party to the contract'. On the interpretation of the Directive with respect to arbitration clauses in consumer contracts, see the ECJ Judgment in *Asturcom Telecomunicaciones SL* of 6 October 2009, Case C-40/08, EU:C:2009:615 and ECJ Judgment in *Elisa María Mostaza Claro v. Centro Móvil Milenium SL* of 26 October 2006, Case C-168/05, EU:C:2006:675. See also, CJEU Judgment in *Katalin Sebestyén v. Zsolt Csaba Kővári, OTP Bank, OTP Faktoring Követeléskezelő Zrt, Raiffeisen Bank Zrt* of 3 April 2014, Case C-342/13, EU:C:2014:1857.

[62] Leyton and Mercer 2004, para 26.086.

[63] Commission Proposal, COM(1999) 348 final, p. 25.

[64] Magnus and Mankowski 2012, p. 711. In general, for criticism on this point in the Brussels I Regulation, see also, Geimer and Schütze 2010, Article 35, n. 14.

revised version deviates slightly from the regulatory scheme of the Brussels I Regulation, where grounds for refusal were contained in separate provisions in Articles 34 and 35. Instead, all the grounds in Brussels Ibs Regulation are consolidated in Article 45. Just as under the Brussels I Regulation, in para 3 it provides that, as a matter of principle, the jurisdiction of the court of origin may not be reviewed, except under the circumstances referred to in para (1)(e). The latter refers to exclusive jurisdiction,[65] as well as disputes in insurance, consumer and employment matters, 'where the policy holder, the insured, a beneficiary of the insurance contract, the injured party, the consumer or the employer was the defendant'. Thus, employment contracts are now placed on the same footing as other transactions involving 'weaker' parties. Besides, the position of a 'weaker' party is protected to a greater extent in the revised Regulation, considering that a violation of jurisdictional grounds may only be an obstacle to recognition if a weaker party was a defendant in the dispute. Conversely, a 'stronger' party will not be able to invoke a violation of the rules on jurisdiction in Sections 3, 4 or 5 in the enforcement proceedings initiated by a 'weaker' party. Such a legal regulation represents a valuable improvement and clarification with respect to grounds to refuse recognition or enforcement.

3.4 Concluding Remarks

Legal instruments on private international law and especially those relating to international jurisdiction and more generally civil procedure illustrate that the EU legislator attaches great importance to the protection of the procedural position of a party with a weaker position in a legal relationship. In particular, the rules on jurisdiction, as well as on the recognition and enforcement of judgments contained in the Brussels I Regulation are meant to ensure that procedural justice is preserved for certain categories of 'weaker parties'—employees, consumers and insurance policy holders or other beneficiaries of insurance contracts.

Such protection of the procedural position of weaker parties is even further enhanced in the revised Regulation. This is particularly achieved by useful adaptations to the relevant provisions relating to tacit prorogation and grounds to refuse recognition and enforcement of judgments. The latter have been adjusted so as to expressly include violations of the jurisdictional rules in disputes arising under contracts of employment. It is also clearly stated that a violation of the jurisdictional rules presents a reason for refusing enforcement or recognition only if this is relied upon by a weaker party. Besides, the scope of application *ratione personae* of the revised Regulation is widened so that consumers and employees may rely on the privileged jurisdictional rules regardless of the domicile of the other party.

[65] Article 45(1)(e)(ii).

Finally, the revised rule on *lis alibi pendens* reversing the priority in deciding on jurisdiction in case of prorogation of jurisdiction does not apply when weaker parties are claimants.

Regrettably the same approach and level of protection for weaker parties is not maintained in other legal instruments unifying the rules of private international law and civil procedure on the EU level. Thus, some EU Regulations do refer to consumers in connection with the rules on jurisdiction, but decisions on jurisdiction in cases involving consumers cannot be 'controlled' in a Member State of the enforcement.[66] More importantly, the recently revised Regulation on Small Claims[67] makes a passing reference to consumers in Recitals (2) and (3), but just like its predecessor contains no provisions which would aim at protecting the procedural position of consumers.

References

Beaumont P, Yüksel B (2010) The validity of choice of court agreements under the Brussels I regulation and the hague choice of court agreements convention. In K. Boele-Woelki et al (eds) Convergence and divergence in private international law, pp 563–577 (At p 575–577)

Boele-Woelki K et al (eds) (2010) Convergence and divergence in private international law. Journal 563–577 (At: 575–577)

Boonstra K (2014) EVO/Rome I beoogt law shopping te voorkomen, maar niet om cherry picking te bevorderen. Tijdschrift voor Recht en Arbeid 6/7(58): *pages*

Camilleri SP (2011) Article 23: formal validity, material validity or both? J Private Int Law 7(2):298

Derks CBG (2011) Toepasselijk recht: hoe gewoon is de gewone werkplek in de internationale arbeidsverhouding? Arbeidsrecht Maandblad voor de praktijk 45:8–11

Even Z (2013) Het toepasselijk recht op arbeidsovereenkomsten. Artikel 6 EVO en 8 Rome I steeds verder ontrafeld. Nederlands Internationaal Privaatrecht 1:13–24

Geimer R, Schütze RA (2010) Europäisches Zivilverfahrensrecht, Kommentar. Art. 35, n. 14

Giuliani M, Lagarde P (1980) Report on the convention on the law applicable to contractual obligations. OJ C 282:1

Hays P (2013) Notes on the European Union's Brussels-I "recast" Regulation—an american perspective. Eur Legal Forum 1:4

Heinze Ch (2011) Choice of Court Agreements, Coordination of Proceedings and Provisional Measures in the Reform of the Brussels I Regulation. Max Planck Private Law Res Paper 11(5):8. http://ssrn.com/abstract=1804111. Last visited 8 Oct 2014

[66] Regulation (EC) No. 805/2004 of the European Parliament and of the Council of 21 April 2004 creating a European Enforcement Order for uncontested claims, OJ L 143, 30.04.2004, pp. 5–39 and Regulation (EC) No. 1896/2006 of the European Parliament and of the Council of 12 December 2006 creating a European order for payment procedure, OJ L 399, 30.12.2006, pp. 1–32.

[67] Regulation (EC) No 861/2007 of the European Parliament and of the Council of 11 July 2007 establishing a European Small Claims Procedure as amended in Regulation (EU) 2015/2421 of the European Parliament and of the Council of 16 December 2015 amending Regulation (EC) No 861/2007 establishing a European Small Claims Procedure and Regulation (EC) No 1896/2006 creating a European order for payment procedure OJ of 24 December 2015, OJ L 341 of 24.12.2015, p. 1, which will apply as from 14 July 2017.

Kropholler J, von Hein J (2011) Europäisches Zivilprozessrecht – Kommentar zu EuGVO, Lugano-Übereinkommen 2007, EuVTVO, EuMVVO und EuGFVO

Laagland FG (2012) Grenzeloze problemen bij grensoverschrijdende arbeid. Arbeidsrechtelijke Annotaties 11(3):63–78

Lazić V (2013a) The revised *Lis pendens* rule in the Brussels Jurisdiction regulation. Rev Eur Law 2:5–27

Lazić V (2013b) Enhancing the efficiency of dispute settlement clauses in the European Union. In: Bodiroga-Vukobrat N et al (eds) Legal culture in transition—supranational and international law before national courts, Logos Verlag, Berlin, 2013, pp 184–188

Lazić V (2014) Procedural Justice for 'Weaker Parties' in Cross-Border Litigation under the EU Regulatory Scheme. Utrecht Law Review 10(4):100–117. doi:http://doi.org/10.18352/ulr.293

Leyton A, Mercer H (2004) European civil practice. Para. 26.086

Magnus U, Mankowski P, Calvo Caravaca A-L, Carrascosa Gonzalez J (2016a) In: Magnus U, Mankowski P (eds) Brussels Ibis regulation. Sellier, Munich, p 2016

Magnus U, Mankowski P, Nielsen P (2016b) In: Magnus U, Mankowski P (eds) Brussels Ibis regulation. Sellier, Munich, p 2016

Magnus U, Mankowski P (2012) European commentaries on private international law. *Brussels I Regulation* (2nd edn)

Trstenjak V, Beysen F (2011) European consumer protection law: Curia Semper Dabit Remedium? CML Rev 48:95–124

Van den Eeckhout V (2014) De ontsnappingsclausule van art. 6 lid 2 EVO. Hoe bijzonder is de zaak Schlecker? Tijdschrift Recht en Arbeid 31(4):3–8

van Hoek AAH (2011) Heiko Koelzsch tegen Groothertogdom Luxemburg. Ars Aequi ...:650–658

Vassilakakis E (2014) International jurisdiction in insurance matters under regulation Brussels I. In Essays in honour of Spyridon VI. Vrellis, pp 1079 *et seq*

Weber J (2011) Universal jurisdiction in third states in the reform of the Brussels I Regulation. Rabels Zeitschrift 75:620 et seq

Chapter 4
The Enforcement of Monetary Final Judgments Under the Brussels Ibis Regulation (A Critical Assessment)

Marta Requejo Isidro

Abstract EU Member State judgments given in legal proceedings instituted on or after January 10, 2015, in civil or commercial matters, will be enforced in another Member State according to the Brussels Ibis Regulation, Regulation (EU) no 1215/2012. The Brussels Ibis Regulation provides for a new framework where a declaration of enforceability is no longer required in the Member State addressed; with the abolition of exequatur the focal point of the system shifts to enforcement proceedings. While the Brussels Ibis Regulation specifies a few rules that directly impact national enforcement rules, many others of its intended rules require the assistance of the national lawmakers to be implemented. Whether this represents a true step forward towards the free movement of decisions, meaning less costly and time-consuming cross-border litigation, remains to be seen.

Keywords Regulation Brussels I recast · Exequatur · Enforcement · Final judgments · Harmonisation (lack of) · National implementation · Diversity

Contents

M. Requejo Isidro (✉)
University of Santiago de Compostela (Spain),
Luxembourg City, Luxembourg
e-mail: marta.requejo@mpi.lu

V. Lazić and S. Stuij (eds.), *Brussels Ibis Regulation*, Short Studies in Private International Law, DOI 10.1007/978-94-6265-147-0_4

4.1 Introduction

In a legally compartmentalised world, where enforcement is the monopoly of public authorities, the so-called *exequatur* works as a bridge to allow enforcement in one State of a judgment issued in another. In this sense, exequatur is a tool to facilitate cross-border movement of decisions.

At the same time, exequatur is an instrument for controlling the regularity of a foreign decision; therefore it represents a potential obstacle to it being accepted in other legal systems. In the context of the EU (and before, the EC) this second view of exequatur has prevailed. All throughout Europe recognition and enforcement of foreign judgments have traditionally been subjected to compliance with specific requirements to be checked within the framework of a specific proceeding, at the end of which the exequatur order was granted—or refused. Exequatur, being thus an intermediate step between the delivery and the actual enforcement of a judgment, has always been perceived as an additional burden for cross-border proceedings. From the very beginning simplifying exequatur has been a goal for the European lawmaker.[1] The milestones along the way towards this objective are well-known: the Brussels Convention of 27 September 1968 on jurisdiction and enforcement of judgments in civil and commercial matters, and its successor, Regulation (EC) No 44/2001 of 22 December 2000 on jurisdiction and recognition and enforcement of judgments in civil and commercial matters. The third stage in this evolution would have been the complete abolition of exequatur; it was accomplished in several regulations of sectorial scope,[2] and supported by the Commission in its proposal for a recast of the Brussels I Regulation.[3]

[1] Article 220 Treaty of Rome, 25 March 1957.

[2] Regulation (EC) No 805/2004 of 21 April 2004 creating a European Enforcement Order for uncontested claims; Regulation (EC) No. 861/2007 of 11 July 2007 establishing a European Small Claims Procedure; Regulation (EC) No. 1896/2006 of 12 December creating a European Order for Payment Procedure, and Regulation (EC) No. 4/2009 of 18 December 2008 on jurisdiction, applicable law and enforcement of decisions and cooperation in matters of maintenance obligations (for Member States also parties to the 2007 Hague Protocol). More restrictively, also Council Regulation (EC) No. 2201/2003 of 27 November 2003 concerning jurisdiction and the recognition and enforcement of judgments in matrimonial matters and the matters of parental responsibility, repealing Regulation (EC) No 1347/200.

[3] Proposal for a Regulation of the European Parliament and the Council on jurisdiction and the recognition and enforcement of judgments in civil and commercial matters (Recast), COM (2010) 748 final.

The Commission's submission was endorsed only partially: in the current Brussels I Regulation (Brussels Ibis Regulation, Brussels *Ibis*) exequatur has disappeared as a procedural intermediate stage; a decision enforceable in a Member State shall be enforceable in other Member States without any declaration of enforceability being required. However, the grounds offered to the judgment-debtor to resist exequatur under the Brussels I Regulation subsist, albeit as a means to oppose enforcement.

The Commission's proposal tending to completely do away with exequatur for decisions on civil and commercial matters had met much resistance in academia; the "dangers de la porte ouverte"[4] in this regard were profusely denounced. However, most of the criticism focused on the removal of the grounds to fight an application for exequatur, especially of the public policy clause; less attention was paid to the interface between the Brussels Ibis Regulation and national rules on enforcement.[5] This paper focuses on the latter point, i.e., it intends to analyse the procedural aspects of the new system, together with its impact on the national rules; and to assess them.[6]

4.2 The System: Description

4.2.1 The New System in a Nutshell

The basic underlying principle of Chapter III, section 2, of the Brussels Ibis Regulation is that of equivalence or assimilation of Member States decisions; it is reflected both in the wording of the provisions and the accompanying recitals.[7] A judgment given in a Member State which is enforceable in that Member State shall be enforceable in the other Member States without a declaration of enforceability being required (Article 39). It should be enforced under the same conditions as a

[4] The expression is borrowed from López de Tejada 2013, Deuxième Partie, Titre I. Academic antagonism to the Commission's proposal led to countless comments and papers. Among many others Kramberger Škerl 2011, pp. 461–490, and Schack 2011, pp. 1345–1358, both in favour of keeping the public policy scope mechanism to defend intrinsic EU values. Kramer 2012, p. 132, supports the public policy clause to fight globally condemned crimes such as corruption (i.e., to deny recognition or enforcement of judgments delivered by corrupted courts). Kuiper 2010, pp. 23–51, concentrates on the *ordre public* of the forum.

[5] Footnote 4 above; nonetheless, see also López de Tejada 2013, p. 285 ff (on "Les incertitudes de l'insertion"); also Timmer 2013, p. 136.

[6] For the sake of simplicity our departing point will be a final monetary judgment. Provisional enforcement as well as enforcement of other instruments is briefly addressed.

[7] See Article 39, Article 40, recitals 26, 28. The principle of extension of effects is also endorsed, although less enthusiastically: see Article 54. Some authors also allude to the "principle of adaptation", to be found under Article 54: Nuyts 2013a, para 2; *id.* 2013b, para 15. In our view adaptation is not a principle, but a necessity, which according to Article 54 shall follow the principle of extension of effects.

judgment given in the Member State addressed (Article 41), upon production of a copy of the judgment which satisfies the conditions necessary to establish its authenticity and a certificate to be issued by the court of origin (Article 42, Article 53). However, the Brussels Ibis Regulation provides for several grounds to refuse the enforcement of judgments on the application of any interest party (Article 45 and Article 46).[8] The design of the procedure for refusal of enforcement is left to the law of the Member State addressed, except for some harmonised rules provided for by the Brussels Ibis Regulation itself (Article 47 ff).

4.2.2 What Exactly Does the Abolition of Exequatur Mean in Terms of Enforcement?

The suppression of the exequatur procedure does not necessarily entail immediate enforcement of the foreign decision.[9] On the one hand, enforcement will follow the forum rules (Article 41.1). In some countries a claim for enforcement is needed, and an additional proper procedure, even entailing the possibility of a hearing, takes place.[10] Also, enforcement may be delayed if the debtor is accorded a period of grace.[11] In addition, if the forum law so provides, the debtor may already resist enforcement at this first stage or/and by appealing the enforcement decision on the basis of procedural or substantive grounds of the law foreseen by the Member State addressed[12]; whether provisional enforcement during this period is allowed and under which circumstances depends on the *lex fori*.

On the other hand the new Regulation itself envisages a delay in enforcement by imposing service of the certificate issued pursuant to Article 53 on the person against whom enforcement is sought prior to the first enforcement measure (Article 43). A translation may also be requested by same person, and again, no measures of enforcement may be taken other than protective measures until that translation has been provided to the person against whom enforcement is sought.[13]

---

[8] The claimant is also entitled to ask for a declaration that no grounds for refusal of recognition (meaning those of Article 45) exist. According to the Regulation, the procedure will be the same as the one provided for the implementation of Article 46 (refusal of enforcement).

[9] As some writings seem to suggest: see Nuyts 2013a, no. 2, 3.

[10] *Acción ejecutiva*: Articles 517 ff Ley de Enjuiciamiento Civil (LEC). Spain seems nevertheless to be one of the few Member States where an intermediate judicial intervention in needed.

[11] In Spain, Article 548 LEC: enforcement is not allowed until 20 days have elapsed since the decision on the merits becomes final. A discretional (i.e., non-automatic) *délai de grace* exists in other countries, such as France, Article 1244-1 to 1244-3 Code Civil.

[12] Only to the extent nonetheless that they are not incompatible with the grounds referred to in Article 45: see Article 41.2, recital no. 30. On the doubts about what the compatibility requirement really entails see below under Sect. 4.4.2.2.

[13] Both rules are meant to protect the judgment debtor against risks potentially concurring at the stage of the enforcement, derived from the cross-border nature of the dispute.

Other factors may contribute to postpone enforcement. In the first place, as stated in Article 54, if the foreign decision contains a measure or an order unknown in the law of the Member State addressed, that measure or order shall be adapted to a measure or an order known in the law of that Member State which has equivalent effects attached, and which pursues similar aims and interests. This adaptation will quite probably require time, and even the need for an explanation on the measure itself: its nature, its scope and effects. Besides, it may be contested by any party before a court (Article 54.2).

Secondly, the vicissitudes suffered by the decision in the State of origin will affect its fate at the enforcement stage in another country, as reflected in Article 44.2. Suspension of enforceability in the State of origin entails suspension of enforcement proceedings in the Member State addressed; such a consequence is not left to the discretion of the enforcing authority, although it will not happen *ex officio* (i.e., it depends on the request by the person against whom enforcement is sought).[14]

Finally, the application for refusal of enforcement (in all its possible stages: first instance, appeal, second appeal if it is provided, see recital 31) may also impact the actual enforcement of the foreign decision according to Article 44.1. Upon request of the debtor the enforcing authority is given the option to limit enforcement to the adoption of protective measures, to make enforcement conditional on the provision of such security as it shall determine, or to suspend the enforcement proceedings. As a result the enforcement of the foreign decision, even if it is a final one, may become provisional.

In view of the preceding assertions the actual immediate implications of Article 39 seem to be limited to Article 40. i.e, to the power to proceed to any protective measures which exist under the law of the Member State addressed. The provision takes up Article 47.2 Brussels I; it allows for the adoption of measures such as bank attachments or seizure without realisation of the assets;[15] the notice of imminent attachment of a debt,[16] or measures to identify and track the assets of the debtor.[17]

---

[14] No reference is made to the consequences on the enforcement of an ordinary appeal lodged against the judgment in the Member State of origin (or to the time for such an appeal not having expired yet).

[15] See Landsgericht Bonn, 04.03.2003, RIW, 2003, p. 388. On a freezing order as a protective measure within Article 47 Brussels I regulation see *Banco Nacional de Comercio Exterior SNC v. Empresa de Telecomunicaciones de Cuba SA*, [2007] EWCA Civ 662, [2007] I.L.Pr. 51.

[16] For instance the German § 845 ZPO, "1. Based on an enforceable deed of title, the creditor may have a notice served on the third-party debtor and the debtor, even prior to the attachment, that the attachment is imminent, which is to include the notice to the third-party debtor that he is to not make payment to the debtor, and the notice to the debtor to forgo any disposition over the claim, in particular its collection" (translation: bmjv.de).

[17] For instance Article 551.3.2 and Article 554 LEC, in Spain. See also Article 14 Regulation (EU) No 655/2014 of the European Parliament and of the Council of 15 May 2014 establishing a European Account Preservation Order procedure to facilitate cross-border debt recovery in civil and commercial matters.

4.2.3 Does the Abolition of Exequatur Interfere with National Enforcement Proceedings?

The initial response to this question would be "no". According to Article 41, the procedure for enforcement of judgments given in another Member State shall be governed by the law of the Member State addressed, and enforcement will take place under the same conditions applied to national judgments. However, the rules add a caveat: "Subject to the provisions of this Section", meaning section 2 of Chapter III (2.3.1.). In addition, the same provision states that the Brussels Ibis Regulation allows the judgment debtor to resist enforcement on some specific grounds available under the Brussels Ibis Regulation, as well as on arguments provided by national law, to the extent that they are not incompatible with the latter; according to recital 30 they should, if possible, all be invoked in the same procedure (2.3.2.).

4.2.3.1 Brussels Ibis Regulation Rules on Enforcement Procedure

Section 2 of Chapter III sets some rules with direct impact on the enforcement of a domestic court decision abroad. To start with, the Brussels Ibis Regulation decides on the documents to be delivered to the competent authority in the required State (Article 42), thus amending any national provision on the same issue. Notably, an exequatur decision is no longer needed; the foreign decision plus the certificate[18] provide the required enforceable title. Unlike the situation under the Brussels I Regulation, the certificate is now compulsory, and very thorough; its importance has not gone unnoticed in academia.[19]

Secondly, other rules in the Brussels Ibis Regulation entail an amending effect: namely those relating to suspension of enforceability in the State of origin (Article 44.2); to the potential consequences of an application for denial of enforcement in the Member State addressed (Article 44.1); and to the need to adapt measures contained in the judgment to enforce, if they are not known in the Member State where enforcement is required (Article 54). Besides, the rules embedded in Article 43, aiming at the protection of the person against whom enforcement is sought, may also have repercussions in the course of enforcement: the certificate issued

[18] The compulsory nature of the certificate supports its characterisation as part of the enforcement title. However, it would also entail consequences which may not be acceptable within the EU legal and policy framework: for instance, its inaccuracy could build a defence of the debtor against enforcement *in the Member State addressed*, based on the lack of enforceability of the title. Ramos Romeu 2006, 126, discusses (and rejects) this interpretation regarding the EEO Regulation, in the light of Article 10; but this is precisely the provision missing under the new Regulation.

[19] Pohl 2013, p. 113. That's why the lack of certain information therein is the more stricking: see below, under 4.1.1.

pursuant to Article 53 has to be served on the person against whom enforcement is sought prior to the first measure of enforcement; a translation of the foreign decision may be required by the judgment debtor and while it is being produced no enforcement measures are permitted.

It is worth noting that some of the Brussels Ibis Regulation's rules on enforcement are comprehensive, in the sense that they do not leave any margin, or very little, for local variations: this is the case for documents that accompany the request for enforcement, notably for the certificate, which has to be produced in the form provided for in Annex I. The implementation of other rules has conversely been left to the national lawmaker or to national practice, thus opening the door to national divergence. For instance, service of the certificate foreseen in Article 43 has to be done prior to the first enforcement measure, but no indication is given as to how long "prior" this must be (recital's 32 reference to a "reasonable time" does not really help).

4.2.3.2 Denial of Enforcement on the Grounds of Article 45

The Brussels Ibis Regulation itself is quite unspecific regarding the design of the application for refusal of execution. It states the grounds for request in Article 45, which contents-wise follows quite closely the Brussels I Regulation. Procedural issues are very briefly addressed in Article 47 ff. A general referral is made to national law, with the usual caveat "in so far as it is not covered by this Regulation". This actually means very little. The Brussels Ibis Regulation only imposes the following: a mandate to national law to provide for at least one possibility of appeal, a second one being not compulsory (Article 47.1, 49, 50); the documents to be provided by the applicant (Article 47); an un-specific mandate to decide "without delay" on the application (Article 48); and the faculty accorded to the judge to suspend the procedure for refusal of enforcement, no matter its stage, if an ordinary appeal has been lodged against the judgment in the Member State of origin or if the time for such an appeal has not yet expired (Article 51).

The question as to how to procedurally implement the possibility given to the debtor therefore remains open. Theoretically two options seem available: either to try to implement the application within the enforcement proceedings currently in force, i.e. as designed by the national lawmaker with domestic decisions in view;[20] or to set out an independent declaratory proceeding, which would probably be similar to the former exequatur.[21] In the following pages we will see examples of both approaches.

---

[20] This is a possible reading of recital 30. Vice versa, it could be read as suggesting the relocation of the national grounds to oppose enforcement of the proceedings where the grounds provided for by the Regulation to same aim are to be argued.

[21] This is likely to be the solution where in compliance with article 75 of the Regulation a Member State has stuck to the authorities already competent for the exequatur under the Brussels I Regulation.

4.3 National Implementation of the System

The actual application of the Brussels Ibis Regulation in the Member States requires further actions by the Member States' lawmakers; for instance, a decision has to be made on the competent authority to deliver the certificate of Article 53 accompanying the decision to be enforced abroad. Most of the steps to be made at the national level affect the Member States as addressed States, i.e., as States of enforcement. In this regard some of the difficulties that States will face pre-existed the Brussels Ibis Regulation, but the fact that they were known does not imply that they have received a satisfactory answer. Under the new Regulation additional, up-to-now inexistent doubts will arise, relating mainly (but not only) to the application for denial of enforcement and the procedure to deal with it. In view of the divergent systems in force throughout Europe it should be borne in mind from the outset that not only the answers may differ from one Member State to another, but the above-mentioned doubts themselves will have unequal relevance or interest.

4.3.1 National Reactions

The need to adapt the national rules for a swift implementation of the recast soon became evident. It is therefore not surprising that amendments were made in some Member States even before the 10th January 2015. Germany, Ireland, the UK and Poland belong to the "diligent" countries.

4.3.2 Germany

In Germany several in-force Acts were amended by the *Gesetz zur Durchführung der Verordnung (EU) Nr. 1215/2012 sowie zur Änderung sonstiger Vorschriften*, of July 8, 2014.[22] The provisions added to the ZPO (§ 1110 to § 1117) specify the authority in charge of issuing an Article 53 certificate (§1110); by way of a *renvoi* to the pertinent rules of the ZPO they establish the procedure for delivering the document (with or without the debtor being heard: § 1111, sec. 1), and for contesting the decision issuing the certificate (§ 1111, sec. 2). Article 39 of the Recast finds its way into the German enforcement system via § 1112, which eliminates the *Vollstreckungsklausel* otherwise requested for foreign decisions to be considered enforceable titles in Germany. § 1114 entrust the adaptation of a foreign unknown enforcement measure to the *Gerichtsvollzieher* and the *Rechtspfleger;* the adaptation can be contested. § 1115 deals with the application for a foreign

[22] BGBl. 2014 I 890. A description and critical study of the provisions is to be found in Schlosser and Hess 2015, Articles 53 ff.

decision to be denied recognition or enforcement: competent court (venue and functional jurisdiction), procedural aspects (motivation of the order, need for a hearing), effect on the enforcement of the decision on the merits. The potential impact of enforceability being suspended in the State of origin is addressed in § 1116, which actually goes slightly further than the Brussels *Ibis* in as far as it also foresees the case of enforceability being limited. Finally, § 1117 gives an answer—in an affirmative sense- to the very sensitive question of whether objections to the enforcement of the claim based on grounds which arose after the last opportunity to invoke them before the (foreign) court, can be addressed in Germany, at the enforcement stage. The competent court in this regard will coincide with the one before which the application for refusal of enforcement is to be lodged, according to § 1115.

While the German lawmaker can be praised for his timely reaction to the new European procedural rules, the solutions opted for have already met criticism from the academia. Some of these critical views do not necessarily apply to other Member States systems as they actually address particularities pertaining to the German legal setting: this is the case with allocation of the competence to decide on applications for denial of enforcement to the *Landgericht*, thus revoking the current attribution to a specialised chamber of the *Oberlandsgericht*; scholars fear that the debtor may profit from the lack of experience of the national authority currently in charge.[23]

Other shortcomings of the new ZPO when combined with the Brussels Ibis Regulation may also be experienced in other countries; we will address them below.[24]

4.3.2.1 UK, Ireland[25]

In the UK several Regulations have been introduced aiming to facilitate the application of the Brussels Ibis Regulation from January 10th, 2015.[26] The accompanying Explanatory Note states explicitly that the main change introduced by the Brussels Ibis Regulation, thus requiring consequential amendment of national laws, concerns removal of exequatur. Provisions governing or referring to exequatur (registration) have therefore been erased or amended. No mention is

---

[23] Hess 2014, p. 279. The LG had been the competent authorities to grant the exequatur under the Brussels Convention. In this regard the Regulation (as implemented in Germany) looks like a step back: *loc. ult. cit.*; also, Linke and Hau 2015, para 14.25.

[24] Below, under 4.2.

[25] Amendments have also been introduced in Scotland by the Act of Sederunt (Rules of the Court of Session Amendment) (Regulation (EU) No. 1215/2012) 2015, in force from February 7, 2015, in consequence of the coming into force of the Brussels Ibis Regulation. Most of the reform consists nevertheless in the introduction of forms for applications.

[26] The Civil Jurisdiction and Judgments (Amendment) Regulations 2014.

made to a procedure to apply for refusal of enforcement. Adaptation of unknown foreign measures may be made by the Court on its own initiative, or on application.

In Ireland several Regulations coming into force on January 10, 2015, to be cited as European Union (Civil and Commercial Judgments) Regulations 2015, have been made to give full effect to the Brussels I recast. Foreign enforceable decisions from another Member State are declared to have the same force and effect as an Irish judgment, and may be enforced as if they were a High Court judgment. Applications for refusal of recognition or enforcement of foreign judgments shall be made to the High Court; partial refusal is possible. The suspension of enforceability of the foreign judgment in the Member State of origin shall cause suspension of enforcement in Ireland on application of the person against whom it is sought. Adaptation of a foreign unknown enforcement measure requires an *ex parte* application to the Master of the High Court; there is no reference to the possibility of appealing the order.

4.3.2.2 Poland

In Poland an amendment to the Code on Civil Procedure was adopted in order to adapt it to several European Regulations, including the Brussels I recast; it entered into force on January 10th, 2015. The new provisions—Article 1153(13) to 1153(25)- incorporate the new Regulation's mandates on adaptation of foreign measures, and those related to the impact of the vicissitudes of the decision at the State of origin on its enforcement in another Member State. Article 1153(23) and (24) set out the rules on venue and appeal when the person against whom enforcement is sought applies for refusal of enforcement.

4.3.3 National (Absence of) Reaction

Spain provides an example of the lack of reaction to the new Regulation.[27] There has so far been no legislative action consequent to the entering into force of the new regulation[28]; the Spanish authorities have nevertheless complied with the obligation set out in Article 75.

[27] But also Belgium and France. The fact that the application for refusal of enforcement entails an exam beyond mere formal requirements has led French scholars to propose coming back to the solution under the Brussels Convention, thus to the President of the Tribunal de Grande Instance: Cuniberti 2013, p. 28. The *juge de l'exécution* could nevertheless provide an alternative, for the sake of efficiency: *id. loc.*

[28] Proposals for the modification of the Ley de Enjuiciamiento Civil (LEC) were before the Parliament at the time of writing, which did not include any reference to the Regulation. An amendment to the LEC was enacted on July 30, 2015, addressing some of the points we described in the text.

Should an application or a claim for enforcement of a Member State decision be lodged in Spain, under the current situation Articles 517 ff Ley de Enjuiciamiento Civil (LEC) would apply.[29] A number of questions would immediately arise, starting with venue: the normal criterion for domestic cases is a functional one, meaning that the same court that decided on the merits at the first instance will also be the enforcement court (Article 545.1 LEC). For obvious reasons the same solution cannot apply to enforcement of a foreign decision. In the absence of a particular solution, several possibilities seem to be open: either Article 545.3 LEC, applicable to enforcement based on titles other than judicial decisions (as it is not possible to assimilate the foreign judicial decision to a domestic one for the purposes of venue), arbitral awards or mediation agreements; LEC Final Provision number 21.5, establishing the venue for enforcement of a EEO; or Article 955 LEC, which actually deals with the jurisdiction to decide on requests for recognition and enforcement of foreign judgments.

Regarding the application for refusal of enforcement on the grounds foreseen by the Brussels Ibis Regulation, lack of a specific procedure allows for two theoretical options: the first would be to implement the opportunity given to the debtor by the Brussels Ibis Regulation within the enforcement legal framework as it is, regardless of the fact that it has been conceived with a view to enforcing national decisions. The second possibility would be to resort, in a kind of (admittedly disputable) analogy, to Article 564 LEC, thus to opening up a process on the merits for the debtor to argue on the basis of facts and events not included in the causes of opposition to enforcement, which are nevertheless relevant for the rights of the enforcement debtor, and which arose after the preclusion of the opportunity of presenting them at a trial.

Should the rules currently in force on ordinary enforcement[30] apply, the judgment-debtor would not be heard before the writ of enforcement is granted by the judge, and the decree with the specific enforcement measures is issued by the registrar. Once the judgment-debtor is served he is allowed to object to both. Therefore, the application for refusal of enforcement on the grounds of Article 45 Brussels Ibis Regulation would be possible then[31]; subsequently the Article 53 certificate has to be served on the person against whom enforcement is sought before the writ of enforcement is released.

---

[29] A (not very precise, and only updated to September 2013) translation is to be found at http://www.mjusticia.gob.es/cs/Satellite/Portal/es/servicios-ciudadano/documentacion-publicaciones/publicaciones/traducciones-derecho-espanol?param1=1288775993122.

[30] As opposed to provisional enforcement. The current rules on provisional enforcement are largely unsuitable to implement the Regulation recast: objections are admitted against specific measures, but not against the *despacho de ejecución* as such, Article 528.3; no appeal is allowed against the decision on the objections to enforcement, Article 530.4. As already stated above, Footnote 6, for the sake of simplicity this paper only addresses final decisions.

[31] The creditor is entitled to contest to the objection, i.e., the proceedings are contradictory at this stage (Article 529.2 for provisional enforcement; Articles 559.2, 560 for ordinary enforcement).

The registrar, as the authority in charge adopting the specific enforcement measures, will probably have the task of adapting an unknown foreign enforcement measure foreseen in the foreign judgment. Appeal before the judge should be ensured by Article 551.5 LEC, which already provides for it in order to discuss the registrar's decree.

Under the Spanish rules, enforcement may be resisted for substantive as well as for procedural reasons; however both types of objections are limited. Only two substantive grounds are admitted namely -payment, and the prescription (*caducidad*) of the action for enforcement: see Article 556 LEC. The procedural grounds are listed in Article 559, although admittedly the categories mentioned therein accommodate a diversity of arguments. At any rate, the fact that the lists are exhaustive can obviously not prevent the debtor from invoking the objections now provided for by Article 45 of the new Regulation. However it is legitimate to ask whether they are some kind of third "extra" independent set of grounds to be added to the already existing ones, or whether they should be categorised among the latter; and, in this case, whether they should be seen as procedural objections or as substantive ones. Should the second proposal prevail, an acceptable classification would be that of grounds leading to the radical invalidity of the writ of enforcement if the title does not meet the legal requirements for enforcement (Article 559.3, i.e., procedural objections). Scholars have nevertheless already given the opposite answer regarding a similar question under Article 21 EEO Regulation.[32]

Regarding appeal against a decision on an application for refusal of enforcement, the communication from Spain to the Commission in compliance with Article 75 Brussels Ibis Regulation allows for a first and a second appeal against a decision on denial of enforcement based on Article 45. However, under the rules currently in force in Spain a first appeal will be possible before the *Audiencia Provincial* for both parties (Article 561.3); but a second appeal is not foreseen. It is worth noting that under the Brussels Regulation, where a (somewhat) similar situation arose,[33] a cassation appeal had to be admitted on the basis of the primacy

[32] Indeed, the question is not completely new: see Garcimartín Alférez 2006, para 125; Ramos Romeu 2006, p. 127, following F. Gascón Inchausti; also, on Article 22.1 EPO Regulation, S. García Cano 2008, para 202. It is interesting to note that the grounds for opposition are treated successively (procedural ones in the first place; substantive grounds will only be addressed at a second stage), and even differently (a hearing may take place if required by the parties to discuss substantive grounds). Actually, the idea that the grounds of Article 45 are akin to substantive objections, i.e., *objections on the merits addressed against the claim itself*, has been endorsed by some national case law: see Hoge Raad 05.03.2002, cited by Van der Grinten 2006, p. 75, Footnote 11, public policy cannot be invoked in an appeal against the granting of an exequatur when it could have been invoked in the proceedings in the Member State of origin if an appeal had been lodged.

[33] The exequatur decision in Spain takes the form of an *Auto*; appeal on cassation for *autos* is not admitted in Spain as a general rule. However, being imposed by the Brussels I Regulation it had to be accepted in Spain.

of EU law. Should this also be the case for the new Regulation, it has to be clear that the only grounds allowing for cassation will be those foreseen by Article 45, and not the domestic ones.

Finally, should objections be made against enforcement on the basis of Article 45 Brussels Ibis Regulation, the question will arise as to how to adapt the Spanish system to the options offered to the enforcement authority according to Article 44.1. To a certain extent, Article 44.1.1 and Article 44.1.2 could be implemented via Article 561.3.[34] However, suspension or stay of proceedings (Article 44.1.3) will be difficult to instrument, as it is a rare possibility in the case of ordinary enforcement which requires a specific legal authorisation (Article 565 LEC). The objection of the person against whom enforcement is sought does not suspend the enforcement (Article 556.2); should the court dismiss her objections, the appeal does not justify the stay of enforcement (Article 561.3, sec. 1; conversely enforcement will be stayed if the objections are accepted, Article 561.3 sec. 2 LEC). Suspension may also be decreed if the provisions for enforcement adopted by the court or the registrar are not consistent with the judicial enforcement title (Article 563.2 LEC), and in case of appeal against a final decision (Article 566 LEC).[35]

4.4 Assessment

Assessment of the enforcement rules of the Brussels Ibis Regulation involves a double perspective: the first perspective addresses concrete aspects and highlights the absence of sufficient instructions to apply and/or to implement some relevant rules—in other words, deficient harmonisation while also pointing critically to a somewhat debtor-biased regime (4.1); the second focuses on the system as a whole and evidences how already existent uncertainties have been fostered upon the abolition of the exequatur, without matching solutions or remedies being provided for (4.2).

4.4.1 Specific Related Criticism

4.4.1.1 *Lacunae* and Insufficient Harmonisation

The Brussels recast has left relevant issues pending. To begin with, the relationship between recognition and enforcement is unclear. An applicant for a decision that there are no grounds for refusal of recognition as referred to in Article 45 is

[34] The rule provides for the up-keeping of the protective measures already adopted, upon security given by the creditor.

[35] Appeal under final decisions is limited to very specific circumstances (*revisión* or *rescisión de sentencia firme dictada en rebeldía*).

redirected by Article 36.2 to the "procedure provided for in Subsection 2 of Section 3"; however, this procedure, being conceived for the refusal of enforcement, may not be suitable for other purposes.[36] Besides, what the refusal of recognition means in a later application for denial of enforcement (or vice versa) is not settled[37]: Of course, it would make no sense to refuse recognition on one of the grounds foreseen by Article 45, and to set aside a later application for denial of enforcement based on the same ground.[38] However, how or even whether the outcome of one proceeding is to be reflected, or taken into account, in the other, has not been not addressed in the Brussels Ibis Regulation.

Secondly, the Brussels Ibis Regulation's design of the certificate is not completely convincing; a fact the more striking in light of the relevance of the document within the new system.[39] Annex I provides for a detailed form where nevertheless important indications are lacking, such as whether the underlying decision is final.[40] Also, relevant data such as the statutory interests will be indicated in the form by reference to the applicable law—a piece of information that will certainly not be easy to handle by the enforcement authority if it happens to be a foreign law. Additionally, the Brussels Ibis Regulation does not include any mechanism related to rectification or withdrawal of the certificate.[41] While the lack of any provision to this avail should not be understood as an exclusion of those possibilities, it would open the door to the local rules in each Member State, thus to non-harmonised solutions.[42]

Thirdly, only some of the vicissitudes of the decision at the State of origin have been taken into account in order to determine their consequences on the Member State addressed: Article 44.2 only foresees one possible case, namely suspension of enforceability.[43]

In addition several provisions of the new Regulation are shaped as open-ended rules: this is the case of Article 43, which imposes no deadline on service of the certificate on the debtor; recital 32 does not really help much by indicating that the document shall be served on that person "in reasonable time". Similarly, Article 48 on the application for refusal of enforcement orders the court to decide "without delay"; no further instruction is given.

---

[36] Gascón Inchausti 2014, para 20.

[37] Linke and Hau 2015, para 14.24.

[38] Linke and Hau 2015, para 14.24.

[39] Above, under 2.3.1.

[40] This may be a compulsory mention to be included in the decision according to national law: see in Spain Article 208 LEC. However, it would have made sense to have it in the certificate.

[41] Nor does it provide for a control by the authority at the State of origin, as imposed by Article 10 EEO Regulation. The fact that such exam can still be performed at the initiative of the debtor in the Member State addressed accounts for the difference of the Regulations in this point.

[42] Resort to the EEO rules may help in this regard.

[43] Above, Footnote 14. Linke and Hau 2015, para 14.27. See also Schlosser and Hess 2015, on Article 51.1. See the better solution of para 1116 ZPO.

Finally, many other issues are left to the national lawmaker, opening the door wide to non-unified solutions throughout Europe. Most relate to the application for refusal of enforcement according to Article 45: the procedural design will be substantially decided by each Member State. In all likeliness it could not be otherwise: it is, as scholars have pointed out, a logical consequence of the suppression of exequatur and the migration to the procedural stage.[44] However, the diversity of national law on enforcement will immediately impact the functioning of the Brussels Ibis Regulation; non-negligible differences are to be expected.

4.4.1.2 Where Enforcement Authorities and Parties Stand

How does the Brussels Ibis Regulation affect the respective positions of the "key players" of a cross-border setting: the enforcement authority; the creditor; the person against whom enforcement is sought?

Regarding the first category, it is well known that the status of enforcement authorities or agents of the Member States diverges largely in many points (education and training, status -civil servant, liberal or mixed-, activities, jurisdiction, responsibilities, organisation), thus a general assessment of the effect of the Brussels Ibis Regulation on them is not possible. In a more limited way some critical remarks have been already made on the tasks to be assumed by the enforcement authority upon the abolition of exequatur.[45] For instance, adaptation of unknown foreign measures, which was considered as one of the classical purposes of exequatur[46] seems to be a concern in light of the (anticipatable) absence of expertise of national enforcement authorities.[47] Whether this expertise is lacking or not will depend on each national enforcement system: in France or Belgium, for instance, in the absence of a specific provision the task is to be performed by the *huissier de justice*.[48] In Germany criticism has been addressed against the national lawmaker and § 1114 ZPO: the adaptation of an unknown enforcement measure falls upon

[44] Gascón Inchausti 2014, para 44.

[45] Timmer 2013, p. 140. Actually, a similar mistrust of the domestic enforcement bodies had been expressed by AG Kokott in case C-92/12 PPU, *Health Service Executive*, delivered on 28 March 2012, para 68–75: they "would not really be in a position to undertake any assessment of a foreign judgment submitted to them, in particular to examine the conditions governing the enforceability of the judgment and to infer from it the nature and extent of the enforcement to be effected".

[46] Nuyts 20013a, para 3; Bureau and Muir-Watt 2014, para 298. This was not the case in other countries, such as Spain.

[47] Some hints have been given by the CJEU in cases C- 394/07, EU:C:2009:219, and C-235/09, EU:C:2011:238.

[48] Van Boxstael 2015, para 80. The *huissiers* hold a *diplôme en droit* and have usually followed further legal studies. Besides, according to the scholars, in case of doubt both the *huissier* and the parties should be allowed to request the intervention of the judge. Whether this will be the *juge des saisies* (Nuyts 2013a, para 3), or the first instance judge (Van Boxstael 2015, para 80) remains to be seen.

the agents of enforcement (the *Gerichtsvollzieher* and the *Rechtspfleger*); they will indeed be able to perform simple adapting tasks such as the calculation of progressive interests, but its more doubtful how they will face more complicated situations requiring a legal background and knowledge of a foreign language, which they currently lack.[49]

Regarding the creditor, *a priori* the winning claimant's prospects of having the decision enforced abroad are improved under the new Regulation. Actually, in the Brussels Ibis Regulation new strategies likely to end up slowing down enforcement are offered to the debtor to the detriment of the creditor. In this regard one of the most criticised new provisions is Article 43: by requiring service of the certificate prior to the first enforcement measure, the "surprise" effect is lost as the debtor is warned of the creditor's intention to enforce the decision in another country.[50] In addition, one may wonder whether the debtor has to be protected in a way that endangers the creditor's chances of recovery; in other words, the cross-border nature of the enforcement[51] does not sufficiently explain why a judgment-debtor needs to know beforehand about the intention of the winning creditor to start enforcement actions against him in another country. Moreover, Article 43 entitles the debtor to request a translation of the judgment; it is for the creditor to supply it, bearing the costs[52]—at least in the first place.[53]

At first sight the situation of the judgment debtor (the person against whom enforcement is sought) is worsened by the Brussels Ibis Regulation. The progressive development of free movement of judgments in Europe allows the conclusion that the debtor's position in cross-border settings has turned from a comfortable shielding behind the frontiers to exposure in a wide geographical area.

But, is the situation of the debtor really so weak? The answer is not conclusive. To begin with, we have alluded to new several provisions included in the Brussels Ibis Regulation aiming directly to protect the due process right of the debtor: the service of the certificate prior to any measure of enforcement is one (Article 43.1). A right to request a translation of the foreign decision in case he was not domiciled

---

[49] Schlosser and Hess, "Article 54", section 4. The criticism comprises also the way chosen by the German lawmaker to protest against the outcome of the adaptation, in that it is considered as a measure of enforcement, and not as a proper decision.

[50] Gascón Inchausti 2014, para 32, highlights the negative impact of the provision on the dynamics of enforcement—the service is likely to trigger debtor's steps to conceal his state. Cuniberti 2013, p. 27, points rather to the inconsistency of the rule with the goal of building up a border-free European area.

[51] See above, Footnote 13.

[52] It is worth noting that according to the Regulation all translations shall be done by a qualified person (Article 57.3); more lenient rules such as Article 144 Spanish LEC do not apply.

[53] It is up to the national lawmaker to pass on the cost to the judgment debtor. Indeed, costs and risks may finally turn against the debtor; the fact remains that in the meantime they also work against the claimant.

in the State of origin is another; worth noting is that, until the translation has been provided, no measures other than protective ones are allowed against the debtor (Article 43.3).

In addition, other provisions not specifically conceived with the debtor in mind may turn to work in his favour—or conversely, undermine the claimant's position. Indeed, the burden of contesting the enforceability of the foreign decision on the grounds provided by Article 45 falls upon the debtor; however, it may also become a strategic opportunity for him to slow down enforcement.[54] Further possibilities in this sense are opened by Article 41 allowing the debtor to contest enforcement on substantive grounds in the Member State addressed[55]; and the appeal referred to in Article 54 against the adaptation of the foreign enforcement measure.[56] Resort to these options does not only mean the prolongation of the procedures, but will usually also entail the need to explain foreign institutions to the national courts, thus increased risks and costs.[57]

4.4.2 Further Uncertainties

4.4.2.1 On a Replacement for the Transitional Role of Exequatur

The Commission's 2010 proposal intending to abolish exequatur encountered great opposition within the academia. Most of the criticism focused on the suppression of the grounds to resist exequatur, particularly the public policy clause. However, removing exequatur entails further consequences, of a procedural nature, perhaps less visible but equally (or more) relevant in practice. Cross-border disputes often generate a disruption between two procedural stages -those of cognizance and enforcement- deeply intertwined between them in all legal systems.[58] As an intermediate step between the State of origin and the State addressed, exequatur works (ideally) as a gateway or link between them, re-connecting the two above-mentioned procedural stages and facilitating the cross-systematic transit of judicial decisions by providing a distinct setting (in the double sense of a *moment* and of a *reference point*) for adaptation, when needed.[59] Absent a declaration of enforceability of a foreign decision traditional questions reappear. That's the case

[54] See above, Footnote 23.

[55] See below the doubts on the actual meaning and scope of this possibility.

[56] The possibility to contest the measure is opened to both parties.

[57] Gascón Inchausti 2014, para 24 in fine.

[58] A very simple example relates to the need for representation and legal counsel at the enforcement stage. In some legal systems representation at this point is not required if it was not compulsory at the cognizance proceedings (see Article 539 LEC). In a cross-border scenario the question arises which forum is to be looked at in order to determine whether the involvement of the professionals is mandatory.

[59] Above, Footnote 46; Timmer 2013, pp. 137–138.

for the starting day to calculate the time-limit to lodge an application for enforcement; without the decree of exequatur there is no "national" *dies a quo* from which the prescription delay is to be calculated.[60] Similar doubts are raised as regards the *delai de grâce* some systems accord to the judgment debtor to voluntarily abide by the judgment.[61]

By way of its homologating function exequatur also helps to establish the dividing line between the subject matters pertaining to *lex fori* and those falling within the scope of *lex causae*[62]; the same can be said regarding the dividing line between the two jurisdictions at stake (Member State of origin, Member State addressed). Both questions are closely related to the scope and interplay of fundamental EU systemic principles, namely the principle of equivalence or assimilation[63] and the principle of extension of effects.[64] While the theoretical delimitation between them is clear (the former principle concerns the procedural aspects of enforcement, the latter the material consequences of the enforceability of the title), implementation in practice is all but easy. Exequatur did not of course do away with all the doubts, but it assisted in shedding some light on the matter.[65]

[60] In most systems that day fixed the starting point for the delay to run. It was nevertheless not the case everywhere: see for Spain the *Sentencia* of the *Tribunal Supremo*, 16.10.2014, ES:TS:2014:4838, at para 4, the relevant moment is finality of the decision in the State of origin; the application for a declaration of enforceability (Articles 38 ff Brussels I regulation) is deemed to be part of the enforcement proceedings themselves for the purposes of prescription on the application.

[61] Automatically (Article 548 Spanish LEC), or upon request of the debtor and discretional for the judge (France, Article 1244-1 to 1244-3 Code Civil).

[62] The *lex cause* being here the legal system of the Member State of origin.

[63] According to case C-415/11, EU:C:2013:164, Aziz, no. 50 ff, equivalence in the context of enforcement is to be understood as follows: "In that regard, in the absence of harmonisation of the national mechanisms for enforcement, the rules (…) are a matter for the national legal order of each Member State, in accordance with the principle of the procedural autonomy of the Member States, on condition, however, that they are no less favourable than those governing similar domestic actions (principle of equivalence) (…)." A further consequence of the principle of equivalence is probably that while it forbids a less favorable treatment of foreign decisions, it does not prevent a better one (inverse discrimination).

[64] The exact meaning of the principle of extension is not easy to ascertain in the light of assertions like the closing ones in no. 66 of case C- 420/07: "In that connection, although recognition must have the effect, in principle, of conferring on judgments the authority and effectiveness accorded to them in the Member State in which they were given (see *Hoffmann*, paras 10 and 11), there is however no reason for granting to a judgment, when it is enforced, *rights which it does not have in the Member State of origin (…) or effects that a similar judgment given directly in the Member State in which enforcement is sought would not have*" (emphasis added).

[65] See Article 21.2 Regulation 4/2009, where exequatur has also been dropped among Member States bound by the Hague Protocol 2007: The competent authority in the Member State of enforcement shall, on application by the debtor, refuse, either wholly or in part, the enforcement of the decision of the court of origin if the right to enforce the decision of the court of origin is extinguished by the effect of prescription or the limitation of action, either under the law of the Member State of origin or under the law of the Member State of enforcement, whichever provides for the longer limitation period".

Therefore, uncertainties which indeed already existed before the recast Regulation may now (i.e., upon the abolition of exequatur) be felt more acutely.[66] An example is the statute of limitations.[67] The competence of the rules in force in the Member State of origin makes sense, as the issue is linked to the enforceability of the title. However, *lex fori* also has a say as a consequence of the exequatur, which confers the right to enforce the foreign decision *in the forum*; that's why the solution has prevailed in some countries.[68] Whether the abolition of exequatur carries with it the possibility to resist enforcement on the basis of the prescription according to *lex fori* should be carefully assessed; in view of the deep divergences within the Member States on the time-limits to apply for enforcement[69] which law applies becomes decidedly a relevant matter of dispute.

4.4.2.2 On How to Handle (National) Objections to Enforcement

The removal of the intermediate stage also imposes an additional effort regarding the distribution of tasks between the jurisdiction where the decision was rendered and the jurisdiction where enforcement is sought. Prior to the Brussels Ibis Regulation several rulings of the CJEU under the Brussels regime had made clear the divide between exequatur and enforcement. According to case 145/1986, a party who has not appealed against the enforcement order at the moment foreseen in the (at that time) Brussels Convention, Article 36, "is thereafter precluded, at the stage of the execution of the judgment, from relying on a valid ground which he could have pleaded in such an appeal against the enforcement order"; the rule must be applied of their own motion by the courts of the State in which enforcement is sought.[70] Conversely, no objections to enforcement, and in particular, no material objections based on grounds arising after the closing of the hearing that was the last opportunity to object[71] can be tried at the exequatur stage.[72] The CJEU solution met different reactions depending on the Member State under consideration: while in Spain it did nothing but support a situation consolidated at the

[66] López de Tejada 2013, para 362 ff.

[67] The period of grace is also an example: see Ramos Romeu 2006, p. 122.

[68] See for instance Civ. 1re, 19.03.1991, *Rev. crit. dr.int. pr.,* 1992, p. 108, note Ancel; the *Sentencia* of the *Tribunal Supremo*, 16.10.2014, ES:TS:2014:4838.

[69] 12 years in Ireland; 5 years in Spain; 30 years in Germany.

[70] CJEC, as. 145/1986.

[71] The prototypical example of substantive objections in this sense is § 767 ZPO. Similar provisions, or rules amounting to the same effect, are to be found in other legal systems: see Bittmann 2008, pp. 182–194.

[72] Case C 267/97, EU:C:1999:213.

national level after a long period of discussion and diverging case law,[73] in other countries it was criticised as a missed opportunity for enhancing the efficiency of the system.[74] In Germany dogmatic considerations also came into play: the material objections foreseen in the ZPO (§767) are considered to target the national decision on the exequatur, and not the foreign title as such.[75]

In the EEO Regulation, where exequatur is abolished, no express rule addresses the fate of the above-mentioned objections. True, the suppression is accompanied by entrusting the Member State of origin with all controls over the decision to be enforced abroad. However, whether this also includes substantive objections to enforcement remained disputed, as demonstrated by the recent OLG Köln decision[76] and the immediate (critical) reaction by scholars.[77]

In Article 22.2 Regulation 1896/2006 the question is approached in relation to payment, leading to a rule in favour of the Member State of enforcement: "1. Enforcement shall, upon application by the defendant, be refused by the competent court in the Member State of enforcement if (…) 2. (…) and to the extent that the defendant has paid the claimant the amount awarded in the European order for payment."

In the Recast Recital 30 and Article 41.2 address the problem following the CJEU in case C-139/10, *Prism Investments*.[78] There the question was whether compliance with a judgment[79] deprives it of its enforceability; *obiter dicta*,[80] the CJEU asserted that "such a ground may (…) be brought before the court or tribunal responsible for enforcement in the Member State in which enforcement is sought. In accordance with settled case-law, once that judgment is incorporated into the legal order of the Member State in which enforcement is sought, national

[73] The confusion between recognition and exequatur, on the one hand, and exequatur and enforcement on the other, has been a recurrent feature of Spanish case law constantly denounced by scholars (see already Remiro Brotóns 1974, p. 305; Domínguez 1981, pp. 162–163), which fortunately happens very seldom nowadays.

[74] López de Tejada 2013, para 350 ff.

[75] Hess 2004, p. 494, with further references; Bittmann 2015, p. 134. In France, the same question has arisen regarding the jurisdiction to accord the *delai de grâce*: the answer depends on the opinion on whether it addresses the debt that has been declared in the Member State of the origin, or whether it targets the effects of the decision on exequatur. See Muir Watt 1995, p. 735 (Note to *Cour d'Appel de Paris (1er Ch.),* 09.03.1995).

[76] The OLG Köln, 21.11.2012 dealt with material objections (those of §767 ZPO) to the enforcement of an Austrian court settlement in Germany: *IPRax*, 2015, p. 158. According to the court's view they should be discussed and decided by the enforcing court, and not by the court in the Member State of delivery of the settlement.

[77] Bittmann 2015, p. 129.

[78] CJEU, as. C-139/10.

[79] The question was framed generally, envisaging grounds other than one of those specified in Articles 34 and 35 of the Brussels I Regulation, which have been advanced against enforcement of the judgment declared enforceable and which arose after that judgment had been delivered.

[80] At no. 40.

legislation of that Member State relating to enforcement applies in the same way as to judgments delivered by national courts". In the same lines, Article 41.1 establishes that the procedure for the enforcement of judgments given in another Member State shall be governed by the law of the Member State addressed, and this includes, according to Article 41.2, the grounds for refusal or of suspension of enforcement under the law of the Member State addressed.

Whether the rule of Article 41.2 will end the debate on "where to discuss what" is uncertain. On the one hand, it has already been negatively assessed in the academia as contrary to one of the main policy goals of the EU in the freedom, security and justice area, namely the free movement of judgments; and also, as likely to meet and create difficulties in practice.[81] Indeed, the solution entails the possibility to reopen the discussion on grounds relating to the *claim* in (potentially) 28 States: the one where the decision at stake was released, and the 27 remaining Member States of the EU.[82]

On the other hand, the possibility given by Article 41.2 to argue the objections against enforcement foreseen in national law is not automatic, but conditional upon their compatibility with the grounds set out in Article 45 of the recast. The exact meaning of the compatibility requirement is unclear—therefore the effective operation of Article 41 is also undecided. The fact that reference is made only to Article 45 should probably not be accorded much weight: it is not plausible that the European lawmaker intends to circumvent other requirements derived from the general duty to respect the Brussels Ibis Regulation's *effet utile*. At any rate, the lack of any mention of the prohibition of reviewing the merits, expressly foreseen in Article 52, is puzzling: the ban on the revision had always been an argument in favour of allocating the discussion on substantive objections to enforcement to the State of origin. Besides, the most likely reason for incompatibility between national law and the system set up in the Brussels Ibis Regulation lays with the objections being perilously too close to a *revision du fond*.[83]

4.4.2.3 Remaining Open Queries

Finally, the removal of exequatur stimulates further discussions. First, on what exactly the enforcement title consists of in the Member State addressed, and

[81] Hess 2014, pp. 279–280. However, a large number of authors are bound to approve the Regulation on this point, as they already had expressed the same view regarding the EEO Regulation: see Bittmann 2015, p. 130.

[82] Garcimartín Alférez 2006, para 124, Footnote 12, supports a distinction between objections based on facts arising after the decision was rendered, and objections addressing the *ab initio* validity or efficacity of the title. However, the proposal would not do away with the plurality of procedures: the new grounds would only be discussed in the State of enforcement; the scope of the decision adopted in their regard would remain limited to that State.

[83] Bittmann (2008), pp. 194–208.

particularly whether the certificate referred to in Article 53 is or is not part of it[84]; a consequence of a positive answer would be the possibility to contest the accuracy of a certificate before a court of the Member State addressed.[85] Second, the abolition of exequatur has not been accompanied by the deletion of the grounds conceived to resist it, therefore the question arises as to how to qualify them: while they aim exactly at the same goal as before, i.e., at controlling the regularity of the foreign decision, what they currently prevent is enforcement of the decision. The relevance of the issue may be none in national systems where a specific procedure to implement the Article's 46 application is introduced, and conversely, substantial where no such a procedure exists, thus the grounds of Article 45 have to be accommodated to local enforcement categories.[86] It is also worth asking whether the CJEU case law on grounds so far conceived as obstacles to exequatur continues to apply to the same grounds in their new role as obstacles to enforcement; a positive answer has already been given in academia.[87]

4.5 Conclusion

At first sight, Chapter III of the Brussels I recast represents a step forward towards free movement of decisions within the EU. As Recital 26 states, the aim of making cross-border litigation less time-consuming and less costly justifies the abolition of the declaration of enforceability prior to enforcement in the Member State addressed, so that a judgment given by the courts of a Member State is treated as if it had been given in the Member State addressed.[88]

However, the favourable impression fades when the instrument is put under further scrutiny.[89] A simple comparison with prior texts suffices to reveal the limited scope of the progress. Indeed, the wording of Article 39 reproduces something already established in previous texts, such as Article 5 EEO Regulation, Article 19 EPO Regulation, Article 20 Small Claims Regulation, or Article 17 Maintenance Regulation; however, while those instruments have completely removed exequatur, both as a procedure and as a control on the regularity of the foreign decision, in the new Regulation the latter function remains (Articles 45, 46 ff). It is precisely

84 Not being a compulsory document the translations cannot be considered as part of the enforcement title. Of the same view, Gascón Inchausti 2014, para 10, Footnote 24.

85 Above Footnote 18.

86 Above, Spain: the need to assimilate the grounds to those foreseen by the rules in force.

87 Gascón Inchausti 2014, para 42.

88 Actually, in a very lucid way the recital uses the conditional form ("a judgment given by the courts of a Member State should be treated as if it had been given in the Member State addressed").

89 Headings in scholarly titles are quite clear in this regard: see Gascón Inchausti 2014, Section 5, "beaucoup de bruit pour rien".

due to this fact that the objective of a more efficient, less costly system, expressly formulated in recital 26, cannot be taken as a matter of fact. Under the new regulation the risk of an attempt to enforce a foreign decision becoming an intricate exploit cannot be excluded. To start with, provisions have been incorporated to protect the position of the debtor facing enforcement in a cross-border setting, at the expense of swift enforcement of the decision, and without a convincing reason to justify them.[90] Moreover -and paradoxically- by shifting the burden of starting the control proceedings to the person against whom enforcement is sought, the recasts offers her even more opportunities than before to resist enforcement in cross-border settings, to the point that the Brussels Ibis Regulation has been accused of being pro-defendant biased.[91] It is not surprising therefore that scholars advise turning to the EEO.[92]

In addition, relevant queries of a procedural nature that found an answer within a system of exequatur have been left unaddressed by the European legislator: for instance, the starting point of the limitation period to apply for enforcement. Old questions, such as where material objections to enforcement should be discussed, are approached, but no convincing (nor definitive) solution is given. New queries appear and remain undecided. This is particularly the case of the application for refusal of enforcement on the grounds provided for by the Brussels Ibis Regulation itself. Only some points of the application have been harmonised for some others only very loose instructions are given by the European lawmaker, while the rest remain to be shaped by each single national legislator; diversity is thus ensured.[93] In this regard, especially when compared to the situation under the Brussels I regulation, the system can hardly be described as user-friendly[94]; the recast constitutes a step backwards.

In our view, whether it could have been otherwise—whether a uniformed design for the application for refusal of enforcement could have been accomplished and whether further coordination between the State of origin and State addressed could have been achieved—may be disputed. Unlike prior European instruments which do away with exequatur, in the Recast the abolition has resulted in enhancing the role of the Member State addressed; in open contradiction to prior decisions of the CJEU, the grounds provided for by the Brussels Ibis Regulation may be argued within the enforcement procedure itself. It is well-known that enforcement is very differently designed in different countries; there are as many systems as Member States. The paucity, sometimes the sheer absence,

[90] The case of the service of the certificate: above under 4.1.2.

[91] Clearly Hess 2014, p. 278, "Die Bevorzugung des Schuldners im Vollstreckungstaat".

[92] Hess 2014, p. 281.

[93] No mandatory deadlines are imposed by the regulation to decide on the application; not even the opportunities to appeal have been harmonised. Above, under Sect. 4.4.1.1.

[94] Diversity works as a deterrent factor when it comes to consider enforcing a court judgment abroad, and complicates the task of the professionals who advise litigants.

of proper instructions or guidance given in the Brussels Ibis Regulation to the stakeholders (courts and practitioners) regarding procedural steps simply reflects the local variety of enforcement rules. The European lawmaker is "rearing his head" in a highly diversified area of law. By doing so it certainly urges the need to achieve some degree of commonality in this domain; a cohesion which actually is the only sensible way to reach the objective of assimilation of national and foreign decisions which is at the core of the European policy in this domain.

References

Bittmann DC (2008) Vom Exequatur zur qualifizierten Klausererteilungsverfahren. Nomos Verlagsgesellschaft. Baden-Baden, München

Bittmann DC (2015) Die Zulässigkeit materiellrechtlicher Einwendungen gegen einen Europäischen Vollstreckungstitel im Vollstreckungsstaat. Praxis des Internationalen Privat- und Verfahrensrecht 35:129–134

Bureau D, Muir-Watt H (2014) Droit International Privé. Presses Universitaires des France, Paris

Cuniberti G (2013) La réforme du règlement Bruxelles I. Droit et Procédures 2013:26–33

Domínguez Cortés (1981) Derecho procesal civil internacional. EDERSA, Madrid

García Cano S (2008) Estudio sobre el proceso monitorio europeo. Aranzadi, Cizur Menor

Garcimartín Alférez FJ (2006) El título ejecutivo europeo. Civitas, Cizur Menor

Gascón Inchausti F (2014) La reconnaissance et l'exécution des décisions dans le règlement Bruxelles I *bis*. In: Guinchard E (ed) Le nouveau règlement Bruxelles I bis. Bruylant, Bruxelles, pp 205–247

Hess B (2004) Europäischer Vollstreckungstitel und nationale Vollstreckungsgegenklage. Praxis des Internationalen Privat- und Verfahrensrecht 24:493–494

Hess B (2014) Urteilsfreizügigkeit nach der VO Brussels Ia: bechleunigt oder aufgebremst? In: Festschrift für P. Gottwald zum 70. Geburtstag, C.H. Beck, München, pp 273–281

Kramberger Škerl J (2011) European public policy (with an emphasis on Exequatur proceedings). J Private Int Law 2011:461–490

Kramer X (2012) Approaches to jurisdiction and foreign judgments and the international fight against corruption. International law and the fight against corruption, Mededelingen van de Koninklijke Nederlandse Vereniging voor Internationaal Recht, Preadviezen, 139 (advisory report for the *Dutch Royal Society of International* Law). T.M.C. Asser Press, The Hague, pp 99–142

Kuiper JJ (2010) The right to a fair trial and the free movement of civil judgments. Croatian Yearb Eur Law Policy 6:23–51

Linke H, Hau W (2015) Internationales Zivilverfahrensrecht. Otto Schmidt, Köln

López de Tejada M (2013) La disparition de l'exequatur dans l'espace judiciaire européenne. Librairie Générale de Droit et de Jurisprudence, Paris

Muir Watt H (1995) Note to Cour d'Appel de Paris (1er Ch). Revue critique de droit international privé 84:735–741

Nuyts A (2013a) Bruxelles I *bis*: presentation des nouvelles règles sur la competence et l'exécution des décisions en matière civile et commerciale. In : Barnich L, Englert H, Nuyts A, Jafferali R, Actualités en Droit International Privé, Bruylant, Bruxelles, pp 77–134

Nuyts A (2013b) La refonte du règlement Bruxelles I. Revue critique de droit international privé 102:1–41

Pohl M (2013) Die Neufassung der EuGVVO- im Spannungsfeld zwischen Vertrauen und Kontrolle, Praxis des Internationalen Privat- und Verfahrensrecht, (vol):109–114

Ramos Romeu F (2006) El título ejecutivo europeo. Civitas, Cizur Menor

Remiro Brotóns A (1974) Ejecución de sentencias extranjeras en España. Tecnos, Madrid

Schack H (2011) The misguided abolition of exequatur proceedings in the European Union. Festschrift für T. Ercinski, LexisNexis Polska Warschau, pp 1345–1358

Schlosser P, Hess B (2015) EU-Zivilprozessrecht, EuGVVO, EuMahnVO, EuBagVO, EuZVO, EuBVO Kommentar. C.H. Beck, München

Timmer LJ (2013) Abolition of *Exequatur* under the Brussels I regulation: Ill conceived and premature? J Private Int Law 9:129–147

Van Boxstael JL (2015) De Bruxelles I à Bruxelles *Ibis*. J des Tribunaux 134:105–108

Van der Grinten P (2006) Abolishing exequatur in the European Union: an alternative. In: Crossing borders (Essays in Honour F. van der Velden). Kluwer, Deventer, pp 71–83

Chapter 5
Provisional and Protective Measures in the European Civil Procedure of the Brussels I System

Ilaria Pretelli

Abstract This article deals with the rules governing the territorial adjudication of interim relief. Firstly, it addresses how the rules introduced already in the 1968 Brussels Convention and taken over in the Brussels I Regulation have been explained and enriched by the ECJ/CJEU. Thereafter, the major changes introduced in the Brussels Ibis Regulation are discussed in connection with the regime of interim relief measures conceived for other relevant EU legal instruments, as the European Account Preservation Order.

Keywords Provisional and protective measures · European civil procedure · Brussels Convention of 1968 · Brussels I Regulation · Brussels Ibis Regulation · Lugano Convention · European Account Preservation Order · Territorial

---

The title of this paper is a wink of the eye towards Luigi Mari, whose enlightened lessons shaped my understanding of the system's philosophy since the earliest years of my studies in Urbino (see Mari 1999). By the expression Brussels I system I refer to all the pieces of legislation generated by the 1968 Brussels Convention (Convention on jurisdiction and the enforcement of judgments in civil and commercial matters (Consolidated version OJ C 097, 11/04/1983, pp. 2–24), namely: the 1988 Lugano Convention (Convention on jurisdiction and the enforcement of judgments in civil and commercial matters of 16 September 1988, OJ L 319, 25/11/1988, pp. 9–48), the Brussels I Regulation (Council Regulation (EC) No. 44/2001 of 22 December 2000 on jurisdiction and the recognition and enforcement of judgments in civil and commercial matters, OJ L 012, 16/01/2001, pp. 1–23), the 2007 Lugano Convention (Convention on jurisdiction and the recognition and enforcement of judgments in civil and commercial matters of 30 October 2007 and its protocols—Protocol 1 on certain questions of jurisdiction, procedure and enforcement—Protocol 2 on the uniform interpretation of the Convention and on the Standing Committee, OJ L 339, 21/12/2007, pp. 3–41) and the Recast (Regulation (EU) No. 1215/2012 of the European Parliament and of the Council of 12 December 2012 on jurisdiction and the recognition and enforcement of judgments in civil and commercial matters, OJ L 351, 20.12.2012, pp. 1–32; hereinafter Brussels Ibis Regulation).

I. Pretelli (✉)
Swiss Institute of Comparative Law, Lausanne, Switzerland
e-mail: ilaria.pretelli@isdc-dfjp.unil.ch

V. Lazić and S. Stuij (eds.), *Brussels Ibis Regulation*, Short Studies in Private International Law, DOI 10.1007/978-94-6265-147-0_5

adjudication · Jurisdiction · Recognition and enforcement of judgments · Measures for taking evidence · Circulation of judgments · *Ex parte* measures · *Inter partes* measures

Contents

5.1 Introduction

Before presenting the Brussels system and the role of provisional measures in its framework and philosophy, I will take advantage of the opportunity to congratulate the Asser Institute on the occasion of its fiftieth anniversary. I am both delighted and honoured to celebrate the creation of the "inter-university institute for international law", dedicated to Tobias Michael Carel Asser. I am here today to represent a much younger sibling of your prestigious Institution: the Swiss Institute of Comparative Law, born no less than seventeen years after the creation of the T.M.C. Asser Instituut in 1965. I would also like to give due attention to the fact that the eminent person who leant his name to the *Instituut* was awarded the 1911 Nobel Peace Prize for his commitment to give a structure to international justice through the Permanent Court of Arbitration, the Hague Conference of Private International Law and the *Institut de Droit International*.

Based on the same philosophy linking peace and justice, the former Article 220 of the original EC Rome Treaty set the foundation for a "European Civil Procedure" and for what may be called the "Brussels I system".

That provision gave rise to the first text of civil procedure rules common to Members of the European Communities: the 1968 Brussels Convention.[1] The idea to develop uniform rules of civil procedure—coexisting with national ones—came as a logical consequence of an inspired intuition by the Convention's drafters.

[1] On the origin and the characteristics of the Brussels Convention see Mari 1999, 1–67.

They shifted from the traditional binary logic of mutual recognition conventions—with the aim to create uniform rules for a State's recognition of a foreign judgement–to a unitary system of rules on jurisdiction—where the focus is on the geolocalisation, so to say, of European disputes.

In other words, the Convention's drafters decided to address the issue of recognition upstream and instead of enumerating the conditions for a *foreign* judgement to be recognised by another Member State, they established a priori common rules for the territorial adjudication of *European* disputes.

There was at that time no real need to shift from the traditional reasoning to some other reasoning: the binary logic functions well in many federal states and primarily in the United States of America. However, the new logic based on the geographical link as a precondition for the exercise of jurisdiction proved to be successful.

Since then, coordination between different systems of civil procedure is carried out by choosing which *European* court, as part of a unified territory, is in *the best geographical position* to ensure *the best administration of justice*. Once identified, the court best placed to hear the case guarantees the most efficient administration of justice by delivering a decision that shall be enforceable in all parts of the unified territory subject to the EU, thus ensuring effective judicial protection for European citizens.

This logic also characterises the regime of provisional measures.

5.2 The *Acquis* on Interim Relief Measures and Its Impact in the Recast

The rules governing the territorial adjudication of interim relief have remained unchanged since the Brussels Convention of 1968.

With the exception of the rewording due to the necessity of making a reference, respectively, to Contracting States or States bound by the Convention and Member States, not a single comma appears to differ in the texts of Articles 24 Brussels Convention and Article 24 Lugano Convention, Article 31 Brussels I Regulation, Article 31 2007 Lugano Convention and Article 35 Brussels Ibis Regulation.[2]

This means that all the problematic issues revealed by the case law and concerning provisional and protective measures could be dealt with by way of the interpretation of the first rule. These include: (i) the definition of provisional and protective measures and the possible inclusion of measures allowing the taking of evidence in that notion; (ii) the identification of the possible connecting factors "justifying" the delivery of a provisional and protective measure; (iii) the possibility to enforce provisional and protective measures abroad and, in particular, the regime of *ex parte* measures.

---

[2] For a synoptic view refer to Ancel et al. (2015), Lynxlex: From Brussels to Lugano, a panoramic table, http://www.lynxlex.com last accessed on 4.10.2016.

As previously explained by the ECJ, it is perfectly coherent with the Brussels I system that a creditor may only obtain an exportable protective measure from the judge who will hear the substance of his case and no other.[3] In this respect, the new Article 35 Brussels Ibis Regulation allows a plaintiff to seek a more efficient and swiftly enforceable measure in the jurisdiction of any other European court: that is addressing his request to a judge capable of directly enforcing the sought interim relief in his jurisdiction.

It is indeed difficult to imagine any reason that could possibly justify a request for interim relief abroad (i.e. issued by a court that has no jurisdiction on the merits) when the relief needs to be enforced at home (in the jurisdiction that decides on the merits). Obviously, the judge empowered with jurisdiction on the substance is better placed to decide on the interim protection, since he or she may evaluate not merely the *fumus boni iuris* and the *periculum in mora* but also the merits of the case.

In plus stat minus.

On the other hand, it has been pointed out that the circulation of interim relief may be even more important than the circulation of final judgments themselves, for several reasons.[4] First, because transnational disputes are usually longer than purely internal ones and judges need more time to issue a final decision since they need to enter the insidious lands of comparative and private international law. In addition, the need to notify acts abroad and/or to take evidence abroad, with all the well-known series of obstacles to a successful communication created by the diversity of legal culture (and thus of legal expectations), and the diversity of the legal language—short of language *tout court*—are all factors capable of increasing the time which is necessary for a transnational proceeding as compared to a purely internal one.

It is not difficult, in light of the case law, to see the additional difficulties occurring in the event of "procedural strategies" that exploit the flaws of the system. Just as in the case of *forum shopping*, a debtor may benefit from procedural advantages from a legal system that he knows well and he is thus encouraged to use (or even abuse) in order to frustrate the execution of decisions taken abroad. Interim relief may play a significant role in such transnational strategies where the "surprise effect" of the national measure may be increased by the ignorance of the measure itself by the "foreign" counterparty. On the other hand, it has been observed that the regime of provisional measures may create a "market" of provisional measures within the area of freedom, justice and security that would not be without beneficial effects as regards access to justice.[5]

---

[3] Bogdan 2012, p. 125 ff., Sandrini 2012, 273 ff.

[4] Garcimartín 2014/2015, pp. 57–58.

[5] *Ibidem* and Honorati 2012, p. 543 ff. and Schlosser 2007, p. 288 ff., 312 ff. In contrast, Nioche 2012, p. 301 argues that *forum shopping* of interim relief measures may virtually generate parallel proceedings resulting in unmanageable situations, even within the Brussels I system.

5.3 Provisional, Including Protective, Measures

5.3.1 The Lowest Common Denominator of Member States' Interim Relief Measures

Comparative law shows a great heterogeneity of measures having both a provisional and protective character. Indeed, the measures of seizure and injunctions provided for by national laws differ widely from one country to another, up to a point where it often becomes very difficult or even impossible to "translate"—even in a purely linguistic form—an interim measure into another legal language, not to say to compare it to any other measure provided for in the other(s) country(ies) involved in the legal battle. Here in the Netherlands the *kort geding* provides for an excellent example: is it not a measure that may only be appropriately referred to in Dutch and in no other language? This kind of relief may have many possible and alternative functions: conservatory, anticipatory, for securing evidence etc. Some of these effects may inevitably be "lost in translation" with the consequence of affecting their "freedom of movement".

From a methodological point of view, the first step taken by the ECJ in this respect was that of drawing a European notion of "provisional and protective measures".[6] In more recent years, the ECJ's notion has been used for the first tentative European uniform measure: the European Account Preservation Order (EAPO).[7]

At the European level, however, even a literal interpretation confronts the interpreter with the twenty-four official languages in which European legislation is drafted. It goes without saying that few lawyers will be able to confront more than a handful of versions and, in this respect, we will also limit ourselves to some observations on the most diffuse of these languages.

Within the English version of the Brussels I system it is common to refer to "provisional *including* protective measures." This corresponds to the German linguistic versions of the original Regulation and its Recast[8] whereas the French and

---

[6] This effort is not recognised by Nioche 2012, p. 18 ff. who excludes the existence of an autonomous notion of provisional and protective measures. The author suggests to simply characterise provisional and protective measures through the use of a negative definition that would include all measures *not* covered by *res judicata*. For a first comprehensive definition of provisional measures in light of ECJ case law (albeit until 1999) see Mari 1999, pp. 714–723 and Kaye 1999, pp. 3022–3062.

[7] See Regulation (EU) No. 655/2014 of the European Parliament and of the Council of 15 May 2014 establishing a European Account Preservation Order procedure to facilitate cross-border debt recovery in civil and commercial matters, OJ L 189, 27.6.2014, p. 59 ff.

[8] Article 35 Brussels Ibis Regulation: *einstweilige Maßnahmen einschließlich Sicherungsmaßnahmen* while Article 31 Brussels I Regulation reads *einstweilige Maßnahmen einschließlich solcher, die auf eine Sicherung gerichtet sind.*

the Italian versions are more evocative of two distinct kinds of measures: one being characterised as provisional, the other as protective.[9]

Since the versions are all official and their interpretation cannot differ from one country to another within the EU, it is important to clarify whether provisional and protective measures are two alternative categories or whether precautionary measures may only be a sub-category of provisional measures. The question of whether the European concept includes measures of a protective nature that do not have a provisional character must be answered in the negative. Rather, the adjectives "provisional" and "protective" bring to mind the traditional characteristics of the measures granting precautionary protection: the *fumus boni iuris* (protective nature) and the *periculum in mora* (provisional nature).

These two substantial elements are common to the extraordinary variety of *escamotages*—so to say—conceived by national legislators in order to ensure the efficiency and effectiveness of justice. This circumstance is easily explained by the common Roman roots of European provisional/protective measures and by the resilience of Roman legal notions over the centuries. Insofar, despite the plethora of national forms of interim relief, the two aforementioned elements are recurrent as umpteenth proof of the persistence of Romanist structures in contemporary legal thinking and in the shaping of European law.

While keeping intact the heterogeneity of measures available within Member States' procedural systems, the Court of Justice has progressively highlighted the criteria that make it possible to characterise relief available in a national procedural system as a "provisional measure" within the meaning and for the purposes of Articles 24 Brussels Convention, 31 Brussels I Regulation, 35 Brussels Ibis Regulation, 24 1988 Lugano Convention, 31 2007 Lugano Convention, whose texts are identical. These criteria all eventually reveal one element that can be taken as the lowest common denominator of all the possible forms of interim, anticipatory, precautionary and provisional relief available under European national legal systems.

5.3.1.1 Instrumentality

The very first clarification by the ECJ as regards the notion of provisional and protective measures came in the context of the Reichert/Köchler case,[10] in which the Court excluded the possibility that the French *action paulienne* regulated by

---

[9] In French, the need to specify that provisional measures *include* protective ones does not seem to be felt: the wording is *mesures provisoires* ou *conservatoires*. See for example recital 33 of the Recast. In Italian the title of section 10 of the original Brussels I Regulation reads: "*Provvedimenti provvisori* e *cautelari*" whereas Article 31 reads: *Provvedimenti provvisori* o *cautelari*, the same wording may be found in section 10 and Article 35 of the Recast. All emphasis added.

[10] Case C-261/90—Mario Reichert, Hans-Heinz Reichert and Ingeborg Kockler v Dresdner Bank AG., ECLI:EU:C:1992:149 following a previous decision in the same instance (Case C-115/88—Mario P.A. Reichert and others v Dresdner Bank—ECLI:EU:C:1990:3, where the *pauliana* had been (wrongly) characterised by the plaintiff as a matter relating to rights *in rem* in immovable property).

Article 1167 of the *code Napoléon* could be characterised as a "provisional or protective measure".

The German Reichert spouses were heavily indebted to Dresdner Bank and the latter sought to recover its credit through a former property belonging to the couple which was discovered in France. It turned out that the asset located in the French region of *Provence* had been given by Mr and Mrs Reichert to their adult child as a gift.

The French *action paulienne*, of Roman origin,[11] corresponds *mutatis mutandis* to the German *Gläubigeranfechtung* (which literally means annulment by the creditor), and allows creditors to sue a third party (alien to the relationship between creditor and debtor but) related to the debtor as a successor in title to a specific property.[12] It is a cause of action that allows creditors—whether in reality or by fiction—to seize assets no longer belonging to their debtor who sold or gave them away in an attempt to secure them from the creditor's enforcement.

In the Reichert case, Dresdner Bank thought it more convenient to sue its debtors in France rather than in their *forum*, thus seeking heads of a possible French jurisdiction in the framework of the Brussels Convention.[13] In so doing it gave an opportunity to the ECJ to verify the possibility to characterise the *pauliana* as a form of interim relief for the purposes of Article 24 Brussels Convention. The ECJ delivered a negative answer because the action named *paulienne*, as well as comparable national versions, was not instrumental to the protection of rights litigated in other jurisdictions. Rather, actions like the *pauliana* imply a thorough analysis of the merits and not a rapid inspection of a *fumus boni iuris*; moreover, they ensure conclusive protection to the creditor's substantive rights. Once successful, the plaintiff is satisfied and the defendant is deprived of the right he was previously enjoying: this kind of relief is not temporary nor reversible.[14]

The lack of instrumentality of the French *action paulienne* is an insurmountable obstacle to its characterization as a *provisional* measure.

The functional link between a national measure and the future decision on the merits is also revealed by the two *De Cavel* judgments.[15]

[11] Ankum 1962, offers an in-depth analysis of Roman and medieval sources of the *pauliana*.

[12] For a comparative analysis, Pretelli 2010, pp. 55–117 in Italian and, for a synthetic overview in English, Pretelli 2011, pp. 589–600.

[13] Namely, the bank tried a European characterization of the *pauliana* as an action in matters of: real estate for the purposes of Article 16-1 Brussels Convention; torts for Article 5-3 Brussels Convention; provisional and protective measures in order to make use of Article 24 Brussels Convention; and the enforcement of judgments for Article 16-5 Brussels Convention. It is still uncertain if the bank would have found the alternative sought to the *forum rei* in the *forum contractus* as later suggested by an Italian judgment of the *Corte di cassazione*: Pretelli 2004, p. 612 ff.

[14] In many legal systems it is even acknowledged that the decision has a constitutive character and may even be compared, to a certain extent, to a constructive trust. See Pretelli 2011, pp. 599–600.

[15] Case 143/78—Jacques de Cavel v Louise de Cavel, ECLI:EU:C:1979:83 and Case 120/79—Louise de Cavel v Jacques de Cavel, ECLI:EU:C:1980:70.

In both decisions, the ECJ excluded the contention that a provisional and protective measure of a civil nature could fall under the material scope of Article 24 Brussels Convention in a case where the measure was instrumental to the settlement of a divorce.

> The case arose from the divorce of a Franco-German couple in the context of which the judge of family matters at the *Tribunal de Grande instance de Paris* had ordered the "putting under seal of furniture, effects and other objects in the flat at Frankfurt-am-Main belonging to the parties and the freezing of the assets and accounts of the [wife] at two banking establishments in that city" (*De Cavel I*, point 2). Before the German Courts the husband had requested the enforcement of the French provisional measure under the Brussels Convention then in force. The German Courts referred the question to the ECJ which subsequently made it clear that: "ancillary claims ... come within the scope of the convention according to the subject-matter with which *they are concerned* and not according to the subject-matter involved in the principal claim" (*De Cavel II*, pt. 9, emphasis added). However, on the other hand, the Court further added that "an application in the course of divorce proceedings for placing assets under seal did not come within the scope of the convention, *not on account of its ancillary nature*, but because it appeared that, having regard to its *true function*, it concerned, in that case, rights in property arising out of the spouses' matrimonial relationship" (*De Cavel II*, pt. 9 emphasis added).

It thus became clear that the "provisional" nature of the measure is a corollary of its instrumentality and does not stand per se as an inherent characteristic of the measure: a provisional measure may well become a final one provided that the subsequent decision on the merits allows for this. In other words, the effects of a relief measure available in a national procedural context must be limited "in time" because of the functional link of the interim measure to the substantive rights that the measure seeks to protect.

> The expression "provisional, including protective, measures" within the meaning of Article 24 must therefore be understood as referring to measures which, in matters within the scope of the Convention, are intended to preserve a factual or legal situation so as to safeguard rights the recognition of which is sought elsewhere from the court having jurisdiction as to the substance of the matter.[16]

The interim measure needs to serve the protection of a substantive right and thus it only stands as long as it is necessary for the judge to decide the issue once and for all: "Provisional means preliminary to further proceedings for final judgments on substance".[17]

5.3.1.2 Measures for the Taking of Evidence

The same definition, limits and conditions may be applied to interim relief aimed at preserving evidence. Here, too, "instrumentality" is the lowest common

[16] C-261/90—Reichert and Kockler (note 10), pt. 34.

[17] Kaye 1999, p. 3026, see also his comments on the following rulings: Case C-261/90—Mario Reichert (supra note 9); Banque Cantonale Vaudoise v Waterlily Maritime Inc. [1997] 2 Lloyd's Rep. 347 (UK); Re an Italian Cargo of Adultered Wine [1991] I.L.Pr. 473 (Germany); Oblique Financial Services Ltd. v The Promise Production Co. Ltd. [1994] I.L.R.M. 74 (Ireland).

denominator of Article 24 Brussels Convention measures (as well as of Article 24 Lugano Convention, 31 Brussels I Regulation, 31 2007 Lugano Convention and 35 Brussels Ibis Regulation). Also in the case of measures for preserving evidence the advantages of direct enforcement justify the adoption of the measure by a judge not empowered with jurisdiction on the merits.

The *leading case* on this subject is "St-Paul dairy"[18], a case raised in very peculiar circumstances. In the framework of a 100 % Belgian dispute,[19] a Dutch order was requested and issued by the *Rechtbank te Haarlem*. The measure sought was the provisional hearing of a witness resident in the Netherlands. According to Dutch law, the measure is conceived as a preliminary step "to enable [an] applicant to decide whether to bring a case, determine whether it [is] well founded and assess the relevance of evidence which might be adduced in that regard" (pt. 16). Since the Netherlands did not have jurisdiction as to the substance and no proceedings were pending in Belgium, it was impossible for the ECJ to see the hearing of the witness in the Netherlands as instrumental to "avoid causing loss to the parties as a result of the long delays inherent in any international proceedings" (pt. 12). In the absence of any *periculum in mora*, in a case that had no substantial connection with the Netherlands, nor had it ever been brought in front of a judge, the statement that "the grant of such a measure could easily be used to circumvent, at the stage of preparatory inquiries, the jurisdictional rules set out in Articles 2 and 5 to 18 of the Convention" (pt. 18) appears obvious.

As for any other interim relief, those aimed at taking evidence benefit under the same conditions of the extension given to their scope of application by Article 35 Brussels Ibis Regulation (and by Article 31 2007 Lugano Convention, as well as, previously, by Articles 24 Brussels Convention, 24 Lugano Convention, 31 Brussels Ibis Regulation in their respective scope of application).

A judge not having jurisdiction as to the substance may order interim relief for preserving evidence whenever the measure is sought "to preserve a factual or legal situation so as to safeguard rights the recognition of which is otherwise sought from the court having jurisdiction as to the substance of the case" (pt. 13).[20]

This test is commonly referred to as "double-condition test" and is based on the following rationale: any judge deprived of jurisdiction as to the substance may grant a provisional measure on the basis of his or her own legal system, because he or she will limit him or herself to verifying the *fumus boni iuris* of the request in a situation of *periculum in mora*, thus only whenever the measure *needs* to be taken

[18] Case C-104/03, St. Paul Dairy Industries NV v Unibel Exser BVBA, ECLI:EU:C:2005:255.

[19] *Ibidem*. See point 7 of the decision: "With regard to the substance of the dispute between Unibel and St. Paul Dairy, the order for reference states that it is common ground that both parties are established in Belgium, the legal relationship at issue in the main proceedings is governed by Belgian law, the court having jurisdiction to hear the matter is the Belgian court and no case on the same subject has been brought in the Netherlands or in Belgium".

[20] The ECJ explicitly referred to its previous statements in pt. 34 of *Reichert and Kockler* (note 10), and pt. 37 of *Van Uden* (note 29).

within his or her jurisdiction.[21] No other justification seems to be acceptable to depart—in order to request interim relief—from the Court that has jurisdiction as to the substance of the case. Unless the measure *needs* to be taken *presto* within another jurisdiction, no other court seems better placed to hear the arguments in favour of granting interim relief.

5.3.2 A Semantic Evolution? The References to the IP Directive

No apparent or invisible semantic evolution appears between the lines of the Recast. In this respect, what seems to be a semantic clarification appears in Recital 25 as regards measures for the taking of evidence.

Recital 25 of Brussels Ibis Regulation reads:

> The notion of provisional, including protective, measures should include, for example, protective orders aimed at obtaining information or preserving evidence as referred to in Articles 6 and 7 of Directive 2004/48/EC of the European Parliament and of the Council of 29 April 2004 on the enforcement of intellectual property rights. It should not include measures which are not of a protective nature, such as measures ordering the hearing of a witness. This should be without prejudice to the application of Council Regulation (EC) No. 1206/2001 of 28 May 2001 on cooperation between the courts of the Member States in the taking of evidence in civil or commercial matters[22]

Let us turn, for a definition of provisional, including protective, measures, to Article 6.2. and 7.1 of the Directive 2004/48/EC on the enforcement of intellectual property rights (hereinafter IP Directive).

The former urges Member States to adapt, whenever necessary, their own internal legislation to the following specific needs of copyright protection:

> Member States shall take such measures as are *necessary to enable the competent judicial authorities to order*, where appropriate, on application by a party, *the communication of* banking, financial or commercial *documents under the control of the opposing party*, subject to the protection of confidential information.[23]

[21] *E multis* see Mari 1999, p. 729 on the *acquis Mietz* with regard to Article 24 Brussels Convention: "Posto dunque che il rifiuto dell'*exequatur* è diretto a colpire un provvedimento abnorme sotto il profilo della competenza [...], i provvedimenti [cautelari] sono conformi all'Article 24—vale a dire legittimamente emanabili sul base del ricorso al diritto nazionale—solo se possono essere attuati senza bisogno dell'*exequatur* in un altro Stato contraente".

[22] Directive 2004/48/EC of the European Parliament and of the Council of 29 April 2004 on the enforcement of intellectual property rights (OJ L 157, 30.4.2004) in the text resulting from the subsequent *Corrigendum* published in the OJ L 195, 2.6.2004, pp. 16–25.

[23] *Ibidem*, Article 6, emphasis added. See Stamatoudi 2014, pp. 573 ff.

The norm seems to suggest that, in addition to the existing national forms of interim relief for the taking of evidence, Member States shall ensure the availability, within their borders, of measures that roughly correspond to the English "worldwide disclosure order".[24] One may be tempted to argue, following this instruction, that measures such as the worldwide disclosure order are to be characterised as interim relief measures also for the purposes of Article 35 Brussels Ibis Regulation. However, as stated above, differently from the Directive on intellectual property rights, the Recast does not unify the judicial protection of specific substantive rights. Therefore, jurisdiction to issue a "worldwide disclosure order" within the framework of the Brussels I system will continue to depend on the results of the aforementioned "double-condition test".

In Article 7 of the Directive we find further indications:

> Member States shall ensure that, even before the commencement of proceedings on the merits of the case, the competent judicial authorities may, on application by a party who has presented reasonably available evidence to support his/her claims that his/her intellectual property right has been infringed or is about to be infringed, order prompt and effective *provisional measures to preserve relevant evidence* in respect of the alleged infringement, subject to the protection of confidential information. Such measures may include the detailed description, with or without the taking of samples, or the physical seizure of the infringing goods, and, in appropriate cases, the materials and implements used in the production and/or distribution of these goods and the documents relating thereto. Those measures shall be taken, if necessary without the other party having been heard, in particular *where any delay is likely to cause irreparable harm to the right holder or where there is a demonstrable risk of evidence being destroyed.*[25]

One must bear in mind, that this rule concerns solely *ex parte* measures and their regime.

In light of the identity of the text of Article 35 and its predecessors, and in light of Recital 25, we may therefore conclude that the answer to the question of whether the Recast has modified the meaning of *provisional, including protective, measures* within the existing European civil procedure of the Brussels I system seems to be negative.

---

[24] On recognition and enforcement of the English worldwide freezing order in the framework of the recast see van Rest 2014, p. 351 ff. See Cruz City 1 Mauritius Holdings v Unitech Ltd and others [2014] EWHC 3704 (Comm) with reference, *inter alia*, to Credit Suisse Fides Trust SA v Cuoghi [1997] 3 All ER 724, at 730, and [1998] QB 818 at 827 suggesting that "protective measures should be granted by those courts best able to make their orders effective. In relation to orders taking direct effect against the assets, this means the courts of the state where the assets are located; and in relation to orders *in personam*, including orders for disclosure, this means the courts of the state where the person enjoined resides".

[25] *Ibidem*, emphasis added.

5.3.3 *Echoes of the Recast in the European Account Preservation Order*

After the IP Directive, a brand new unified interim relief was created by Regulation (EU) No. 655/2014 (hereinafter EAPO Regulation)[26] under the name of European Account Preservation Order (hereinafter EAPO).[27]

The EAPO is an interim relief instrument that may be requested before a court in a European Member State in order to secure the outcome of a "cross-border case". A "cross-border case", for the purposes of the EAPO Regulation, occurs in two hypotheses: (i) when it is dealt with by a court located in one Member State whereas "the bank account concerned by the Order is maintained in another Member State" and, (ii) when the creditor asking for the relief is domiciled in one Member State and "the court and the bank account to be preserved are located in another Member State" (Recital 10).

The EAPO can function either as interim relief, aimed at securing "the enforcement of a later judgment on the substance of the matter prior to initiating proceedings on the substance of the matter and at any stage during such proceedings" (Recital 11). However, it may also be used as a measure for the enforcement of a previous judgment.

In both cases, it is instrumental to the enforcement of a judgment, whether already existing or yet to be pronounced.

Jurisdiction needs to be justified by the verifiability of a "close link between the proceedings for the Preservation Order and the proceedings on the substance of the matter" (Recital 13).

The EAPO Regulation is clear and drastic in stating that such a link may only be expressed by the identity of the court issuing the EAPO and the court judging the case on the merits (Article 6).

It is just as clear and radical in stating that the EAPO needs to respond to a situation of *periculum in mora* since the issuing of an EAPO obliges the creditor to initiate proceedings on the merits "within 30 days of the date on which he lodged the application or within 14 days of the date of the issue of the Order, whichever date is the later" (Article 10-1) and obliges him or her "to provide proof of such initiation to the court with which he lodged his application for an Order" whenever there is no coincidence between the two courts.

Had the creditor not initiated proceedings or not informed the Court having issued the EAPO of the commencement of proceedings, then the EAPO is subject to revocation by the Court of its own motion or automatically (Article 10-2 and Recital 16).

26 Regulation (EU) No. 655/2014 (note 7).

27 A special regime governs EAPOs issued for the recovery of consumers' debts.

In sum, the basic principles lying at the heart of the need to which Article 35 Brussels Ibis Regulation responds inspired the construction of the EAPO regime, that allows ex parte measures from the competent court (art. 11).

5.3.4 Characterization in the Absence of a Taxonomy

Mietz[28] and *Van Uden*[29] prompted further clarification on the characterization of interim relief, in connection with the Dutch *kort geding*.

The ECJ, in charge of progressively making the Brussels I system a workable and efficient system of territorial adjudication of disputes in Europe, has avoided constructing a "European taxonomy" of interim measures for the purposes of Article 24 Brussels Convention (and its successors). This may explain why the ECJ has not felt the need to take a position on the "nature" of the *kort geding*. In both decisions there is no dogmatic classification of the *kort geding* as a provisional measure falling within the scope of Article 24 Brussels Convention or outside it.

Certainly, a classification of all interim measures existing under the national laws of Member States would not have been undemanding. In addition, it seems that for the ECJ, it was not useful for the efficient and proper functioning of the Brussels I system. In the framework of the Recast, it seems to have been equally unnecessary.

Regardless of its "true nature", the *kort geding* may well fit within Article 35 Brussels Ibis Regulation (*brevitatis causa*) or not fit within the scope of that rule, depending on its "true function" in a given case, as explicitly stated by the ECJ.[30]

In proceedings governed by the Brussels I system, a judge may extract from his or her national procedural law the power to grant interim relief if and only if the double-condition test leads to a positive result: namely, if the true function of the relief is to prevent future problems with the enforcement of the final decision (or to prevent the risk that relevant evidence becomes unavailable); and if the measure is to be enforced in a jurisdiction different from the one empowered to decide on the merits.

This verification takes place on a case by case basis and not through an *a priori* classification. A European taxonomy of national forms of interim relief is not needed for the system to perform correctly.[31]

---

[28] Case C-99/96 Hans-Hermann Mietz v Intership Yachting Sneek BV, ECLI:EU:C:1999:202.

[29] Case C-391/95 Van Uden Maritime v Kommanditgesellschaft in Firma Deco-Line and Others, ECLI:EU:C:1998:543.

[30] The reference is to the second *Reichert* case (note 10) at pt. 9, quoted *supra* section 2.1.1.1.

[31] Cf. Recital 13 of Regulation (EU) No. 655/2014 (note 7): "proceedings on the substance of the matter should cover any proceedings aimed at obtaining an enforceable title on the underlying claim including, for instance, summary proceedings concerning orders to pay and proceedings such as the French *procédure de référé*." Here, the references to national procedures seems to have been added as mere examples, rather than as a tentative sketch of a primitive taxonomy.

5.4 Enforcement of Provisional Measures Abroad

5.4.1 The Double-Condition Test as a Detector of the Instrumental Character of a Measure

In deciding *Mietz*,[32] the ECJ has highlighted the distinction to be made between the jurisdictional power to grant provisional and protective measures that belongs to the Court having jurisdiction as to the substance (jurisdictional power grounded on the Brussels system) and the jurisdictional power to grant interim relief that belongs to the Court not having jurisdiction as to the substance (jurisdictional power grounded on national law).

> The case pitted Mr Mietz against Intership Yachting after disagreements over the "contract of sale" of "an Intership boat model 1150 G, which would have to undergo several changes". Subsequent disagreements between the parties led to the delivery of a Dutch judicial order, directed to Mr Mietz, to pay the sum of 143,750 DM plus interest. The judgment was pronounced under Articles 289 to 297 of the Dutch Code of Civil Procedure, which provide, upon application for a *kort geding*, for the adoption of urgent measures. It was declared provisionally enforceable. The ECJ took note of the following: *i)* "Articles 289 to 297 of the Netherlands Code of Civil Procedure deal with a form of procedure known as *kort geding*, which allows the President of the *Arrondissementsrechtbank* to grant enforceable measures 'in all cases which, having regard to the interests of the parties, require an immediate measure on grounds of urgency"(pt. 34); *ii)* "under Article 292 of the ... Code, 'interim decisions are without prejudice to the main proceedings' [and] *Kort geding* may be instituted without the need to bring substantive proceedings before the court having jurisdiction. The President of the *Arrondissementsrechtbank* may, however, refer the parties back to the ordinary proceedings" (pt. 35); *iii)* "Under Article 289 of the Netherlands Code, *kort geding* may be instituted at very short notice and, in accordance with Article 295, an appeal must be lodged within two weeks, on pain of being declared inadmissible" (pt. 37).

The instrumental character of the *kort geding* permitted its characterization as an interim relief because, in the circumstances of the case, the Court considered, on the one hand, that the effects of the *kort geding* were reversible and, on the other, that it concerned assets located within the jurisdiction of the "interim" judge (see especially pt. 42).

When the jurisdictional power to grant a relief exists "solely by virtue of the jurisdiction provided for under Article 24", the reversibility of effects is of crucial importance. It is essential not to undermine a possible decision on the merits dismissing the case. For the same reason, it is essential for the measure to be taken outside the territory of the judge entrusted with jurisdictional power as to the substance of the case, so that the measure does not need any enforcement abroad.

In a system of uniform *fora*, it is possible to seek an interim relief elsewhere than in the jurisdiction entrusted with the power to decide the issue on the merits only if "the measure ordered relates ... to specific assets of the defendant located

[32] *Supra* (note 28).

or to be located within the confines of the territorial jurisdiction of the court to which application is made" (*Mietz*, pt. 2 of the operative part).

These assumptions had already been set in *Van Uden*,[33] making it clear that Article 24 Brussels Convention "may confer jurisdiction on the court hearing that application even where proceedings have already been, or may be, commenced on the substance of the case and even where those proceedings are to be conducted before arbitrators". In other words, Article 24 Brussels Convention had the function of extending the scope of application of national rules on the adjudication of interim relief in connection with proceedings pending abroad. In those circumstances, the ECJ set the "Double-condition test" according to which Article 24 Brussels Convention permitted the obtaining of interim relief from a jurisdiction deprived of the power to decide the merits subject to two cumulative conditions: the reversibility of the measure's effects and the existence of a genuine link between the measure and the jurisdiction. Also, the clarifications on the genuine nature of the required link is made through a reference (albeit implicit) to enforcement: the ECJ states that in case of interim payment orders, a European judge may order the payment whenever it may be enforced through "specific assets of the defendant located or to be located within the confines of the territorial jurisdiction of the court to which application is made" (pt. 5 of the operative part).

Both conditions reveal once more the aforementioned aspects of the instrumental character of the measure. As to the first condition, it is certainly obvious to acknowledge that no irreversible measure may be said to be instrumental for a future decision on the merits, since an irreversible measure affects the outcome of the decision on the merits. As to the second condition, the "genuine" character of the link between a measure and a territory cannot but be appreciated in light of the "true function" of the relief which is (or at least should be) that of securing the decision on the merits.

Rather obviously, the genuine character of such a link is easy to ascertain, and may even be ascertained *a priori*, whenever the measure is issued by the same Court that will eventually decide on the merits. On the other hand, the nature of the link is more difficult to understand when the measure is sought elsewhere: in this case the reasons for the plaintiff's choice are inevitably those of benefiting more rapid enforcement.[34] For what other legitimate reason would a claimant seek interim relief in a Member State other than the one where the final decision will be taken?

---

[33] *Supra* (note 29).

[34] Mari 1999, pp. 713–740. See, however, Dickinson 2010, pp. 557–558, identifying the courts better placed to grant specific interim relief according to the measure's characteristics, and Garcimartín 2014/2015, p. 66 on interim relief *in personam*.

5.4.2 *Enforcement of Provisional Measures in the Recast*

A specific regime for the enforcement of provisional measures is prescribed by Article 42-2 of the Recast. In this respect, the regulation maintains what is described as a two-track system, because it provides a different regime for the movement of the protective measure, depending on whether the decision is issued by the judge responsible for the merits or by a different judge.[35]

Recital 33 of the Recast explicitly states:

> Where provisional, including protective, measures are ordered by a court having jurisdiction as to the substance of the matter, their free circulation should be ensured under this Regulation.[36] However, provisional, including protective, measures which were ordered by such a court without the defendant being summoned to appear should not be recognised and enforced under this Regulation unless the judgment containing the measure is served on the defendant prior to enforcement. This should not preclude the recognition and enforcement of such measures under national law. Where provisional, including protective, measures are ordered by a court of a Member State not having jurisdiction as to the substance of the matter, the effect of such measures should be confined, under this Regulation, to the territory of that Member State.

The main noticeable differences between the enforcement regime of a provisional measure and the general regime of Article 42-1 concern the formalities of the certificate accompanying the decision. The latter needs to include a certification that: "(i) the court has jurisdiction as to the substance of the matter; (ii) the judgment is enforceable in the Member State of origin".

The order issued must contain a specific statement by the judge as to its competence.

One may wonder how it would be possible, in the current system, to challenge such a statement. One possibility is certainly to refer to the irreconcilability of judgments for the purposes of Article 45(c) and/or (d) of the Brussels Ibis Regulation.[37]

---

[35] Domej 2014, p. 543, Garcimartín 2014/2015, p. 59, Heinze 2011, p. 602, Honorati 2012, p. 526.

[36] See C-39/02, Maersk Olie, pt. 46: "As is pointed out in the Report on the Brussels Convention (OJ 1979 C 59, p. 71, point 184), Article 25 of that Convention is not limited to decisions which terminate a dispute in whole or in part, but also applies to provisional or interlocutory decisions."

[37] See C-80/00 Italian Leather SpA—WECO Polstermöbel GmbH & Co., ECLI:EU:C:2002:342 whose operative part, at pt. 1, contains the following decisions: "On a proper construction of Article 27(3) of the Convention of 27 September 1968 [...] a foreign decision on interim measures ordering an obligor not to carry out certain acts is irreconcilable with a decision on interim measures refusing to grant such an order in a dispute between the same parties in the State where recognition is sought". See Hess 2008, p 518 ff.

5.4.3 Territorial Justification of Relief under Article 35

Precautionary measures issued on grounds of Article 35 Brussels Ibis Regulation are not able to cross the borders of the issuing State and, in particular, they may not be imposed on the judge who has "wider" jurisdictional power since he or she is responsible for a decision on the merits of the dispute. Logically, the first shall not interfere with or impose a measure on the second.

> In *Van Uden*,[38] one of the parties had already initiated proceedings before arbitrators, thus there was no longer any possibility of accessing a court empowered with jurisdiction on the substance of the dispute. Therefore, the only judge available for provisional measures was the judge empowered with jurisdiction by his or her national law, a jurisdiction that could be exercised for the purposes of Article 24 Brussels Convention (and now 35 Brussels Ibis Regulation).

One problem concerns cases in which the interim relief decision is issued *ex ante* and no European judge has exclusive jurisdiction concerning the dispute.[39] In most of these cases, by virtue of the special rules on jurisdiction that add facultative *fora* to the *forum rei*, jurisdictional authority lies in the hands of more than a European judge. Normally, the judge issuing the interim relief will be deemed to have jurisdiction on the substance.[40] As a consequence, the issued relief measure shall be able to circulate within the Brussels I system.

However, a problem will appear if the judge—even though *a priori* empowered with jurisdiction concerning the dispute—is not seized *a posteriori* by the claimant.

What if the claimant, having obtained the interim relief in State A, then having succeeded in obtaining its enforcement in State B, subsequently starts proceedings in State B and not in State A?

And what if the claimant, having obtained the interim relief in State A, then having succeeded in obtaining its enforcement in State B, subsequently starts proceedings in State C?

What could possibly justify the choice of addressing a judge who has no power to decide on the merits of the case or no authority to enforce the relief sought?

Significantly, the EAPO Regulation excludes the possibility that a judge not empowered with jurisdiction as to the substance may ever issue an EAPO. As a logical consequence, if the national interim relief is an EAPO issued prior to the commencement of proceedings and if such following proceedings are initiated in a

---

[38] *Supra* (note 29).

[39] On the concept of exclusive jurisdiction in the Brussels I system see Mari and Pretelli 2013/2014, p. 218.

[40] Dickinson 2010, p. 546, Garcimartín 2014/2015, p. 61, Heinze 2011, p. 608, Layton and Mercer 2004, para 23.019, Leible 2010, Article 31, No. 18. Note that Honorati 2012, p. 539, contends that the judge may only take *ex ante* measures under Article 35 Brussels Ibis Regulation.

jurisdiction which is different from the one which had issued the EAPO, the latter must be revoked (Article 33-1 of the EAPO Regulation).[41]

Similarly, the majority of authors argue that the measure *ex ante* taken by the judge empowered *in abstracto* but having "lost" jurisdiction as a consequence of the claimant bringing the case elsewhere "should be revoked or cease to have effect".[42]

5.4.4 No Enforcement Abroad of Ex Parte Measures by Surprise

The Recast differentiates the regime for the enforcement of *ex parte* measures in line with the *Denilauler* decision[43] from the recent provisions adopted for the EAPO regime. Article 2(a) includes in the definition of "decision" for the purposes of Chap. 3 on recognition and enforcement: "provisional, including protective, measures ordered by a court or tribunal which by virtue of this Regulation has jurisdiction as to the substance of the matter"; but excludes any "provisional, including protective, measure which is ordered by such a court or tribunal without the defendant being summoned to appear, *unless* the judgment containing the measure is served on the defendant prior to enforcement".

Article 42-2(c) adds to the formal requirements for the enforcement of provisional measures, including protective measures, a specific condition for *ex parte* measures. Such a condition "codifies" the *Denilauer* case.[44]

> Couchet Frères, the creditor of Denilauler, had obtained from the *Tribunal de Grande Instance* of Montbrison a freezing order based on Article 48 of the French Code of civil procedure and named *saisie conservatoire*. Under French procedural law, a *saisie conservatoire* may be ordered at the request of the creditor and without the debtor having been summoned to appear. The order authorised the creditor to freeze the account of the debtor at a bank in Frankfurt am Main. It was declared provisionally enforceable and, on that basis, the creditor started proceedings in Germany in order to obtain, on the one hand, an *exequatur* of the *saisie conservatoire* and, on the other, a *Pfandungsbeschluss*: the German order allowing the seizure of the account. The order was enforced and later served on the debtor who immediately appealed against it before the *Oberlandesgericht* Frankfurt am Main. Upon the request of the latter, the ECJ concluded that "Judicial decisions authorizing provisional or protective measures, which are delivered without the party against which they are directed having been summoned to appear and which are

[41] Article 33 reads: "Remedies of the debtor against the Preservation Order—1. Upon application by the debtor to the competent court of the Member State of origin, the Preservation Order shall be revoked or, where applicable, modified on the ground that: (a) the conditions or requirements set out in this Regulation were not met; [...]".

[42] Garcimartín 2014/2015, p. 62.

[43] Case 125/79 Bernard Denilauler—SNC Couchet Frères, ECLI:EU:C:1980:130, see *infra* at 3.2.2.

[44] *Supra* (note 43).

intended to be enforced without prior service do not come within the system of recognition and enforcement provided for by title III of the Brussels Convention".[45]

In connection with this dispute the ECJ determined the following principles: Article 24 Brussels Convention (just as Article 35 Brussels Ibis Regulation today) does not prevent the creditor from obtaining a freezing order by surprise without the other party having been summoned to appear. Neither does Article 24 Brussels Convention (just as Article 35 Brussels Ibis Regulation today) prevent enforcement abroad of *ex parte* measures issued by the Court empowered with jurisdiction on the merits. However, the surprise effect can only be pursued within the borders of the legal order issuing the interim relief. In sum, in *Denilauler*, the creditor should have directly requested an *ex parte* freezing order in Germany, had he wished to freeze those assets by surprise.

As a consequence, the Recast prescribes, for *ex parte* measures to circulate, that the claimant, in addition to providing the Court with a judgment and the related certificate, include proof of service of that judgment, precisely because the "surprise effect" is not exportable. The logic of this exclusion was further explained in connection with the decision in the case of *Hengst Import*: the system is based on the fact that a failure to respect the rights of the defence is (as was the case in the Brussels Convention) a ground for refusal, pursuant to Article 45, n. 1 letter b) Brussels Ibis Regulation.[46]

Despite this rationale and the need of guaranteeing consistency in the system in force, some authors have criticised the development of the Recast, observing that proof of service does not guarantee respect for the principle of *audi et altera parte* on which the ECJ had based its decisions in *Denilauler* and *Hengst*, but it merely frustrates the surprise effect.[47]

5.5 Conclusions

If the ECJ has remedied, in connection with its case law, the *lacunae* of the Brussels I system that are due to the absence of a European comprehensive legal order, the codification of ECJ case law often results in fragmentary definitions and rules. This is visible, for example, in the definition of interim relief given by

---

[45] See the operative part of *Denilauler* (note 43).

[46] Case C-474/93 Hengst Import BV—Anna Maria Campese, ECLI:EU:C:1995:243 at pt. 16 "it must first be noted that the provisions of the Convention as a whole, both in Title II on jurisdiction and in Title III on recognition and enforcement, manifest an intention to ensure that, within the scope of the objectives of the Convention, proceedings culminating in judicial decisions are conducted in such a way that the rights of the defence are observed". The case concerned the enforcement in the Netherlands of the Italian *Decreto Ingiuntivo*, an *ex parte* measure that is served on the defendant in order to allow him or her to challenge it in order to avoid subsequent imminent enforcement.

[47] Garcimartín 2014/2015, p. 68, von Hein 2013, p. 108 and Domej 2014, p. 546.

Recital 33 giving excessive attention to the characterisation of measures for the taking of evidence instead of attempting to sketch a comprehensive and systematic concept. A closer look reveals, however, that, the problem is merely one of legislative technique, since the philosophy of the system does appear logically coherent.[48]

Provisional, including protective, measures are all those national measures of interim nature, so by definition temporary, limited in time and reversible. The concept that emerges from the aforementioned ECJ's decisions is clarified by the logic of the system: the anticipatory or satisfactory character of European interim relief measures is irrelevant, since their essence lies in their instrumentality to the main cause of action. In this respect, their protective nature and whether they intervene *ante* or *post causam* is not of paramount importance, when compared to the existence of a *periculum in mora*, a criterion frequently recalled to assess the provisional character of measures aiming at the taking of evidence.

In line with the ECJ case law, the option of classifying each national measure, in order to assert its characterisation as interim relief, has not been taken up by the Recast. In light of the above, an abstract *a priori* characterisation of typical national measures is definitely unnecessary. Rather, attention must be paid to the true function of the measure in every given dispute.

Provisional measures benefit in the Recast of a specific procedure of enforcement. Article 42-1 prescribes specific formalities for the certificate accompanying the decision. These include a certification that: "(i) the court has jurisdiction as to the substance of the matter; (ii) the judgment is enforceable in the Member State of origin". Moreover, a specific rule now exists for *ex parte* measures taken *inaudita altera parte*. For these measures to be enforced abroad, the claimant needs to serve the judgment prior to the enforcement of the measure.

References

Ankum JA (1962) De geschiedenis der "actio pauliana" (L'histoire de l'action paulienne). Tjeenk Willink, Zwolle

Bogdan M (2012) The proposed recast of rules on provisional measures under the Brussels I regulation. In: Lein E (ed) The Brussels I review proposal uncovered. British Institute of International and Comparative Law, London, pp 129–133

Dickinson A (2010) Provisional Measures in the Brussels I Review: Disturbing the Status Quo? J Private Int Law:519–542

[48] Case C-302/13 flyLAL-Lithuanian Airlines AS v Starptautiskā lidosta Rīga VAS and Air Baltic Corporation AS, ECLI:EU:C:2014:2319, pt. 57: "the provisional and protective measures at issue in the main proceedings do not consist in the payment of a sum but simply in the monitoring of the assets of the defendants in the main proceedings".

Domej T (2014) Die Neufassung der EuGVVO, Quantensprünge im europäischen Zivilprozessrecht. Rabel J Comp Int Private Law 78(3):508–550
Garcimartín F (2014/2015) Provisional and Protective Measures in the Brussels I Regulation recast. Yearb Private Int Law XVI:57–83
Heinze C (2011) Choice of court agreements, coordination of proceedings and provisional measures in the reform of the Brussels I regulation. Rabel J Comp Int Private Law 75(3):581–618
Hess B (2008) In: Hess B, Pfeiffer Th, Schlosser P (eds) The Brussels I Regulation 44/2001. Application and Enforcement in the EU, Beck, Munich, pp 518–537
Honorati C (2012) Provisional measures and the recast of Brussels I regulation: a missed opportunity for a better ruling. Rivista di diritto internazionale privato e processuale 3:525–544
Kaye P (1999) Law of the European Judgments Convention. Barry Rose Law Publishers Ltd., Little London, vol. IV
Layton A, Mercer H (2004) European Civil Practice, 2nd ed. Sweet & Maxwell, para 23–001
Leible S (2010) in Rauscher Th (ed.) Europäisches Zivilprozess- und Kollisionsrecht EuZPR/EuIPR, Sellier: Article 31 para 1
Mari L (1999) Il diritto processuale civile della Convenzione di Bruxelles. Il Sistema della Competenza, Padova Cedam
Mari L, Pretelli I (2013/2014) Possibility and Terms for Applying the Brussels I Regulation (Recast) to Extra-EU Disputes. Yearb Private Int Law XV:211–253
Nioche M (2012) La décision provisoire en droit international privé européen. Bruylant, Brussels
Pretelli I (2004) Arrêt de la Cour de cassation d'Italie, (Section réunies) du 7 mai 2003 (trad. fr.) et note. Revue critique de droit international privé (vol.):612–632
Pretelli I (2010) Garanzie del credito e conflitti di leggi. Editoriale Scientifica, Naples
Pretelli I (2011) Cross-border Credit Protection against Fraudulent Transfers of Assets. Yearb Private Int Law XIII:589–640
Sandrini L (2012) Coordination of substantive and interim proceedings. In: Pocar F, Viarengo I, Villata F (eds) Recasting Brussels I. CEDAM, Padova, pp 273–284
Stamatoudi I (2014) In: Stamatoudi I, Torremans P (eds) EU Copyright Law: A Commentary, Edward Elgar, Northampton, MA, USA
von Hein J (2013) Die Neufassung der EuGVVO, RIW:97–111
van Rest C (2014) Erkenning en tenuitvoerlegging van (ex parte) voorlopige en bewarende maatregelen op grond van de EEX-Verordening en de Herschikking van de EEX-Verordening. Een analyse aan de hand van de Engelse Freezing Order, Nederlands Internationaal Privaatrecht 2: 351–356

Chapter 6
Brussels Ibis in Relation to Other Instruments on the Global Level

Vesna Lazić and Steven Stuij

Abstract This chapter will discuss the relationship between the Brussels Ibis Regulation and other international conventions which regulate the recognition and enforcement of foreign judgments or arbitral awards in civil and commercial matters. Since a number of such conventions are in force, a possible collision with the Brussels Ibis Regulation may occur. As to the preceding Brussels I Regulation, the Court of Justice has already addressed the problem of conventions that may concur with the Regulation. This raises the question whether this case law remains untouched by the entry into force of the Brussels Ibis Regulation. Also, the relationship of Brussels Ibis with the Hague Convention on Choice-of-Court Agreements of 2005 will be discussed, since this Convention has not been signed by Member States but instead by the Council on behalf of the European Union. Thus, a different approach to a possible collision between the two instrument may be required. Lastly, the position of the New York Arbitration Convention of 1958 will be dealt with. Though explicitly excluded from the substantive scope

This publication is meant as a replacement for the paper by P. Beaumont, who spoke about this topic during the Conference and whose opinions are not reflected in this contribution.

V. Lazić (✉) · S. Stuij
T.M.C. Asser Institute, The Hague, The Netherlands
e-mail: V.Lazic@asser.nl

S. Stuij
e-mail: S.Stuij@asser.nl

V. Lazić
Utrecht University, Utrecht, The Netherlands

V. Lazić
University of Rijeka, Rijeka, Croatia,

V. Lazić and S. Stuij (eds.), *Brussels Ibis Regulation*, Short Studies in Private International Law, DOI 10.1007/978-94-6265-147-0_6

of Brussels Ibis, arbitration has still been subject to some debate *vis-à-vis* its position in light of the Brussels I regime. The recent *Gazprom* case is an interesting example in this respect, which will be looked at in more detail.

Keywords Foreign · Judgments · Recognition and enforcement · Choice-of-court agreements · Arbitral awards · Brussels ibis regulation · Hague convention on Choice-of-Court agreements 2005 · New york arbitration convention 1958 · CM

Contents

6.1 Introduction

This contribution will look into the relationship between the Brussels Ibis Regulation[1] and other international conventions which regulate the recognition and enforcement of foreign judgments or arbitral awards in civil and commercial matters. At the moment, a number of such conventions are in force which may concur with the Brussels Ibis Regulation. With respect to the Regulation's predecessor—the Brussels I Regulation—the Court of Justice has already addressed the problem of concurring instruments. It will be interesting to see whether this case law remains untouched by the entry into force of the Brussels Ibis Regulation or whether a change has been brought about in this respect.

But apart from the Brussels Ibis Regulation's relationship with conventions concluded by Member States, it is questionable whether this would hold true with respect to the position of the Hague Convention on Choice-of-Court Agreements

[1] Regulation (EU) No. 1215/2012 of the European Parliament and the Council of 12 December 2012 on jurisdiction and the recognition and enforcement of judgments in civil and commercial matters, OJ L 351, p. 1.

of 2005. For this Convention has not been signed by Member States but instead by the Council on behalf of the European Union. Does this circumstance make a difference? Would the case law of the Court of Justice still have a bearing on the application of this Convention?

Another matter to be dealt with is the position of the New York Arbitration Convention of 1958. Though explicitly excluded from the substantive scope of Brussels Ibis,[2] arbitration has still been subject to some debate *vis-à-vis* its position in light of the Brussels I regime. The recent *Gazprom* case[3] is an interesting example in this respect, which will be looked at in more detail.

In order to find answers to the aforementioned questions, we will first look into the case law of the CJEU—or the ECJ as it used to be called—concerning Article 71 of the Brussels I Regulation. We will also briefly address the changes that Brussels Ibis has brought about in this respect (Sect. 6.2). Furthermore, the position of the Hague Convention of 2005 will be addressed, since this convention seems to have a special position in relation to both Brussels I and Brussels Ibis (Sect. 6.3). After the conventions on the recognition and enforcement of judgments have been discussed, the focus will be on the recognition and enforcement of arbitral awards as regulated by the New York Convention of 1958 (Sect. 6.4). More specifically, the latter's interaction with the new Brussels Ibis Regulation will be scrutinised. Final remarks can be found in the conclusions (Sect. 6.5).

6.2 Article 71 of the Brussels I Regulation and Its Relationship with Other International Instruments

As has been said in the above, the Brussels Ibis Regulation contains a provision in its Article 71 stipulating under what circumstances it will give way to other conventions on international jurisdiction or the recognition and enforcement of foreign judgments in civil and commercial matters. In order to look at the particularities of this provision, though, it will be expedient to address the Court of Justice's case law on the interpretation of the predecessor of Article 71, namely Article 57 of the Brussels Convention of 1968. After all, the interpretation given to these instruments will still be necessary in order to maintain the continuity between the three instruments.[4]

[2] See Article 1(2)(d).

[3] CJEU Judgment of 13 May 2015, Case C-536/13 (*Gazprom OAO v. Lietuvos Republika*) ECLI:EU:C:2015:316 (hereinafter: *Gazprom* judgment).

[4] See Recital 34 of the Brussels Ibis Regulation: 'Continuity between the 1968 Brussels Convention, Regulation (EC) No. 44/2001 and this Regulation should be ensured, and transitional provisions should be laid down to that end. The same need for continuity applies as regards the interpretation by the Court of Justice of the European Union of the 1968 Brussels Convention and of the Regulations replacing it.'

To start with the Brussels Convention, the Court of Justice interpreted Article 57 thereof in the *Tatry* case. In this case, the Court was confronted with the allegation that the Brussels Convention of 1968 and the Brussels Arrest Convention of 1952 concurred on the issue of *lis pendens*. One of the parties invoked the rule of the Arrest Convention that prohibits parties from arresting assets in multiple states in the same case once an arrest has been made,[5] stating that this rule contained a kind of '*lis pendens*' rule. The question arose whether Article 57 of the Brussels Convention should be interpreted as meaning that in case of conflicting instruments the application of the Brussels Convention is always precluded by the specialised convention or that it is only precluded in cases governed by it and not in those in which it does not apply. We take this to mean that the question was whether the specialised convention would only apply 'partially', i.e., *insofar* it collides with the Brussels Convention, or that it will apply *in toto*, i.e., completely instead of the Brussels Convention.

Without agreeing on the merits of this line of argument—the Court ruled that the litigious rule of the Arrest Convention was not to be equated with *lis pendens* in the sense of Article 22 of the Brussels Convention of 1968—the Court did determine that Article 57 of the Brussels Convention only precludes its application in cases governed by a specialised convention. Basically, this comes down to a 'partial' preclusion of the Brussels Convention, since only insofar as the specialised convention contains similar rules on—in this case—*lis pendens*, should the former instrument apply. For other matters, the Brussels Convention's applicability would not be precluded. The Court held that Article 57 is only intended as an exception to the general rule that, normally, the Convention takes precedence over other instruments with the purpose of ensuring compliance with the rules of specialised conventions.[6] The application of the provisions of the Brussels Convention is solely precluded *vis-à-vis* questions that are governed by a specialised convention.[7]

However, the Brussels Convention has been succeeded by the Brussels Regulation since the ECJ's judgment in *Tatry*. With the entry into force of the Brussels I Regulation, the character of the Brussels regime, including its provision on its relationship with other instruments, has changed from a convention into a regulation. This circumstance could lead to a number of questions. Does the Brussels regime, having become part of EC law, impact on the way in which the concurrence of different international instruments is dealt with? In the situation of Article 71 of the Brussels Regulations, though, the concurrence was one of a convention and a Regulation, the latter having direct effect and being directly

[5] Article 3(3) of the Arrest Convention of 1952.

[6] ECJ Judgement of 6 December 1994, Case 406/92, (*The owners of the cargo lately laden on board the ship "Tatry" v the owners of the ship "Maciej Rataj"*), ECR 1994, I-05439, ECLI:EU:C:1994:400, (hereinafter: *Tatry* judgment) para 24.

[7] *Tatry* judgment, para 25.

applicable, and being the result of a 'normal' majority voting process instead of unanimity. What did the—albeit slightly—changed wording of Article 71 Brussels I Regulation amount to?[8]

In *TNT v Axa,*[9] the European Court of Justice had the opportunity to answer these questions. This case concerned the concurrence of the Brussels I Regulation and the Convention on the Contract for the International Carriage of Goods by Road ('CMR'). The CMR contains provisions on *lis pendens*[10] and on the recognition and enforcement of judgments,[11] just like the Brussels I Regulation.[12] The question arose to what extent the CMR would take precedence over the Brussels I Regulation. Reiterating the case law on Article 57 of the Brussels Convention, the Court considered that Article 71 of the Regulation is meant to make an exception to the precedence that the Regulation will normally have over other conventions in order to ensure compliance with the rules of such specialised conventions. The application of rules of the Brussels Regulation concerning issues governed by specialised conventions was therefore precluded.[13]

Although the ECJ thus applied its case law under the Brussels Convention on Article 71(1) of the Regulation, it nevertheless put some restrictions on the application of specialised conventions insofar as such an application would compromise the principles that underlie judicial cooperation in civil and commercial matters in the European Union. According to the ECJ, these principles concern the:

> '[…] free movement of judgments in civil and commercial matters, predictability as to the courts having jurisdiction and therefore legal certainty for litigants, sound administration of justice, minimisation of the risk of concurrent proceedings, and mutual trust in the administration of justice in the European Union.'[14]

According to the Court, Article 71(1) cannot purport to be an application of specialised conventions that violates these principles. The application of such a convention cannot lead to less favourable results for the internal market than the application of the Brussels I Regulation would, so the Court held.

---

[8] In Article 71 of Brussels I, the wording of the provision no longer contained the phrase 'or will be parties'. Thus, only existing (and not future) conventions would take precedence over the Brussels I regulation. This makes sense in the light of the fact that the legislative competence of the EU in the matter of judicial cooperation in civil matters was moved from the so-called 'third pillar' to the 'first pillar'. In doing so, the EU would also have exclusive competence to negotiate conventions or agreements with third states on matters on which it had internal exclusive competence, based on the 'ERTA' (or 'AETR') doctrine. See for more information on this Kuijper 2011, p. 97 ff.

[9] ECJ of 4 May 2010, Case C-533/08, (*TNT Express Nederland BV v AXA Versicherung AG*), ECR 2010 I-04107, ECLI:EU:C:2010:243, (hereinafter: *TNT v AXA*).

[10] Article 31(2) CMR.

[11] Article 31(3) CMR.

[12] Articles 27 and 32 ff., respectively.

[13] *TNT v AXA*, para 48.

[14] *TNT v AXA*, para 49.

It is interesting to see that the ECJ in *TNT v AXA* addressed both the rules on *lis pendens* and the rules on recognition and enforcement.[15] As to the former, the Court held that rules on *lis pendens* that are contained in a specialised convention can only be applied insofar as they are 'highly predictable', would 'facilitate the sound administration of justice' and that they would minimise the risk of parallel proceedings. The Court referred in that respect to recitals 11, 12 and 15 of Brussels I.

In the specific context of the recognition and enforcement of foreign judgments, the ECJ put emphasis on the principles that are laid down in recitals 6, 16 and 17 of the Brussels I Regulation's preamble. From these recitals, the ECJ inferred two main principles that should be observed when applying a specialised convention's rules on recognition and enforcement. These are the principle of the free circulation of judgments and the principle of mutual trust in the administration of justice. In the latter context, the ECJ expressly spoke of a '*favor executionis*'. The ECJ held that these principles should be respected within the European Union, also when a specialised convention applies. Thus, the assertion by one of the parties that the recognition and enforcement mechanisms of the CMR did not take precedence over the Brussels I Regulation, was not followed. The regime of the recognition and enforcement of this Convention still applied, albeit with certain restrictions. More specifically, the ECJ ruled that Article 31(3) of the CMR, providing for the recognition and enforcement of judgments, can only be applied if it would make it possible for the aims of the free movement of judgments and of mutual trust in the administration of justice within the EU.

The *TNT v AXA* judgment has met some criticism. It has been argued that the judgment of the Court of Justice was contrary to the intentions of the Council in order to allow Member States to comply with their obligations under international law.[16] This intention is evidenced by recital 25 of the Brussels I Regulation[17] and in the Jenard Report on the Brussels Convention.[18] Also, it has been contended that the Court violated the *lex specialis* principle.[19] Others, though, have argued that the judgment was necessary to prevent an undermining of the Brussels I regulation.[20] It has also been said that the restrictions that the ECJ has made in *TNT v*

[15] Haak 2010, section 3.

[16] See, e.g., Van den Oosterkamp 2011, pp. 193–194, and Mankowski, in: Magnus & Mankowski, Brussels Ibis Regulation, Article 71, para 8–12, more specifically para. 10 as regards the ratio of Article 71.

[17] This recital reads as follows: 'Respect for international commitments entered into by the Member States means that this Regulation should not affect conventions relating to specific matters to which the Member States are parties.' See also Van den Oosterkamp 2011, pp. 193–194. In Brussels Ibis, this can be found in Recital 35.

[18] See Jenard Report, pp. 60–61.Van den Oosterkamp 2011, pp. 193–194.

[19] Van den Oosterkamp 2011, pp. 193–194.

[20] Kuijper 2011, p. 94.

AXA were of a more theoretical or dogmatic nature, and that in practice the CMR would actually meet the standards set by the ECJ.[21]

The ECJ's judgment was repeated in the *Nipponkoa* case.[22] In this case, the Court was again confronted with the question of how Article 71 of Brussels I should be interpreted in case of concurrence with the CMR. The matter concerned the conflict of rules on *lis pendens*. The ECJ reiterated its judgment in *TNT v AxA* by holding that the application of Article 71 of Brussels I—and thus of a specialised convention instead of the Brussels Regulation—may not purport to be a violation of the principles underlying the Regulation.[23] Article 71 Brussels I should be interpreted as meaning to preclude the interpretation of a convention in a way that does not ensure the observance of the underlying principles under conditions at least as favourable as the one of the Brussels I regime.[24]

However, in *Nipponkoa* the Court of Justice of the EU went farther. One of the questions concerned the problem of whether two concurring proceedings had the 'same cause of action'. The one concerned an action for indemnity, the other was a so-called action for a 'negative declaration', which means that the potentially liable person initiates proceedings for a declaratory judgment stating that he is not liable for the damages that have occurred. The question of to what extent this would constitute a 'same cause of action' has been raised in the past. Some jurisdictions, like the German, consider an action for negative declaratory relief ('*negative Feststellungsklage*') as not having the same cause of action as an action for indemnity.[25] If this view had been followed by the Court, it would have meant that the *lis pendens* rule does not apply, whilst the opposite view would have entailed that the court last seized will need to stay the proceedings and will have to wait for the first seized court to rule on its jurisdiction. In *Nipponkoa*, the Court chose the latter option by holding that Article 71 of Brussels I precludes an interpretation of Article 31(2) of the CMR according to which such concurring actions—i.e., one for indemnification and one for a negative declaratory relief—do not have the 'same cause of action'. This somewhat complicated wording means that the application of a specialised convention may not lead to the conclusion that such action, normally regarded as having the 'same cause of action' under the Brussels I Regulation's regime, would be regarded as different actions

---

[21] See Mankowski, in: Magnus & Mankowski, Brussels Ibis Regulation, Article 71, para 12. Although it is questionable whether this position would hold in the light of the Nipponkoa judgment.

[22] CJEU Judgement of 19 December 2013, Case C-452/12, (*Nipponkoa Insurance Co (Europe) Ltd v. Inter-Zuid Transport BV, intervening parties: DTC Sushuisterveen BV*), ECLI:EU:C:2013:858 (hereinafter: *Nipponkoa* judgment). Critical of this decision is Mankowski 2014.

[23] *Nipponkoa* judgment, paras 36–37.

[24] *Nipponkoa* judgment, para 39.

[25] See Hoeks 2011, p. 471.

under that specialised convention. This probably relates to the requirement set forth by the Court of Justice in *TNT v AXA*, namely that the application of a specialised convention should keep the risk of concurring proceedings to a minimum.[26]

A recent judgment of the CJEU on the interpretation of Article 71 of Brussels I can be found in the *Gazprom* case.[27] This case concerned the recognition and enforcement of an arbitral award rendered by the Stockholm Chamber of Commerce. Therefore, this case will be discussed in more detail in Sect. 6.4.5.

The case law of the Court of Justice shows that Article 71 of the Brussels I Regulation still allows specialised conventions to take precedence over the Brussels regime, even though the instrument is now shaped in the form of a Regulation and thus concerns a piece of European legislation instead of a convention. Nevertheless, the Court of Justice has introduced some safeguards in order to prevent the aims and objectives on which the Regulation is based from being undermined by an 'absolute' precedence of specialised conventions over the Regulation. Therefore, the Court restricted the application of Article 71 by requiring compliance with a given set of principles to be taken into account. This leads to the question of to what extent the Brussels Ibis Regulation has brought about a change in this situation. The case law of the Court of Justice seems to remain untouched by the entry into force of the Brussels Ibis Regulation. For the wording of its Article 71 is equal to the one of its predecessor in Brussels I. Also, when reading the preliminary documents accompanying the Recast, it seems that the legislator did not intend to bring changes to the system since no reference is made in this respect. From this, the conclusion can be inferred that the case law of the CJEU on Article 71 is still reflecting the state of the law in view of specialised conventions to which Member States are a party. Some other provisions of Brussels Ibis about the confluence of conventions and the Regulation have in fact a different wording compared to their predecessors in Brussels I. One of them is Article 69 which will be discussed in more detail in the subsequent Section.

---

[26] See *TNT v AXA*, para 49.

[27] *Gazprom* judgment. For a comment on this judgment, see Van Zelst 2015, p. 269 ff. Before *Gazprom*, the CJEU applied the *TNT/AxA* and *Nipponkoa* case law to the CMR again in *Nickel & Goeldner* (Judgment of 4 September 2014, Case C-157/13, ECLI:EU:C:2014:2145), without finding a violation of Brussels I. *Gazprom* is not the most recent case anymore. In the meantime, the CJEU has rendered the *Brite Strike* judgment (Judgment of 14 July 2016, Case C-230/15, ECLI:EU:C:2016:560), in which Article 71 of Brussels I was again interpreted. This judgment could not be taken into account in this contribution's main text anymore. It suffices to note that the CJEU applied the requirements as developed in *TNT/AxA* and *Nipponkoa*.

6.3 The Hague Convention on Choice of Court Agreements of 2005

6.3.1 The Hague Convention: Status and Scope

The Hague Convention on Choice of Court Agreements (hereafter: the Hague Convention) entered into force on 1 October 2015.[28] On that date, three months had passed since the deposit of the approval by the Council on behalf of the EU as a so-called Regional Economic Integration Organisation ('REIO').[29] Thus, the requirement of Article 31(1) that the Convention will enter into force on the first day of the month following the expiration of three months after the deposit of the second instrument of ratification, acceptance, approval or accession, was fulfilled. Mexico had already deposited its instrument of accession to the Convention on 26 September 2007.[30]

The Hague Convention 2005 can be seen in the broader light of the so-called 'Judgments Project' which the Hague Conference has embarked upon and which is still under consideration.[31] This project, originally initiated by the US delegates to the Conference in 1992, aims at providing for an international instrument that would regulate the recognition and enforcement of foreign judgments. Since there were some difficulties in coming to a mutual agreement on the issues of jurisdiction and enforcement, the idea came up to find some common ground on a more commonly accepted basis for jurisdiction in civil and commercial matters, such as party autonomy, and to arrange the recognition of judgments of courts that have based their competence upon a choice of court agreement.[32]

The Hague Convention has a restricted scope *ratione materiae*. For this instrument only regulates matters of international civil procedure insofar as an exclusive choice of court agreement is concerned (Article 1(1)). In Article 2 of the

[28] See, for more general information on this Convention, Lazić 2007, p. 214 ff.; Wagner 2009, p 100 ff.; Beaumont 2009, p. 125 ff.; Garnett 2009, p. 161 ff.; Hartley 2013, p. 18 ff. (for a background to the Convention).

[29] The EU signed the Convention on 1 April 2009 and approved it in the Council Decision of 4 December 2014 on the approval, on behalf of the European Union, of the Hague Convention of 30 June 2005 on Choice of Court Agreements (2014/887/EU), OJ L 353 10 December 2014, p. 0005. Article 2 thereof stipulated that the deposit would take place within one month of 5 June 2015 by the President of the Council or someone empowered by him for that purpose.

[30] So far, there are no other States that have approved, ratified or accessed the Convention. The US signed the Convention on 19 January 2009 but has not yet ratified it. Recently, Singapore (25 March 2015) and the Ukraine (21 March 2016) have signed the Convention as well.

[31] Recently, the Draft for a Proposal for a Convention on recognition and enforcement was published on the Hague Conference website, see www.hcch.net under 'Projects'.

[32] The history of the project can be read on the Hague Conference's website (www.hcch.net), under 'Projects'/ 'Legislative projects'/ 'Judgments'. See also Wagner 2009, pp. 102–110.

Convention, a vast list of issues concerning international jurisdiction is excluded from the scope of the Convention. As has been noted by Hartley, Article 2 of the Hague Convention makes a distinction between, on the one hand, the nature of the agreement that has been excluded from its substantive scope and, on the other, the nature of the matter which is at stake.[33] In the second group, there are matters which are also excluded from the subject-matter of the Brussels I and Brussels Ibis Regulations, such as the status and legal capacity of persons, wills and successions, matters related to insolvency, and, not without significance, arbitration. It is beyond the scope of this contribution to touch upon these issues in too much depth, apart from arbitration.[34]

It is also required that the case should be of an international character. In order to determine the international nature of the case, the Convention uses different criteria depending on the question whether it concerns jurisdiction or recognition and enforcement. When jurisdiction is at issue, the international character of the case is determined by the fact that parties are not resident in the same state and whether the relationship of the parties and all other relevant elements are connected to more than one State. In short, if the only international element is the choice of a foreign court, the case is not regarded as an international one (Article 1(2)). In the case of the recognition and enforcement of a judgment, this requirement of internationality is met when the judgment is given by a foreign court (Article 1(3)).[35] In both cases, the court chosen and/or the court whose judgment is to be recognised and enforced should be the court of a Contracting State. It is not required that the residence of the parties (or of one of them) is situated in a Contracting State.[36] As we will see, the residence of the parties does play a role in delineating the application of the Convention with other international instruments.

6.3.2 Relationship with Other Conventions or REIO Legislation

The question arises as to which solution has been provided if the 2005 Hague Convention conflicts with other international instruments. This matter is regulated by Article 26 of the Convention, which comprises a rather complicated regime to cope with the relationship of the Hague Convention *vis-à-vis* other conventions or pieces of legislation. This provision, which is rather difficult to read,[37] consists of

---

[33] Hartley 2013, p. 78.

[34] See, for an overview, Lazić 2007, p. 233 ff. Hartley 2013, pp. 77–78 and 83–86.

[35] See also Lazić 2007, p. 219 ff.

[36] Kramer 2006, p. 111, 112.

[37] Wagner 2009, p 134, Kramer 2006a, p. 116 and Kramer 2006b, p. 169 (who points out at the the use of multiple negations in this provision). Vlas refers to the provision's 'comprimise' character in this respect, see Vlas 2006, p. 94.

6 paragraphs, of which only the latter 5 allow for other treaties to take precedence over the Hague Convention.[38] These rules are also referred to as 'give way rules' in the Hartley/Dogauchi report.[39] The first paragraph of Article 26 merely stipulates that the Convention will be interpreted in a way that is compatible with other treaties, regardless of the fact that those treaties were concluded before or after the Hague Convention.

Focusing more on the so-called 'give way rules' of Article 26, it should be noted at the outset that Article 26(6) is the most important paragraph in the context of the Brussels I or Brussels Ibis Regulation.[40] It stipulates that under certain circumstances the Hague Convention will not affect the rules of a so-called 'Regional Economic Integration Organisation', which is, until now, only the European Union. It does not matter whether or not these rules predate the Hague Convention. Article 26(6) reads as follows:

> 'This Convention shall not affect the rules of a Regional Economic Integration Organisation that is a Party to this Convention, whether adopted before or after this Convention:
>
> a. where none of the parties is resident in a Contracting State that is not a Member State of the Regional Economic Integration Organisation;
> b. as concerns the recognition or enforcement of judgments between Member States of the Regional Economic Integration Organisation.'

Although the double negation contained in Article 26(6)(a) does not contribute to its legibility, this provision can be understood as requiring that all the parties to the dispute should be resident in a Member State of the Regional Economic Integration Organisation at hand in order for the concurring instrument to apply. In the case of the Brussels Ibis Regulation this would mean that the parties should be resident in a Member State of the EU, except for Denmark.[41]

What is the relevance of this provision in the current state of affairs? Since Mexico and Singapore are the only Contracting States so far that do not belong to a REIO, the Convention would only apply when at least one of the parties is resident in Mexico or Singapore. So in the case of a Mexican buyer who brings an action against a German seller before the French courts on the basis of a choice of court agreement designating these courts as the competent courts to hear the case, the French court should determine its jurisdiction on the basis of the Convention and not the Brussels Ibis Regulation.

It should be noted that the provision does not say that all parties should be resident outside a REIO Member State. Otherwise this provision would have entailed that the Hague Convention applies when the parties are resident in a

[38] Wagner 2009, p. 134.

[39] Hartley/Dogauchi, Explanatory report, para 269 ff. See also Hartley 2013, p. 111, 114–125.

[40] Vlas 2006, p. 91, 92 (in the context of the Brussels I Regulation). Some authors refer to Article 26(6) as a 'disconnection clause', zie Ahmed and Beaumont 2016, p. 3 and Van Calster 2016, p. 130.

[41] Wagner 2009, p. 137.

Non-Contracting State. This would have jeopardised the extended scope of application of the Brussels Ibis Regulation in relation to choice of court agreements. For the Brussels Ibis Regulation does not require that the parties to such an agreement are domiciled in an EU Member State,[42] meaning that also non-EU parties can make a valid choice of court under that Regulation. So if, for example, a Chinese buyer and a South African seller have agreed upon the competence of the French courts to settle their disputes, the Brussels Ibis Regulation would apply and not the Hague Convention.[43]

The emergence of the residence of the parties in Article 26(6)(a) does give rise to a specific question. If the residence of the parties is not a factor to be taken into account when looking at the personal or territorial scope of application of the convention,[44] why does it play a role when it comes to the 'give way rule' in view of the Brussels Ibis Regulation?[45] In the other sections of Article 26 of the Hague Convention the residence of the parties is not mentioned at all. It is arguable that the provision contained in Article 26(6) is not so much a 'give way rule', but rather a further restriction of the geographical scope of the Hague Convention. For the application of Article 26(6)(a) it is required that (a) there is a REIO, which (b) has enacted specific legislation with the same subject-matter as the convention, and (c) which has a 'universal scope' as regards choice of court agreements, and (d) prefers to have its REIO legislation applied to intra-REIO jurisdictional matters. That is why there is a special 'give way rule' for REIOs having enacted legislation with the same subject-matter as the convention. Also, it explains why the (almost unintelligible) double negation in Article 26(6)(a) comes down to the exclusion of cases in which the parties are either resident in the EU or in a non-Contracting State and why the concept of 'residence' is used, contrary to the other 'give way rules' of Article 26. It is a rather complex way of stating that the Brussels Ibis Regulation applies to EU Member State courts when the parties are resident in the EU and/or in a non-Contracting state.

---

[42] See Article 6(1) in conjunction with Article 25(1) of Brussels Ibis. This is a change with regard to Article 23 of Brussels I, which stipulated that one of the parties had to be domiciled in an EU Member State. Under the Brussels I Regulation, national law would have applied in a case where both parties were domiciled in a State which was neither a Contracting State, nor an EU Member State. See example (v) given by Vlas 2006, p. 92, 93.

[43] For Article 4 in conjunction with Article 25 of Brussels Ibis stipulates that there is no need that one of the parties is domiciled in a Member State of the EU in case of a choice of court agreement.

[44] Unless it concerns the international character of the case, i.e., when both parties are resident in the same Contracting State. See Vlas 2006, p. 87–88.

[45] Despite the neutral language of Article 26(6), the only REIO so far is the EU, and the only 'conflicting instrument' under this provision is, thus, the Brussels Ibis regulations.

Since there is only one REIO, the Convention could just as well have stipulated that the Convention applies when a court of a Contracting State has been chosen, unless this is an EU Member State's court and none of the parties is resident in a Contracting State which is not an EU Member State. Or, more neutrally put, a Member State of a REIO with specific legislation on the matters mentioned in Article 1. Of course it is possible that REIOs other than the EU will enter the arena of the Hague Conference's unification efforts. Until now, this has not happened so that the 'give way rule' of Article 26(6)(a) basically comes down to a restricted personal or territorial scope of the convention. Either way, it is obvious that the incorporation of Article 26(6) amounts to a rather sophisticated 'coordination' in neutral wording of two instruments on international jurisdiction based on choice of court agreements.[46]

Article 26(6)(b) concerns the situations in which both the Hague Convention and the legislation of a REIO would concur in case of the recognition and enforcement of a foreign judgment. This 'give way rule' does not seem to give rise to any problems. [47] In the current situation, this would come down to the situation in which the courts of the one EU Member State are confronted with a judgment of the courts of another Member State. In that specific intra-European situation, the Hague Convention 'gives way' to the Brussels Ibis Regulation. So when a German court is confronted with a French court's judgment, the latter will apply the rules on recognition and enforcement of the Brussels Ibis Regulation. Even when the jurisdiction of the French court was based on the Hague Convention, since one of the parties resided in Mexico, the judgment will still be recognised and enforced according to Brussels Ibis. In a more overall view, the Convention may take precedence when jurisdiction is concerned, as it will still step back for a REIO's legislation in the stage of recognition and enforcement.

It has been argued by some that this may, in some exceptional cases, lead to a discrepancy. Hartley, for instance, has noted that the Hague Convention, contrary to the Brussels regime, does not restrict choice of court agreements in the field of insurance matters.[48] What if an EU court has based its jurisdiction on the Hague Convention, because one of the parties is domiciled in Mexico, and its judgment has to be recognised in another EU Member State? What if, using the example above, the French court's judgment has to be recognised in, say, Belgium? The Belgian court, looking at the Brussels Ibis regulation, will normally have to look whether Article 10 ff. of that regulation have been violated if the defendant is a policy holder, an insured, a beneficiary or an injured party. If so, the court should deny the recognition of the said judgment. Hartley has contended that in that case, the Belgian court should still recognise the judgment and to disregard the provision of Article 45(1)(e)(i) Brussels Ibis in this respect, as the protective

[46] Vlas refers to it as a 'comprimise text', see Vlas 2006, p. 94 and points out that this provision has been 'extensively discussed during the Twentieth Session' (Vlas 2006, p. 91, footnote 22).

[47] Idem Hartley 2013, p. 126, para 6.63.

[48] Hartley 2013, p. 124, para. 6.58. See also the Hartley/Dogauchi Report, para. 302.

jurisdictional rule of Articles 14 and 15 Brussels Ibis is not applicable.[49] However interesting this debate may be, the fact remains that it is no longer an issue—at least not to a great extent. Since when approving the Hague Convention the EU has made a Declaration on the basis of Article 21 of the Convention.[50] This Declaration excludes certain types of insurance contracts from the scope of the Hague Convention, in order to make it comply with the protection offered to the insured party under the Brussels Ibis regime.[51] The chance that a real 'gap' exists between the substantive scopes of both instruments is therefore rather small.

6.3.3 Relationship with Articles 69 and 71 of the Brussels Ibis Regulation

The question arises as to the relationship with Articles 69 and 71 of Brussels Ibis. Article 69 of the Brussels Ibis Regulation stipulates that this regulation shall, as between the Member States, supersede the conventions that regulate the same issues, save for Articles 70 and 71. Since Article 69 simply speaks of conventions 'as between the Member States', and not of conventions which are concluded by the Member States, the wording could in principle apply to the Hague Convention of 2005 as well. However, EU law should not be interpreted grammatically, but as to its function and purpose, so that it will be unlikely that Article 69 is meant to have the Brussels Ibis regulation take precedence over the Hague Convention.

Another matter concerns Article 71 of the Brussels Ibis Regulation. Mankowski has asserted that the Hague Convention can be the test for the problem of concurring EU conventions.[52] Two options have been argued: the analogous application of Article 71—putting the Hague Convention on a par with specialised conventions—or the application of Article 67—which regards the Hague Convention as a part of EU law.[53] Can the Hague Convention, however, be regarded as a 'specialised convention' in the sense of Article 71? Also, Article 71 concerns conventions to which the 'Member States are parties', whilst the Hague Convention has been concluded by the Council on behalf of the EU. This means that the Member States are bound by the Convention, but not necessarily that they are 'parties' in the sense of Article 71. Looking at the history of this provision in the preceding instruments,[54] this provision was originally meant to preserve the Member States' com-

[49] Hartley 2013, p. 124, para. 6.58-6.60.

[50] To be found in Annex I to the Council Decision of 4 December 2014 on the approval, on behalf of the European Union, of the Hague Convention of 30 June 2005 on Choice of Court Agreements, OJ L 353 10.12.2014, p. 005.

[51] Hartley 2013, p. 126, para 6.63 ff.

[52] Mankowski, in: Magnus & Mankowski, 'Brussels Ibis Regulation', Article 71, para 14.

[53] Mankowski, in: Magnus & Mankowski, 'Brussels Ibis Regulation', Article 71, para 13.

[54] Article 57 of the Brussels Convention of 1968 and Article 71 of the Brussels I Regulation.

pliance with their international commitments and, since the entry into force of Brussels I, only the 'existing' international commitments in this respect.[55] It is therefore difficult to conceive that the Hague Convention of 2005 will fall within the ambit of Article 71 Brussels Ibis.

But besides the issue of a teleological interpretation of EU law, it is also a matter of the hierarchy of legal norms within the EU's constitutional framework. The difference between the case law of the Court of Justice concerning Article 71 of the Brussels I Regulation and Article 57 of the Brussels Convention of 1968, on the one hand, and the concurrence with the Hague Convention, on the other, is that the latter convention was concluded by the EU itself. The EU is bound by its obligations under international law, including those deriving from international agreements. Article 216(2) of the TFEU expressly stipulates that agreements concluded by the Member States are binding upon the EU institutions and the Member States. This can be distinguished from the obligations under international law that the Member States themselves may have.[56] Basically, the EU had, when approving the Hague Convention, wilfully deviated from the system under Brussels Ibis by adhering to this new system in cases when one of the parties to the dispute is resident outside the EU.

This is evidenced by both the preamble and the explanatory memorandum to the proposal for a Council Decision approving the Hague Convention which give indications that the EU intended to have the Hague Convention take precedence over the Brussels I or Brussels Ibis Regulation. To start with the latter, the Explanatory Memorandum to the Proposal addressed the relationship between the Brussels I Regulation and the Convention and therefore referred to Article 26(6) of the Hague Convention of 2005. Based on this provision, the Proposal stated that 'the Convention affects the application of the Brussels I Regulation' in matters of jurisdiction and recognition and enforcement in situations as mentioned in Article 26(6) and that 'the Convention will prevail over the jurisdiction rules of the Regulation except if both parties are EU residents or come from third states, not Contracting Parties to the Convention'.[57] Moreover, the Proposal even stated that the application of the Convention will diminish the application of the Brussels I or Brussels Ibis Regulation, but thought this to be 'acceptable in the light of the increase in the respect for party autonomy at international level and increased legal certainty for EU companies engaged in trade with third State parties'.[58]

---

[55] The fact that Article 71 of Brussels I does not, contrary to its predecessor, speak of 'future' conventions anymore, shows that this 'give way rule' is only meant for existing conventions. The EU has the power to conclude new conventions in this field of law on the basis of the 'ERTA' (or 'AETR') doctrine. See CJEU 7 February 2006, Opinion 1/03, ECR 2006 I-01145, ECLI:EU:C:2006:81.

[56] Wessel 2008, p. 156.

[57] See Proposal for a Council Decision on the approval, on behalf of the European Union, of the Hague Convention of 30 June 2005 on Choice of Court Agreements (COM (2014) 46 final, Sect. 1.3. Idem Van Calster 2016, p. 130–131.

[58] Proposal (COM (2014) 46 final, Sect. 1.3.

Furthermore, the preamble to Council Decision (2014/887/EU) expressly states that the Convention will 'affect' EU secondary legislation, recital 4 saying that:

> The Convention [Hague Convention of 2005, authors] affects Union secondary legislation relating to jurisdiction based on the choice of the parties and to the recognition and enforcement of the resulting judgments, in particular Council Regulation (EC) No. 44/2001, which is to be replaced as of 10 January 2015 by Regulation (EU) No. 1215/2012 of the European Parliament and of the Council.

It is intriguing to observe a number of differences between the situation of concurring instruments as meant in Article 71 of Brussels I and Brussels Ibis, on the one hand, and the position of the Hague Convention of 2005 on the other. In the former case, specialised conventions may take precedence over the Brussels I regime, but this precedence is restricted. After all, the precedence of specialised conventions may not, as the CJEU or—then—ECJ has ruled, violate certain basic principles underlying the Brussels I Regulation. This is completely different in the situation that the Brussels I or Brussels Ibis Regulation concurs with the Hague Convention of 2005. Here, the restrictions put forward by the Court of Justice, such as the *favor executionis*, cannot be found in Article 26(6). If the Hague Convention takes precedence over the Brussels I or Ibis regimes—which will happen only occasionally—it will apply unconditionally.

What is the rationale of this difference? How can it be explained? There are a number of factors that can be taken into account to justify these differences. At first, the Hague Convention may apply unconditionally, but in the Convention itself the interests of the principles underlying the Brussels I and Brussels Ibis regimes are well protected. For the Convention's regime of recognition and enforcement will not apply to what can be called 'intra-European' cases. In case a French court's judgment is to be recognised in Germany, the latter's courts will have to assess the recognition of the judgment on the basis of the Brussels Ibis Regulation, even though the jurisdiction of the French court was based on the Hague Convention.[59]

Another reason for a more 'privileged' position of the Hague Convention of 2005 in comparison with the specialised conventions under Article 71 of the Brussels I or Brussels Ibis Regulation can be found in the fact that the Hague Convention has been concluded by the European Union itself, whilst the specialised conventions that are concurring with Brussels I or Brussels Ibis have been concluded by the Member States. When concluding an agreement itself, the EU might better be able to safeguard the interests of its own legislation, as occurred with Article 26(6) of the Hague Convention which basically keeps the Brussels Ibis Regulation's regime of recognition and enforcement intact. In other words, the EU might be better able to warrant Union-wide interests instead of Member States.

[59] Because one of the parties was resident in Mexico or Singapore.

Moreover, it does not seem to be necessary to apply the same set of restrictions on the application of the Hague Convention of 2005 to the same extent as to a specialised convention under Article 71 of the Brussels Ibis Regulation. The two instruments, both Brussels Ibis and the Hague Convention, have more or less 'converged'. For in matters of jurisdiction, the Brussels Ibis Regulation prescribes a manner of assessing the substantive validity of forum selection clauses in a way which is similar to the manner according to which such clauses are scrutinised under the Hague Convention. This is particularly mentioned in the proposal to the Recast.[60]

Although it is not necessary to apply the restrictions that the Court of Justice has applied when interpreting Article 71 on specialised conventions, it is not excluded that the Court of Justice will not apply these or similar restrictions to the applicability of the Hague Convention as well. After all, this is an international agreement concluded by the EU, so that the Court of Justice has full powers to interpret this instrument.[61] Furthermore, in a more institutional light, it is arguable that the Court of Justice can still become 'active' in its role of safeguarding the main principles underlying Brussels Ibis. It has already deviated from the Council's position on Article 71 of Brussels I.[62] There, the Council did not intend to follow a different approach to specialised conventions than under the Brussels Convention. On the contrary: recital 25 of the Brussels I Regulation expressly mentioned the need for Member States to comply with their international commitments. Nonetheless, the Court of Justice found it necessary to depart from the wording of the provision. If this was to ensure compliance with the principles underlying the Brussels regime, it is not unimaginable that the Court will do so as well *vis-à-vis* the concurrence of the Hague Convention with the Brussels Ibis Regulation.

6.4 The New York Arbitration Convention of 1958

6.4.1 General Remarks

The Brussels Ibis Regulation introduces some helpful clarifications on the interface between the Regulation and arbitration. For the first time there is an express reference to the 1958 New York Convention in Article 73(2). Additionally, the extent of the arbitration exception is clarified in recital (12).

---

60 Proposal for a Regulation of the European Parliament and of the Council on jurisdiction and the recognition and enforcement of judgments in civil and commercial matters (Recast), COM(2010) 748 final, p. 9.

61 Article 267 TFEU.

62 See Van den Oosterkamp 2011, pp. 193–194.

When negotiating the 1968 Brussels Convention[63] it was chosen to exclude arbitration from its substantive scope of application. This deliberate choice was based on the idea that relevant aspects of arbitration were sufficiently regulated in other instruments, notably in the 1958 New York Convention.[64]

The issue of the interaction between the Brussels regime and arbitration occasionally appeared problematic for national courts in the EU Member States and required interpretation by the European Court of Justice (ECJ), later the Court of Justice of the European Union (CJEU). Decisions of the ECJ[65] usually triggered vivid debate on the interaction between the Regulation and arbitration. The discussion on the extent of the arbitration exception particularly intensified following the ECJ judgment in the infamous *West Tankers* case.[66] Therein the ECJ again clearly disapproved of the use of antisuit injunctions prohibiting a party from pursuing legal suits before the courts of the EU Member States. That was for the third time[67] that the ECJ had declared such injunctions incompatible with the Regulation even when they were issued in order to support arbitration.

The *West Tankers* judgment was extensively discussed in the legal literature and often widely criticised, especially in common law jurisdictions. Some authors and courts interpreted this decision so as to imply the binding nature of a decision on the validity of an arbitration agreement in other EU Member States (*infra* 5.2). The Commission heavily relied on this case in its Proposal to amend the provision on the 'arbitration exception' (*infra* 5.3). The Commission's Proposal was rejected, but the Brussels Ibis Regulation introduces important clarifications on the interface between arbitration and the Regulation (*infra* 5.4). Yet the extent of the

[63] 1968 Brussels Convention on jurisdiction and the enforcement of judgments in civil and commercial matters Official Journal L 299, 31/12/1972 pp. 0032–0042.

[64] Convention on the Recognition and Enforcement of Foreign Arbitral Awards of 10 June 1958, United Nations, New York.

[65] E.g., ECJ Judgment of 25 July 1991, Case C-190/89 (*Marc Rich & Co. AG v Società Italiana Impianti PA*) ECR I-3855, ECLI:EU:C:1991:319, *NIPR* 1993, 150, excerpt in 17 p. 233 *et seq.*; ECJ Judgment of 17 November 1998, Case C-391/95 (*Van Uden Maritime BV, trading as Van Uden Africa Line v Kommanditgesellschaft in Firma Deco-Line and Another*) ECR I-7091, ECLI:EU:C:1998:543, NIPR 1999, 77. Some other sources point to multiple potential problems, e.g., Green Paper on the Review of Council Regulation (EC) No. 44/2001 on Jurisdiction and the Recognition and Enforcement to Judgments in Civil and Commercial Matters of 12 April 2009, COM(2009) 175 final, as well as the 'Heidelberg Report' (Hess et al. 2007).

[66] *West Tankers* judgment.

[67] Previous two decisions were ECJ Judgment of 9 December 2003, Case C-116/02, (*Erich Gasser GmbH v. Missat Srl*) ECR I-14693, ECLI:EU:C:2003:657, NIPR 2004, 36 and ECJ Judgment of 27 April 2004, Case C-159/02, 27 April 2004 (*Gregory Paul Turner v Felix Fareed Ismail Grovit, Harada Ltd and Changepoint SA*) ECR I-3589, ECLI:EU:C:2004:228, NIPR 2004, 146. In *Gasser* the ECJ held that the court of a EU Member State having jurisdiction under Article 23 of the Brussels I Regulation was not authorised to issue an anti-suit injunction so as to restrain the party from pursuing litigation before the court of another Member State which had been first seised of the dispute. In *Turner v. Grovit* the ECJ held that the court of a Member State was not to issue an anti-suit injunction so as to restrain a party from pursuing legal proceedings in another Member State on the ground that the proceedings had been initiated in bad faith.

arbitration exception has remained a topical issue especially after the Advocate General expressed his views in the case of *Gazprom*.[68] The discussion on the interface between arbitration and the Brussels I regime has continued after the CJEU rendered its judgment in May 2015[69] (*infra* 5.5).

6.4.2 Reasoning in the West Tankers Judgment[70]—Criticism and (Mis)Interpretation in Literature and Case Law

One of the present authors has already expressed her view on the *West Tankers* judgment in earlier publications[71] and in principle has disagreed with the criticism expressed. The CJEU decision was mainly criticised in the context of inaccurately defining the scope of the arbitration exception in the Regulation. However, the judgment merely confirmed what had already been accepted in previous decisions, notably the *Marc Rich* and *Van Uden* judgments regarding the scope of the arbitration exception and in *Gasser* and *Turner* judgements with respect to anti-suit injunctions. In particular, the Court affirmed that the nature of the subject-matter was crucial when deciding whether or not a dispute falls within the scope of the Regulation. It held that proceedings leading to the making of an anti-suit injunction could not fall within the scope of the Regulation,[72] but that they 'may nevertheless have consequences which undermine its effectiveness'.[73] The anti-suit

68 Opinion of the Advocate General Wathelet of 4 December 2014, Case C-536/13 (*Gazprom OAO v. Lietuvos Republika*) ECLI:EU:C:2014:2414 (hereinafter: Opinion of the Advocate General).

69 *Gazprom* judgment.

70 The vessel 'Front Comor', owned by West Tankers Inc. and chartered to Erg Petroli SpA, collided with a jetty owned by Erg Petroli SpA in Syracuse (Italy). An arbitration clause in the charter party agreement provided for the settlement of disputes by arbitration in London. The compensation for the damage resulting from the collision was paid by Erg Petroli's insurers Allianz SpA and Generalli Assicurazioni Generali. In order to recover damages for its uninsured losses, Erg Petroli initiated arbitration in London against West Tankers. The insurers for their part filed the claim against West Tankers with the court in Syracuse to recover the amounts paid for the damages caused to Erg Petroli under the insurance policy. West Tankers applied to the High Court of Justice of England and Wales seeking a declaration that the insurers were bound by the arbitration agreement in the charter party agreement between West Tankers and Erg Petroli SpA. Additionally, it applied for an injunction restraining the insurers from participating in any proceedings in relation to the dispute except in arbitration, particularly in the proceedings before the Italian court in Syracuse. The case reached the House of Lords which expressed the view that an anti-suit injunction in the present case could not infringe the Regulation, because all arbitration matters were excluded from its scope of application by Article 1(2)(d). It decided to stay its proceedings and referred the following question to the ECJ for a preliminary ruling.

71 Lazić 2012; Lazić 2011.

72 *West Tankers* judgment, para 23.

73 *Id.*, para 24.

injunction in the *West Tankers* case was directed at restraining a party from pursuing an action for damages, which is a matter falling within the scope of the Regulation. Consequently, since the injunction related to the subject-matter within the Regulation's scope, it was held to be incompatible with the Regulation even when issued in support of arbitration. It is rather obvious that a mere invoking of an arbitration agreement in the proceedings concerning the subject-matter falling within the Regulation's scope cannot transpose that subject-matter into an 'arbitration exception'. In other words, the substantive claim is not removed from the scope of application of the Regulation by a mere reference to an arbitration clause contained in the disputed transaction.

Furthermore, the *West Tankers* judgment was often interpreted so as to imply the binding nature of a decision on the validity of an arbitration agreement taken by the court seised of the matter in the proceedings where the arbitration agreement has been invoked.[74] Presumably the somewhat imprecise wording of the judgment in paras 26 and 27 induced some to reach the erroneous conclusion on the binding nature of the decision on the validity of an arbitration agreement. In particular, it is likely that the holding that 'a preliminary issue concerning the applicability of an arbitration agreement, including in particular its validity, also comes within its scope of application'[75] was the basis for the conclusion that consequently a decision made in that respect also falls within the Regulation's scope of application. The same holds true for the wording in para 27 stating that 'the basis of the existence of an arbitration agreement, including the question of the validity of that agreement' comes within the scope of the Regulation. Also the English Court of Appeal in *National Navigation*[76] reached such an obviously incorrect conclusion. It held that, in the light of the *West Tankers* judgment, it was bound by a preliminary decision concerning the validity of an arbitration agreement brought by the court in another Member State seised of the matter. The Court erroneously concluded that it was consequently precluded from ruling on that issue. The *West Tankers* judgment clearly prevented the Court of Appeal in *National Navigation* from issuing an anti-suit injunction, but it did not affect its jurisdiction to rule on the validity of an arbitration agreement. However, a decision refusing to stay court proceedings and to refer the parties to arbitration was appropriate as the right to arbitrate had been waived.[77]

[74] See e.g., Van Haersolte-van Hoff 2011 p. 281; Markus/Giroud 2010, p. 237; Radicati di Brozolo 2011, p. 29; see also, Illmer 2010 p. 748; Moses 2014.

[75] *West Tankers* judgment, para 26.

[76] Decision of the English Court of Appeal in *National Navigation Co. v. Intesa Generacion SA*, [2009] EWCA Civ. 1396, http://www.bailii.org/ew/cases/EWCA/Civ/2009/1397.html.

[77] In the case at hand the right to invoke the arbitration agreement had obviously been waived so that the Court correctly refused to refer the parties to arbitration. Accordingly, the waiver was the true and appropriate reason for the refusal to refer to arbitration and not an allegedly binding nature of the decision on the validity of an arbitration agreement rendered by the court in another Member State as the English Court stated in support of its decision.

Even though the CJEU could have used more careful and more precise wording in paras 26 and 27 of the *West Tankers* judgment, nowhere in the judgment is it stated that a *decision* on the validity of an arbitration agreement fell within the scope of application for the purposes of recognition and enforcement under the Regulation. The wording in paras 26 and 27 merely states that for the purposes of ascertaining jurisdictions over a subject-matter of the dispute a court in a Member State may rule on the validity of an arbitration agreement. Moreover, the reasoning in the EC judgment as a whole presents no solid basis for the conclusion that a preliminary *decision* on the invalidity of the arbitration agreement was to be brought within the scope of the Regulation as some authors seem to suggest. It is clear that a decision on the merits of the case would be within the Regulation's scope of application for the purposes of recognition and enforcement, but not the decision on the validity of the arbitration agreement itself. In earlier publications[78] one of the present authors has already disagreed with what appeared to be a majority view on this issue. Earlier decisions in some Member States correctly held that a decision on the validity of an arbitration itself fell outside the scope of the Regulation.[79] Such a decision cannot be recognized in another EU Member State on the basis of the Regulation. Besides, it does not bind an arbitral tribunal either, so that arbitrators may take a different view on the validity of the arbitration agreement.

The criticism of the *West Tankers* judgment expressed in the literature lies in the essence of the Commission's Proposal[80] to amend the 'arbitration exception'.

6.4.3 Commission's Proposal—Summary

The Commission in its Proposal and the Impact Assessment[81] suggested to amend the 'arbitration exception' under the Regulation. Allegedly, 'the current legal framework does not sufficiently protect the effectiveness of arbitration agreements in the EU'. The necessity to avoid parallel proceedings and to reduce 'the possibilities of undermining arbitration through abusive litigation tactics' so as to enhance the effectiveness of arbitration agreements were the most important reasons for the suggested amendments. The Commission almost exclusively relied on the *West Tankers* judgment when attempting to substantiate its Proposal and the alleged

78 Lazić 2012, p. 24.

79 *See, e.g.*, in Germany, OLG Stuttgart, Dec. 22, 1986, *Recht der Internationalen Wirtschaft*, 1988, p. 480. In France, *Legal Department du Ministère de la Justice de la République d'Irak v Sociétés Fincantieri Cantieri Navali Italiani, Finmeccanica et Armamenti e Aerospazio*, 15 June 2006, *Cour d'appel de Paris* (2007) 1 *Rev Arb* 87.

80 The European Commission's Proposal COM(2010) 748 final.

81 The Impact Assessment Accompanying the Proposal (Commission Staff Working Paper) 18101/10 ADD1 JUSTCIV 239 of 17 December 2010.

problems that called for solutions. The most important changes suggested in the Commission's Proposal[82] are here summarised.[83]

In its Proposal the Commission suggested a 'partial deletion' of the arbitration exception in Article 1(2)(d) with the purpose of allegedly enhancing the effectiveness of arbitration agreements.[84] The proposed amendments were drafted within the framework of provisions of *lis pendens*, in particular Articles 29(4) and 33(3) of the Proposal (Articles 27 and 30 of the Brussels I Regulation).

A major shortcoming of the suggested rule can be seen in the unclear nature of a decision of the court at the seat of arbitration on the validity of the arbitration agreement, i.e., whether or not it would be binding in other Member States.[85] If such a decision were to fall within the Regulation and consequently to be binding in all EU Member States, that would substantially impact on Articles II(3) and V(a) of the 1958 New York Convention.

Additionally, the obligation for a court seised of the matter in one Member State to stay its proceedings in order to enable the court at the seat of arbitration to decide on the validity of an arbitration agreement undermines the *competence-competence* principle. Namely, it would be reasonable that a court seised would be required to stay its proceedings so that the arbitral tribunal may rule on its own jurisdiction, as is provided in Article VI(3) of the 1962 European (Geneva) Convention. However, it is difficult to find a rationale behind the obligation to stay court proceedings in one jurisdiction with the mere purpose that a court in another jurisdiction could decide on the validity of the arbitration agreement. In addition to these obvious shortcomings, there are grave deficiencies in the wording of the Proposal which would have caused serious difficulties in the application and interpretation by national courts in the Member States.[86]

---

[82] The Proposal has been extensively discussed in the legal literature and heavily supported by some authors. See e.g., Illmer 2010; Radicati di Brozolo 2011; Haersolte-van Hoff, (2011) pp. 280 et seq. For criticism of the approach and the wording of the Proposal, see Lazić 2012.

[83] The summary of the proposed amendments is based on the overview presented in an earlier publication, Lazić 2013, pp. 181–209.

[84] To this end, the changes to the text of Article 1(2)(d) regarding the arbitration exception were suggested as follows: '2. This Regulation shall not apply to arbitration, save as provided for in Articles 29, para 4 and 33, para 3.'

[85] Even the members of the 'Expert Group' that has drafted the Proposal have expressed opposite views on the purpose and the intention of the suggested rules concerning the binding nature of the decision on the validity of an arbitration agreement. Some argue that such a decision would not be covered by the Regulation and accordingly would not be binding in other Member States (see, e.g.,, Radicati di Brozolo 2011, p. 29), whereas others have argued that the decision would indeed fall under the Regulation's scope of application and thus be binding in all Member States (see, Illmer 2010, p. 21).

[86] The major shortcomings of the Proposal are scrutinised in Lazić 2012, pp. 19–48; Lazić 2011, pp. 289–298. See also an early publication relating to the ECJ decision in *West Tankers*, Lazić 2009, pp. 130 *et seq.*

6.4.4 Brussels Ibis Regulation

Considering the serious shortcomings in the substance and wording of the suggested changes, it is not surprising that none of them has found a place in the revised text of the Regulation. Instead, a number of very helpful clarifications on the interface between arbitration and the Regulation have been introduced. Thus, it is for the first time that an express reference to the 1958 New York Convention has been made in Article 73(2), providing that '[t]his Regulation shall not affect the application of the 1958 New York Convention.'

The extent of the arbitration exception is further clarified in recital (12). It provides, *inter alia*, that '[a] ruling given by a court of a Member State as to whether or not an arbitration agreement is null and void, inoperative or incapable of being performed should not be subject to the rules of recognition and enforcement of this Regulation, regardless of whether the court decided on this as a principal issue or as an incidental question.' Such clear and unambiguous wording renders moot any further discussion on the uncertainties about the reach and scope the of the arbitration exception under the Regulation, as well as on the allegedly binding nature of a decision on the validity of the agreement of the court seised of the matter. Thereby, the idea that a decision on the validity of arbitration is covered by the Regulation and is accordingly binding in other EU Member States has been clearly rejected. Further wording in recital (12) leaves no doubts in that respect.

As explained previously, the *West Tankers* judgment was often interpreted in the literature so as imply the binding nature of such a decision.[87] This wording in the recital (12) merely confirms what was the rationale of the *West Tankers* judgment: the question of the validity of the arbitration agreement does not remove a subject-matter from the scope of the Regulation and as such this matter remains with its scope, but any decision rendered on validity cannot be subject to recognition under the Regulation.

The recital (12) further provides that nothing in the Regulation prevents national courts from ruling on the validity of an arbitration agreement. Furthermore, a ruling by a court of a Member State on the invalidity of an arbitration agreement shall not preclude the recognition and/or enforcement of that court's judgment rendered on the substance in another Member State. Finally, it reiterates that the New York Convention takes precedence over the Regulation and that the Regulation does not apply to any action or ancillary proceedings related to arbitration, such as, 'the establishment of the arbitral tribunal, the powers of

[87] See e.g., Van Haersolte-van Hoff 2011 p. 281; Markus/Giroud 2010, p. 237; Radicati di Brozolo 2011, p. 29; see also, Illmer 2010 p. 748; Moses 2014. See also the reasoning of Advocate General Wathelet in the *Gazprom* case, paras 127 and 128 indirectly concluding that the CJEU held that the decision on validity would fall within the Regulation's scope of application.

the arbitrators, the conduct of the arbitration procedure or any other aspects of such a procedure, nor to any action or judgment concerning the annulment, review, appeal, recognition and enforcement of an arbitral award.'

In an earlier publication[88] one of the present authors expressed the view that the added wording in the recital (12) answered all queries that may arise in the context of the arbitration exception in Article 1(2)(d) of the Regulation especially those triggered by the *West Tankers* judgment. As such it presents a valuable clarification and a useful tool in the interpretation of this provision. One would have expected that the revised text would have put an end to any further discussion on the interaction between arbitration and the Regulation.

Yet rather soon after the final text of the revised Regulation had been released some well-known objections and previously alleged problems occasionally reappeared in the legal literature. Alleged 'torpedoes' against arbitration, parallel proceedings and consequently conflicting decisions are some repeatedly raised objections.[89] The risk of irreconcilable decisions possibly rendered by a national court and an arbitral tribunal is indeed a major shortcoming. Yet as already explained in an earlier publication,[90] the problem is more potential than real, as the chances of it occurring are rather minimal. The Commission in the Impact Assessment mentioned no examples of irreconcilable decisions, besides the rather peculiar circumstances surrounding the decision in *West Tankers* case. In any case, even if such a problem would ever occur, the Brussels I regime of enforcement does provide for an appropriate solution by an analogous application of Article 34 of the Brussels I Regulation (Article 45 of the Brussels Ibis Regulation) with respect to arbitral awards. Thus, an earlier rendered foreign arbitral award which fulfils the conditions for enforcement under the 1958 New York Convention or a more favourable national law prevents the enforcement of a judgment rendered by a court of a EU Member State either on the basis of Article 34(4) or 34(1).[91] A domestic award prevents the enforcement of a foreign judgment by an analogous application of Article 34(3) of the Brussels I Regulation. The same holds true under the Brussels Ibis Regulation as the same grounds have been taken over in Article 45(1)(a)–(d). Any other interpretation would be contrary to the basic principles of procedural law and public policy. In a similar vein, an earlier rendered judgment by a court of a Member State would present a ground for refusing the enforcement of a subsequently issued arbitral award by

[88] Lazić 2013, p. 25.

[89] See e.g., Nielsen 2014, p. 71. Draguyev 2013.

[90] Lazić 2012, pp. 21–22.

[91] For a more detailed explanation, see Lazić 2012, pp. 21–22 and the literature referred to therein in footnote 8. See also, Lew et al. 2003, p. 503; Schlosser 1981, pp. 388 *et seq.*

relying on the public policy exception under Article V(2)(a) of the 1958 New York Convention.[92]

Another more vividly discussed issue is an alleged alteration of the holding on the incompatibility of anti-suit injunctions by the wording of Recital (12). The discussion is based on an erroneous presumption that the consequence of the *West Tankers* judgment was that decisions on the validity of arbitration agreements fell within the scope of application of the Regulation. The wording of the Recital (12) clearly stating the opposite has been interpreted by some as repealing the *West Tankers* judgment.[93] In addition, the wording excluding all other related matters from arbitration allegedly overturned the *West Tankers* decision on the incompatibility of anti-suit injunctions with the Regulation.[94] The discussion on this issue and more generally on the interface between the Brussels I regime and arbitration again intensified after the opinion the Advocate General Whatelet[95] was released and continued after the CJEU rendered its judgment in the case of *Gazprom*.[96] In particular, the debate on the continuous 'validity' of the *West Tankers* judgment and consequently the permissibility of anti-suit injunctions was reintroduced. Whereas in the *West Tankers* case anti-suit injunctions issued by the courts of a Member State were at stake, the *Gazprom* case concerned anti-suit injunctions issued by an arbitral tribunal.

6.4.5 Gazprom Case

The dispute between Gazprom, a company incorporated under Russian law, and Lietuvos Respublika arose in the context of a shareholders' agreement establishing the legal entity 'Lietuvos dujos AB'. The shareholders' agreement contained

[92] *Contra*, Nielsen 2014, p. 71, expressing the view that since the Brussles Ibis Regulation does not regulate the question of the enforcement of a judgment which is in conflict with an arbitral award, the issue is left to the national law of EU Member States to give priority either to the award or to the judgment. Consequently, it seems that the author suggests that an earlier rendered judgment does not prevent the enforcement of the award under the New York Convention, 'which takes precedence over' the Brussles Ibis Regulation. Some authors are of the opinion that when a court is requested to enforce a foreign arbitral award and a judgment obtained in violation of arbitration agreement it will always enforce the award in view of the express provision of Article 73(2) giving prevalence to the New York Convention over the Brussles Ibis Regulation. Only with respect to domestic arbitral awards is an analogous application of Article 45(1)(c) of the Regulation suggested. See, Lutzi 2015, p. 3.

[93] Dowers and Tang 2015, p. 138. See also the Opinion of the Advocate General Wathelet of 4 December 2014, Case C-536/13 (*Gazprom OAO v. Lietuvos Republika*), paras 126–128.

[94] For more particulars, see *infra*, under 4.5.1.

[95] Opinion of the Advocate General Wathelet of 4 December 2014, Case C-536/13 (*Gazprom OAO v. Lietuvos Republika*) ECLI:EU:C:2014:2414 (hereinafter: Opinion of the Advocate General).

[96] *Gazprom* judgment.

an arbitration clause providing for dispute settlement according to the Rules of the Stockholm Chamber of Commerce. The parties thereto were Gazprom, E.ON Ruhrgas International GmbH, a company established under German law, and the State Property Fund acting on behalf of the Republic of Lithuania, the latter being subsequently replaced by the Ministry of Energy of the Republic of Lithuania. In the application to the Regional Court in Vilnius, the Ministry sought an investigation as to whether the activities of Lietuvos dujos AB, its general manager and a number of members of its board of directors were improper.

Gazprom initiated arbitration at the Arbitration Institute of the Stockholm Chamber of Commerce. It took the view that the Ministry had breached the arbitration clause in the shareholders' agreement and requested the arbitral tribunal to issue an order prohibiting the Ministry from continuing the proceedings before the Vilnius Regional Court. The arbitral tribunal rendered an award declaring a partial breach of the arbitration clause and ordering the Ministry to withdraw or limit some of its claims filed before the Lithuanian court. The Ministry continued the litigation and Gazprom, for its part, applied for the recognition and enforcement of the arbitral award containing an anti-suit injunction in separate proceedings. Gazprom's request for recognition was rejected at two instances and finally reached the Supreme Court of Lithuania. The Court submitted 3 questions to the CJEU for a preliminary ruling which be summarised as follows: can the court having jurisdiction under the Regulation refuse to recognise an award prohibiting a party from bringing certain claims or ordering to limit those claims before the court in that Member State as it restricts that court's right to determine its own jurisdiction?

6.4.5.1 Opinion of the Advocate General

In his Opinion of 4 December 2014, Advocate General Wathelet curiously enough held that the *West Tankers* judgment was to be regarded as having been overruled in view of recital (12). Allegedly, anti-suit injunctions in support of arbitration became permissible as they were to be considered as 'ancillary proceedings' and as such were excluded from the Regulation's scope by the wording in the fourth paragraph of recital (12). He argued that '[n]ot only does that paragraph exclude the recognition and enforcement of arbitral awards from the scope of that regulation, which indisputably excludes the present case from its scope, but it also excludes ancillary proceedings, which in my view covers anti-suit injunctions issued by national courts in their capacity as court supporting the arbitration'.

It is not clear where to find the basis for the holding that the EU legislator wanted to reverse the *West Tankers* judgment and that anti-suit injunctions can be qualified as 'ancillary proceedings' as referred to in the recital (12). If that had been the intention of the EU legislator then this would have been expressly stated in the revised Regulation. At least it would have been mentioned as an example of 'ancillary proceedings' in the recital (12) especially in view of the considerable debate that the judgment prompted in the legal literature, as well as the ECJ's previous rulings on the incompatibility of anti-suit injunctions in the *Gasser* and *Turner* judgments. More importantly, the use of anti-suit injunctions in support of arbitration is certainly not a 'typical' example of proceedings 'ancillary' to arbitration. Such orders are generally an unknown concept in civil law jurisdictions. Even in common law legal systems it does not seem that support for arbitration by upholding arbitration agreements is the primary function of anti-suit injunctions, although they can be and often are used with the purpose of facilitating and supporting arbitration. For example, in the 1996 English Arbitration Act containing *inter alia* provisions on court intervention and support for arbitration there is no mention of anti-suit injunctions. Obviously, the English courts must rely on other sources and concepts of English law when issuing anti-suit injunctions in support of arbitration. Finally, that issue was directly addressed in the *West Tankers* judgment where the Court expressly stated that although anti-suit injunctions could be considered as ancillary proceedings related to arbitration and as such are excluded from the Regulation's scope 'they may nevertheless have consequences which undermine its effectiveness, namely preventing the attainment of the objectives of unification of the rules of conflict of jurisdiction in civil and commercial matters and the free movement of decisions in those matters.'[97] What is not easily discernible is what is the basis for the conclusions of the Advocate General that the revised Regulation allegedly reversed the ruling on the incompatibility of anti-suit injunctions?

The Advocate General seems to find further support for his holding in an erroneous presumption that the consequence of the *West Tankers* judgment was that decisions on the validity of arbitration agreements were to fall within the scope of application of the Brussels I Regulation.[98] The inappropriateness of such an inter-

---

[97] *West Tankers* judgment, para 24.

[98] Opinion of Advocate General Wathelet para 126 reads as follows: 'Indeed, while the wording of the regulation's provisions were not altered, the second paragraph of that recital states that '[a] ruling given by a court of a Member State as to whether or not an arbitration agreement is null and void, inoperative or incapable of being performed *should not be subject to the rules of recognition and enforcement laid down in this Regulation, regardless of whether the court decided on this as a principal issue or as an incidental question*'. It continues in Para 127 as follows: 'The passage in italics shows that the verification, as an incidental question, of the validity of an arbitration agreement is excluded from the scope of the Brussels I Regulation (recast), since if that were not so the rules on recognition and enforcement in that regulation would be applicable to decisions of the national courts concerning the validity of an arbitration agreement.' In para 128 the Advocate General concluded 'that was not the Court's interpretation in the judgment in *West Tankers* para 26, where it based its position concerning the fact that the proceedings initiated by Allianz and Generali against West Tankers before the Tribunale di Siracusa, in breach of the arbitration agreement, themselves came within the scope of the Brussels I Regulation on the assumption that the verification, as an incidental question, of the validity of an arbitration agreement *was included* in the scope of that regulation.' (Emphasis in the original).

pretation of the CJEU judgment which was unfortunately a majority view in the legal literature has already been addressed.[99]

6.4.5.2 Gazprom Judgment

Considering the views expressed in the Opinion of the Advocate General, the judgment of the CJEU was expected with great interest. The reasoning of the CJEU can be summarised as follows:

(1) The Court upheld and reiterated its holding in the *West Tankers* judgment on the incompatibility of anti-suit injunctions issued by the courts of the EU Member States with the Brussels I Regulation.[100]

(2) It distinguished the case at hand from the *West Tankers* judgment, since the present case concerns the enforceability of anti-suit injunctions contained in an arbitral award.[101]

(3) It further held that 'in those circumstances, neither that arbitral award nor the decision [recognizing it]...are capable of affecting the mutual trust between the courts of the various Member States upon which Regulation [Brussels I] is based'.[102]

(4) The Court distinguished the legal effects of anti-suit injunctions issued by a court in the *West Tankers* case from the effects of an arbitral award in the case at hand as the failure to comply with the arbitral award 'is not capable of resulting in penalties being imposed upon it by a court of another Member State.'[103]

(5) It concluded that the Brussels I Regulation 'must be interpreted as not precluding a court of a Member State from recognizing and enforcing, or from refusing to recognize and enforce, an arbitral award prohibiting a party

---

[99] *Supra*, under 5.2.

[100] In para 34 the Court held that an antisuit injunction 'runs counter to the trust which the Member States accord to one another's legal systems and judicial institutions and is liable to bar an applicant who considers that an arbitration agreement is void, inoperative or incapable of being performed from access to the court before which he nevertheless brought proceedings.'

[101] *Gazprom* judgement, para 35, stating that the question is 'whether it would be compatible with that regulation for a court of a Member State to recognise and enforce an arbitral award ordering a party to arbitration proceedings to reduce the scope of the claims formulated in proceedings pending before a court of that Member State'. Further, it held in para 38 that 'an arbitral tribunal's prohibition of a party from bringing certain claims before a court of a Member State cannot deny that party the judicial protection referred to in para 34 of the present judgment, since, in proceedings for recognition and enforcement of such an arbitral award, first, that party could contest the recognition and enforcement and, second, the court seised would have to determine, on the basis of the applicable national procedural law and international law, whether or not the award should be recognised and enforced.'

[102] *Gazprom* judgment, para 39.

[103] *Ibid.*, para 40.

> from bringing certain claims before a court of that Member State, since that regulation does not govern the recognition and enforcement, in a Member State, of an arbitral award issued by an arbitral tribunal in another Member State.'[104] In other words, it is up to the courts in each Member State to decide whether or not to give effect to such injunctions ordered by arbitrators. In this way, the enforceability of anti-suit injunctions in arbitral awards is given the same 'status' as the enforceability of any other measure ordered by an arbitral tribunal.

Thus, clearly the Court did not alter its holding in the *West Tankers* judgment regarding anti-suit injunctions issued by a court of a EU Member State and it did not follow the reasoning of the Advocate General, even though it did not express reject it. The reasoning of the judgment is generally well received by the arbitration community as being a sound decision[105] and is considered to provide a proper balance in the relationship between arbitration and the Regulation. In any case, nothing in the decision suggests a possible reversal of the *West Tankers* judgment regarding the permissibility of anti-suit injunctions issued by national courts.

Yet although it is 'politically correct', the decision is not free from criticism. First of all, it is regrettable that no reference is made to the revised Regulation and to the Opinion of the Advocate General. That leaves room for further speculation on the 'validity' of the *West Tankers* judgment in the context of the revised Regulation, as well as other alleged problems in the relationship between the Regulation and arbitration.[106] More importantly, the judgment may raise some concerns from a theoretical point of view, particularly on the nature and relevance of EU legislative acts.

Firstly, it seems that the *rationale* underlying the distinction between anti-suit injunctions issued by national courts and those issued by arbitrators lies in the fact that an arbitral award cannot impose sanctions or penalties in case of a failure to comply with the injunction. Consequently, it may be presumed that a court requested to inforce such an injunction contained in an arbitral award is expected not to impose such penalties either. It is regrettable that the judgment does not state this expressly, although this interpretation follows from the rationale of the decision in distinguishing between the injunctions issued by national courts and those by arbitrators. If this holding was to be interpreted differently, i.e., that a national court could impose such sanctions, it would result in exactly the type of anti-suit injunction that was considered incompatible with the Regulation in the *West Tankers* judgment.

Besides, it is conceivable that a failure of a party to comply with the injunction issued by an arbitral tribunal may result in arbitrators drawing inferences that they consider appropriate just as is the case in other cases where provisional measures

104 *Ibid.*, para 44.

105 See e.g., Ojiegbel 2015, p. 75.

106 E.g., Van Zelst 2015.

are ordered by an arbitral tribunal.[107] It is true that arbitrators generally exercise their authority to impose sanctions and issue anti-suit injunctions with restraint in order not to jeopardise the enforceability of the award. The *Gazprom* judgment gives a clear message that no penalties may be attached to such injunctions. The issue of awarding damages for a breach of choice of court and arbitration clauses remains open, i.e. whether or not such decisions impact on the operation of the Brussels I and Ibis Regulations. Awarding the costs of litigation by other courts or by arbitrators poses no problem when such costs cannot be awarded in the proceedings on the merits. However, it may be questioned whether awarding such costs even before litigation on the merits is concluded affects the operation of the Regulation.[108]

The holding that the enforceability of such orders is left to the courts and national law of the Member States results in maintaining double standards of enforcement within the European Union. Thus, probably in common law jurisdictions such injunctions will be effective so as to restrain court proceedings pending there, whereas they are likely to be ineffective in Member States in which anti-suit injunctions are an unknown legal concept. Such a result in itself is acceptable as far as it concerns proceedings pending in a particular Member State: the courts in each Member State are free to decide on which effect is to be attributed to such measures. However, the problem may arise if an injunction restraining court proceedings in one Member State is enforced in another Member State, as an anti-suit injunction is directed towards a party and not towards a foreign court. Thus it is conceivable that a court in a Member State which can assert *in personam* jurisdiction over a party enforces an anti-suit injunction prohibiting that party from continuing litigation in another Member State. It is appropriate to conclude that the reasoning of the *Gazprom* judgment does not apply to such a situation considering that the judgment consistently refers to the effect of injunctions regarding proceedings pending in a Member State where the enforcement of the order is sought.

Finally, from a theoretical point of view it is surprising that the Court held that 'neither that arbitral award nor the decision by which, as the case may be, the court of a Member State recognizes it are capable of affecting the mutual trust between the courts of the various Member States upon which Regulation No. 44/2001 is based'.[109] It is understandable that the Court cannot give an interpretation on the application of the New York Convention or national arbitration law, as these are not EU legislative acts. However, in some other judgments the CJEU has sent some important messages which may be relevant in the context of enforcing arbitral awards. For example, in *Eco Swiss*[110] the Court clearly held that a viola-

107 See e.g., Article 42 NAI Rules ('arbitral tribunal may draw conclusions that it deems appropriate').

108 See the English Court of Appeal in *The Alexandros T* [2014] EWCA Civ 1010.

109 *Gazprom* judgment, para 39.

110 ECJ Judgment of 1 June 1999, Case C-126/97 (*Eco Swiss China Time Ltd v. Benetton International NV*) ECLI:EU:C:1999:269.

tion of EC competition law had to be interpreted as a violation of public policy in the context of proceedings for setting aside an arbitral award. The same holds true for the policy of consumer protection.[111] Although arbitrators as 'private judges' are strictly speaking not bound to apply EU law in contrast to such obligation for state court judges and arbitrators may not submit questions for a preliminary ruling to the CJEU, the courts of the Member States must ensure that arbitral awards do not run counter to certain principles incorporated in EU legislative instruments. That is at least what can be concluded from the relevant CJEU case law. The holding in the *Gazprom* judgment seems to imply that no such obligation is imposed upon the courts when a unification of conflict of law rules on international jurisdiction such as Brussels I Regulation is at stake. Thus, the courts in the EU Member States may not give effect to arbitral awards which violate such principles incorporated in some EU legal instruments unifying substantive law, but they are permitted to give effect to injunctions restraining a party from pursuing proceedings before a national court which does have jurisdiction according to the rules on international jurisdiction unified on the EU level. This implication of the different nature and treatment of various EU legal unifications and may give rise to criticism in the legal literature.[112]

From a practical point of view, the *Gazprom* judgment can be regarded as a sound decision, despite some shortcomings from the theoretical point of view addressed above. It attempts to provide a proper balance between basic principles of 'mutual trust' on which the unification of jurisdictional rules is based and the legal traditions of the Member States. Considering that the *Gazprom* judgment clearly insists that no sanctions may be imposed upon a party in order to comply with an anti-suit injunction it must be concluded that other types of orders would violate basic principles on which the Regulation is based. Finally, nothing in the decision implies that the CJEU intended to alter or overrule the *West Tankers* judgment as the Advocate General had argued.

6.5 Concluding Remarks

The case law of the Court of Justice has shown that there is room for the application of other instruments that touch upon the same matters as the Brussels I Regulation, albeit that it restricted this 'give way rule' in order to protect the most fundamental aims and objectives that the Brussels I Regulation strives for. This has not changed under the umbrella of the Brussels Ibis Regulation.[113]

[111] ECJ Judgement of 26 October 2006, Case C-168/05 (*Elisa Maria Mostaza Claro v. Centro Movil Milenium SL*) ECLI:EU:C:2006:675.

[112] See e.g., Ortolani 2015, pp. 15–17.

[113] See also, Mankowski, in: Magnus & Mankowski 2016, Article 71, para 5.

The Brussels Ibis Regulation expressly gives priority to the 1958 New York Convention and clarifies the extent of the arbitration exception. Most importantly, the recital (12) clearly states that decisions on the validity of an arbitration agreement fall outside the scope of the Regulation. It thereby overrules what appeared to be a majority view in the literature in interpreting the *West Tankers* judgment. Also, all court proceedings ancillary to arbitration, such as the appointment and challenge of arbitrators, setting aside and enforcement proceedings are excluded from the scope of application of the Regulation. The issue of enforcing a conflicting or irreconcilable arbitral award and a judgment can sufficiently be resolved by an analogous application of the provisions of the Regulation relating to the enforcement of conflicting judgments. Even though it relates to the Brussels I Regulation, the finding of the CJEU in the *Gazprom* case is in line with the clarifications introduced in the revised Regulation.

References

Ahmed M, Beaumont P (2016) Exclusive choice of court agreements: some issues on the Hague Convention on Choice of Court Agreements and its relationship with the Brussels I Recast especially anti-suit injunctions, concurrent proceedings and the implications of BREXIT. CPIL Working Paper Series, No. 2016/5 http://www.abdn.ac.uk/law/research/working-papers-455.php

Beaumont P (2009) Hague choice of court agreements convention 2005: background, negotiations, analysis and current status. J Private Int Law 5:125–159

Dowers N, Tang ZhS (2015) Arbitration in EU Jurisdiction Regulation: Brussels I Recast and a New Proposal. GroJIL 3(1):125–146

Draguyev D (2013) Impact of Brussels I's recasting on arbitration: putting enforcement problems on statutory basis (Part II). March 2013, Kluwer Arbitration Blog. http://kluwerarbitrationblog.com/2013/03/05/impact-of-brussels-is-recasting-on-arbitration-putting-enforcement-problems-on-statutory-basis-part-ii/ (accessed 17 June 2016)

Garnett R (2009) The Hague choice of court convention: magnum opus or much ado about nothing? J Private Int Law 5:161–180

Haak KF (2010) Hof van Justitie van de Europese Unie (Grote Kamer) 4 mei 2010, nr. C-533/08. Nederlandse Jurisprudentie; NJ 2010, 482(39):4733–4743 (case comment)

Hartley T (2013) Choice-of-court agreements under the European and international instruments. Oxford University Press, Oxford

Hess B, Pfeiffer Th, Schlosser P (2007) Report on the Application of Regulation Brussels I in the Member States, September 2007. Ruprecht-Karls-Universität Heidelberg, Study JSL/C4/2005/03. Available at: http://ec.europa.eu/civiljustice/news/docs/study_application_brussels_1_en.pdf (accessed 10 October 2016)

Hoeks MAIH (2011) CMR of EEX? Van samenloop, litispendentie, en het vrij verkeer van beslissingen in Europa. Hof van Justitie EU 4 mei 2010, zaak C-533/08 (*TNT Express/AXA*). Nederlands Internationaal Privaatrecht 29(3):468–472

Illmer M, Brussels I and Arbitration Revised—The European Commission's Proposal COM(2010) 748 final. In: Max Planck Private Research Paper No. 11/6. Available at: http://ssrn.com/abstract=1804079 (accessed 10 October 2016)

Kramer XE (2006a) Het nieuwe Haags Forumkeuzeverdrag. Een welkom compromis met vallen en opstaan. Nederlands Internationaal Privaatrecht 24:109–118

Kramer XE (2006b) De forumkeuze als betrouwbaar alternatief voor het arbitraal beding in de internationale handelspraktijk? Het nieuwe Haags Forumkeuzeverdrag. Nederlands Tijdschrift voor Handelsrecht 5:165–172

Kuijper JP (2011) The changing status of private international law treaties of the member states in relation to regulation No. 44/2001. Case No. C-533/08, *TNT Express Nederland BV v. AXA Versicherung AG*. Legal Issues of Economic Integration 38(1):89–104

Lazić V (2007) The Hague convention on choice of court agreements of 2005: scope of application and main rules. In: Knežević G, Pavić V (eds) Državljanstvo i Međunarodno Privatno Pravo. Haške Konvencije/Nationality and Private International Law, Hague Conventions, Službeni Glasnik/Pravni Fakultet Unverziteta u Beogradu/Journal of Belgrade Law Faculty, Belgrade, pp 214–237

Lazić V (2009) The arbitration exception in the Brussels jurisdiction regulation in the light of the judgment of the European court of justice. In Allianz SpA et al. v. West Tankers, Inc, Nederlands Internationaa lPrivaatrecht (NIPR), pp 130 et seq (No. 2, 2009)

Lazić V (2011) The amendment to the arbitration exception suggested in the commission's proposal: the reasons as to why it should be rejected. Nederlands Internationaal Privaatrecht 29(2):289–298

Lazić V (2012) The commission' proposal to amend the arbitration exception in the EC jurisdiction regulation: how "much ado about nothing" can end up in a "comedy of errors" and in anti-suit injunctions Brussels-style'. J Int Arbitr 29(1):19–48

Lazić V (2013) 'Enhancing the efficiency of dispute settlement clauses in the European Union. In: Bodiroga-Vukobrat N, Sander GG, Rodin S (eds) Legal culture in transition—supranational and international law before national courts, Europäisches und internationales Wirtschaftsrecht, Band 4. Logos Verlag, Berlin pp 181–209

Lew JDM, Mistelis LA, Kröll SM (2003) Comparative international commercial arbitration. Kluwer Law International, pp 503

Lutzi T, The Protection of Arbitration Agreements within the EU after West Tankers, Gazprom, and the Brussels I Recast, Conflict of Laws.net. http://conflictoflaws.net/2015/the-protection-of-arbitration-agreements-within-the-eu-after-west-tankers-gazprom-and-the-brussels-i-recast/ (accessed 10 October 2016)

Mankowski P (2014) EuGVVO, Brüssel Ia-VO und Spezialübereinkommen. Überlegungen aus Anlass von EuGH 19.12.2013-Rs. C-452/12, TranspR 2014, 26-Nipponkoa Insurance Co. (Europe) Ltd. v. Inter-Zuid Transport BV. Transportrecht 37(4):129–135

Markus A/Giroud S (2010) A Swiss perspective on west tankers and its aftermath. ASA Bulletin 28(2):230–252

Moses M (2014) Arbitration/Litigation interface: the European debate. Northwest J Int Law Bus 35(1):1–47

Nielsen PA (2014) The recast Brussels I regulation. Nordic J Int Law 83:61–71

Ojiegbel ChP (2015) Arbitral tribunals are not bound by the principle of mutual trust: the CJEU (Grand Chamber) decides in Gazprom case. Int Arbitr Law Rev 18(4):74–79

Ortolani P (2015) Anti-suit injunction in support of arbitration under the recast Brussels I regulation. MPILux Working Paper 6 available at: www.mpi.lu (accessed 10 October 2016)

Radicati di Brozolo L (2011) Arbitration and the Draft Revised Brussels I Regulation: Seeds of Home Country Control and of Harmonisation. J Pvt Inter Law. Available at: http://ssrn.com/abstract=1895303 (accessed 10 October 2016) 7(3):423–460

Schlosser P (1981) Conflits entre jugement judiciaire et arbitrage. Revue de l'arbitrage pp. 371–393

Van Calster G (2016) European Private International Law. Hart Publishing, Oxford and Portland, Oregon

Van den Oosterkamp JS (2011) Zaak C-533/08, TNT Express Nederland BV/AXA Versicherung AG. Sociaal-Economische Wetgeving—Tijdschrift voor Europees en economisch recht, 59(4):190–194 (case comment)

Van Haersolte-van Hoff JJ (2011) The commission's proposal to amend the arbitration exception should be embraced. Nederlands Internationaal privaatrecht 29(2):280–288

Van Zelst B (2015) HvJ 13 mei 2015, zaak C-536/13, *Gazprom/Litouwen*. Over de moeizame relatie tussen het Unierecht en arbitrage. Nederlands Tijdschrift voor Europees recht 21(9):269–273

Vlas P (2006) The Hague Convention on Choice of Court Agreements in Dutch Perspective. In: Van der Grinten P, Heukels T (eds) Crossing Borders. Essays in European and Private International Law, Nationality Law and Islamic Law in Honour of Frans van der Velden. Deventer, Kluwer, pp. 85–94

Wagner R (2009) Das Haager Übereinkommen vom 30.6.2005 über Gerichtsstandsvereinbarungen. Rabels Zeitschrift für ausländisches und internationales Privatrecht 73:100–149

Wessel R (2008) The EU as a party to international agreements: shared competences, mixed responsibilities. In: Dashwood A, Maresceau M (eds) Law and practice of EU external relations—salient features of a changing landschape. Cambrigde University Press, Cambridge, pp 291–308

The manufacturer's authorised representative in the EU is Springer Nature Customer Service Centre GmbH, Europaplatz 3, 69115 Heidelberg, Germany. If you have any concerns regarding our products, please contact ProductSafety@springernature.com

Printed and bound by CPI Group (UK) Ltd, Croydon, CR0 4YY

28/09/2026

02224070-0015